NEWMAN'S CHALLENGE

By the same author

Les tendances nouvelles de l'ecclésiologie

The Relevance of Physics

Brain, Mind and Computers
(Lecomte du Nouy Prize, 1970)

The Paradox of Olbers' Paradox

The Milky Way: An Elusive Road for Science

*Science and Creation: From Eternal Cycles
to an Oscillating Universe*

*Planets and Planetarians: A History of Theories
of the Origin of Planetary Systems*

The Road of Science and the Ways to God
(Gifford Lectures: University of Edinburgh, 1975 and 1976)

The Origin of Science and the Science of its Origin
(Fremantle Lectures, Oxford, 1977)

*And on This Rock: The Witness of One Land
and Two Covenants*

Cosmos and Creator

Angels, Apes and Men

Uneasy Genius: The Life and Work of Pierre Duhem

Chesterton: A Seer of Science

The Keys of the Kingdom: A Tool's Witness to Truth

Lord Gifford and His Lectures: A Centenary Retrospect

Chance or Reality and Other Essays

The Physicist as Artist: The Landscapes of Pierre Duhem

The Absolute beneath the Relative and Other Essays

(continued on p. [322])

Newman's Challenge

STANLEY L. JAKI

WILLIAM B. EERDMANS PUBLISHING COMPANY
GRAND RAPIDS, MICHIGAN / CAMBRIDGE, U.K.

© 2000 Stanley L. Jaki
Published 2000 by Wm. B. Eerdmans Publishing Co.
255 Jefferson Ave. S.E., Grand Rapids, Michigan 49503 /
P.O. Box 163, Cambridge CB3 9PU U.K.

Printed in the United States of America

05 04 03 02 01 00   5 4 3 2 1

Library of Congress Cataloging-in-Publication Data

Jaki, Stanley L.
Newman's challenge / Stanley L. Jaki. — 1st ed.
p.   cm.
Includes bibliographical references and indexes.
ISBN 0-8028-4395-6 (pbk. : alk. paper)
1. Newman, John Henry, 1801-1890.
2. Newman, John Henry, 1801-1890 — Contributions in
doctrine of the supernatural.
3. Supernatural — History of doctrines — 19th century.
I. Title.
BX4705.N5 J35   2000
282'.092 — dc21   99-046845

Contents

Foreword

The chapters forming this book were written, over the last ten or so years, as separate essays. They are reproduced here with minor changes that concern mostly uniformity of style. New material is added only in two places that are duly indicated.

Different as the subjects of these essays may be, they all support the view that Newman is a challenge to some widely entertained images about him. These images are steeped not so much in a careful study of his writings, especially of his letters, as in the presumption that Newman's thought anticipates trends supportive of the "opening" of the Church to the modern world. Insofar as such trends diminish appreciation of the supernatural, they are thoroughly at variance with Newman's fondest aspirations and intellectual efforts. Newman's chief challenge today, as in his own times, aims at the defense of the supernatural.

Of course, the defense of the supernatural for Newman was far more than a mere intellectual enterprise. For him the supernatural was above all an existentially spiritual challenge to be implemented within a plan set by God. Compared with this perspective on Newman, all other facets of his intellectual physiognomy should seem secondary. It would indeed be a great misconception to try to reconstruct the very gist of his message as that of a cultural icon. If it is true that in order to have culture one must have cult, this was eminently held by Newman. His view on culture rested on his search for the true cult. This was the core of the challenge he set for himself before he challenged anyone else on that score.

Chapter 1, that appears here for the first time in print, is an overview of that challenge as set forth in the rest of the book. Chapters 2, 3, 11, 12 and 13 first appeared in *Downside Review*; chapter 4 in *Crisis*; chapter 5 in *Catholic Dossier*; chapters 7 and 10 in *Faith and Reason*; chapter 9 in *Newman Today* (the text of lectures given at a conference sponsored by Wethersfield Institute in 1989); chapter 6 is the text (with notes now added) of the Introduction to my re-edition of Newman's *Anglican Difficulties* (Real View Books, 1994); chapter 12 is a section from my book, *Theology of Priestly Celibacy* (Christendom Press, 1997); chapter 8 is the text, with slight modifications, of my Dawson Memorial Lecture, given at Steubenville University in 1997. Here I wish to express my appreciation to the respective publishers of the original publications for their kind permission to have them here reprinted.

Written as they were with no intention to have them eventually published together, these essays contain a few repetitions. These are, however, such that cannot be repeated often enough, and certainly not when the aim has been from the start to help grasp the gist of Newman's challenge to himself, to his own times, and to all time as long as there will be fallen men ready to rise above themselves with the help of God's grace.

S. L. J.

1

Always challenged and forever challenging

During the last winter of Cardinal Newman's life a Catholic priest in Birmingham took a stand that appeared an act of rank intolerance to the foremen ("masters" they were called) of a factory there. The priest would not yield on his demand that Catholic workers not be obligated to take part in Bible readings which those zealous "masters" regularly imposed on their employees. To break the impasse the "masters" asked Cardinal Newman, the grand old man of Birmingham, to settle the dispute between them and the priest. In doing so they were hardly inspired by the activities of another Cardinal, Manning, who for all his social "liberalism" was a chief representative of theological "conservatism." In soliciting Cardinal Newman's good services those "masters" relied on his reputation as a man of broad views, which in many ways he was, but, as the "masters" were to find out, not with respect to the kind of issue at hand.

Heedless of the inclement weather, Newman hastened to see the "masters" on their premises. Once he was back in the Oratory, he cheerfully remarked that he was glad to live on, if he could be of similar assistance again. But the old Cardinal had done exactly the opposite of what a typical liberal would have done in the circumstances. Instead of showing the slightest readiness to become part of a compromise, he had made the "masters" understand that Catholics could not be expected to compromise in matters of conscience. Catholics were not to be compelled to take part in Protestant devotional practices, for as Catholics they were not at liberty to do so.

Undoubtedly Newman used both reason and sweetness in making the "masters" see his point and agree with it. The almost nonagerian Newman had, of course, a presence that spoke more eloquently than his always eloquent words. That alone, and the opportunity to brag about the fact that the Cardinal paid a visit to them in the factory, may have been enough to bring the "masters" around to his point of view. Still, sweetly as Newman could act whenever he saw that not malice but lack of information confronted him, here too he was true to himself. He again did what he had been doing all his life: he acted as a challenge on behalf of what he thought was God's clear command to man, a command embodied in a very concrete plan of salvation.

Newman's character was indeed the very opposite of that which some contemporary portraits of him seem to convey. He was not the kind of suave gentleman who is ready to use refinement to gloss over stark differences. He was the very opposite of a skillful diplomat who thrives on compromises that invariably end up in glossing over serious issues. He was a far cry from the one for whom the new, the progressive, had an intrinsic advantage over the old, the traditional. He could persuasively urge that "to live is to change and to change often," but only because he had his eyes fixed on what was permanently valid in the old. He espoused the idea of development because he accepted the challenge to be faithful to the type set by a divine plan that no welter of change could ever alter.

Unlike many latter-day reformers, he never challenged anything or anyone just for the sake of challenging. Whenever he challenged, either himself or others, it was only because he knew that there were principles and truths that were never to be challenged in the sense of being circumvented by convoluted reinterpretations. He was not a liberal with an advance form of liberation theology. Had those "masters" sensed in him anything of that sort, they would not have thought even for a moment of turning to him. But they hardly expected him to challenge them on a point far more serious than ever could be implied by a "socialized" Gospel. The challenge was even more serious than the purely liberal or democratic issue that all were equally entitled to follow their own conscience.

Those "masters" were hardly the ones to recall that fifteen years earlier Newman had defended the rights of conscience without giving the slightest concession to doctrinal or moral relativism. Then he had challenged any and all to take most seriously the voice of a conscience that imposed the duty on everyone to search for truth and demanded utter faithfulness to truth from those who had found it. The duty consisted in a single-minded attention to the business of saving one's soul. He had many times stated that he had converted to Rome for the sole reason that it was his duty, too, to secure his eternal salvation. He also noted that no matter how many times he had assured doubting Thomases about his never having had a moment's doubt about having done the right thing, they would not believe him. But his very perseverance remained a sharp challenge to that disbelief.

Challenge in that sense sums up what Newman truly represented and still does. As one who has been recognized by the Church to have practiced the virtues in a heroic way, Newman certainly lived up to the dictates of the most difficult challenge a human being can face: the relentless challenge of dealing with one's own fallen self. This is why he could challenge that old man in others in a way no less thoroughgoing than he faced the challenge posed to himself.

First he responded in full to the voice that challenged him inwardly to live a life ever more centered, as he put in, on an invisible world. It made him commit himself to lifelong celibacy, apart from taking orders in the Church of England. His first plans were to be a missionary in foreign lands. As an Anglican clergyman, he had to face up to the challenge of sinking with the Established Church to the lowlands of the polished naturalism of civilized society. The challenge meant a work to be done, a work that became known as the Tractarian Movement. Its aim was to recover the supernatural (or "Church principles" in the Tractarians' vocabulary). But those principles, when taken with full consistency, brought the challenge of turning to Rome. This challenge, as Newman was to find out, was too much for most of his fellow Tractarians, and inconceivable to other Anglicans.

Contrary to Newman's expectations, the Tractarian Movement made hardly a dent on most of his co-religionists. This in
turn helped him perceive even more clearly that the concretely
and fully supernatural, as ordained and channelled by Revelation, was inseparable from Rome. It posed for him an excruciating
challenge, but he did not shirk from it. It meant for him a self-
imposed exile from Oriel College, his intellectual paradise, then
it demanded from him the parting from most of his friends. Even
his closest relations thought that he had become unhinged. Then
he took up the challenge of implementing his religious vocation.
The result was the introduction of St. Philip Neri's Oratory to
England, which brought him the daily challenges of religious
community life.

About the same time he did not shrink from the task of
challenging his former fellow Tractarians who thought it possible
to be Catholics and still be members of the Church of England.
He gained only a few percent of the Tractarians, who in turn
represented only a few percent of Anglicans. It was a strange
anticipation of what turned out to be an uncannily quantitative
"constant" of the "science" of ecclesiology. This is a point, which
those who cultivate ecclesiology as if it were a science, in
particular in reference to reunion with the Church of England,
would do well to keep in mind as they draw up their ecumenical
formulas and paint rosy expectations.

Relatively easy among the challenges which Newman as a
newborn Catholic had to take up was that of seeking ordination
as a Catholic priest. Nothing was easier for him than to ward off
dreams about the validity of Anglican orders, although at that
time he did not yet feel about them the strong repugnance which
later took hold of him. He wanted to be the sort of Catholic priest
whose chief vocation is to challenge all "the lost sheep of Israel"
and to do so in season and out of season, as Paul urged Timothy
to do. He knew, of course, that he was to live up to that challenge
mainly through speaking to the educated and therefore with a
marked intellectual touch. Although he knew by 1850 that his
calling was to be mainly to half-believers, since society was
rapidly losing its traditional attachment to faith, he accepted

Archbishop Wiseman's challenge to deliver in London a series of talks which he knew would be mostly attended by former comrades-in-arms in the Tractarian Movement. Again, he did not refuse the request of the by the then Cardinal Wiseman to be the keynote speaker at the first Synod of the Catholic Church in England since Reformation times.

His speech, "The Second Spring," ushered in for him a Winter, in which the light was not to break through until much later. But since the Spring was to be genuine, and not a matter of rosy dreams, it brought along spells of storm. One brought the prospect of being jailed. He was fully aware of this as he, still a neophyte priest, rose in court in defense of all priests as he challenged the accusations of Achilli, an apostate priest who delighted overflow Protestant audiences with juicy insinuations of sacerdotal immorality. Newman was not the one to avoid that challenge by recommending a change in the rule of celibacy as some Newmanists would do a hundred years later.

Then there was the challenge of setting up a Catholic University in Dublin, with its endless and thankless duties of explaining things that all too often should have seemed self-explanatory except for those who had to be courted to hear common sense. His major answer to them was that since the Apostolic See wanted that university, there remained no ground for specious excuses not to obey wholeheartedly. His clarion call for obedience and loyalty, his "Cathedra sempiterna," was not remembered a hundred years later when countless Catholic academics made a sport of turning Catholic universities and colleges into breeding places of "loyal opposition."

Then he took up the challenge of translating the Bible, only to find himself let down. No happier was his brief stint as editor of *The Rambler*, where an article of his on the role of laity was the last straw in the eyes of his ecclesiastical critics. He rose to the challenge of remaining obedient to Church authorities. The world, including the Catholic world, saw little of his faithfulness amidst the challenges of daily drudgery in the Oratory and its School. There he seemed to be buried while still in his prime.

The challenge Kingsley posed to the sincerity of Newman and of the Catholic clergy seemed to come out of the blue.

Newman's response to it, the *Apologia pro vita sua*, made literary, theological, and social history. It became impossible in England to treat Catholics with contempt and get away with it without running the risk of being taken for an outmoded bigot. More importantly, no reader of the *Apologia* could seriously doubt that it was solely a sincere search for the supernatural that had made Newman turn his back to the Church of England and embrace the Church of Rome.

And since he turned to Rome only because he saw in it the fulcrum on earth of God's very plan of salvation, he never challenged Rome's decision that no Catholic college was to be set up in Oxford. A great sacrifice it must have been for him as he felt that to run such a college was the only thing he could really do well and feel at home with. But precisely because he accepted the challenge that demanded sacrificing one's human self, years later he did not sound hollow as he urged full obedience not only to policies set by the pope himself but also to those set by all the pope's offices, the Curia, much maligned by "enlightened" Catholics then as now. This should be a painful challenge to some Newmanites, who are so prolific at preaching in his name a newfangled spirituality: Its primary precept is the full development of one's own natural potential, at the practically total disregard of the often "unnatural" demands of the supernatural.

For a long time after Newman's death only a few Newman scholars tried to take that supernatural edge from the challenge which Newman's life and thought continued posing. The modernist image which Bremond first painted of Newman remained for decades a literary curiosity. Others, like Przywara, overemphasized the existential character in Newman's thinking, his insistence on the concrete as opposed to the general, and his ability to portray and relish the personally experienced faith. Such efforts could not help, at least indirectly, but create the impression that for Newman hierarchical authority, speaking infallibly in the pope, was somehow a secondary matter.

Still, around the centenary of Newman's conversion the great majority of publications on Newman and his thought—and they ran to over ten thousand items—presented a picture that, for want of a better word, was "conservative." Above all, he was still a convert, to put it bluntly, who was respected as such because it was still respectable to go out and make converts. Within a decade or so he began to appear in a light which increasingly distracted from the towering fact of his conversion. The light was the one in which Vatican II began to be bathed, contrary to its official intentions and to the very words of its documents. It became a sign of theological and ecclesiastical sophistication to hail Newman as the chief inspiration of Vatican II and to leave aside the task of listing the factual and documentary proofs on behalf of that shibboleth.

A purpose was thereby served, and the more effectively, the less any effort was made to specify the sense in which Vatican II could be related to Newman's very words, formal and informal. There was a supreme irony in the fact that the publication of Newman's thirty-odd-volume correspondence just began when Vatican II ended. The more the riches of those volumes will be mined, the more fatuous will appear this tying of Newman to the "spirit" of Vatican II, a spirit certainly to be distinguished from its official documents. But the Newman who, even with an eye on the Bible itself, said that a book cannot defend itself from false interpretations would not be surprised.

Theological efforts began to multiply to find Catholic fullness in his Anglican writings and to put an Anglican spin on his Catholic writings. In both cases studied selectivity ruled vis-à-vis what he actually bequeathed. Less and less was he looming large as a convert, let alone as arguably the most important convert since Reformation times. By the time of the centenary of his death, Anglicans were ever bolder to claim him. Most recently, they have inserted Newman into their liturgical calendar, to the greater glory of that ecclesiastical eclecticity in which they are past masters. He is one more item in that spiritual smorgasbord which they take glory in serving up, so that anyone may satisfy his or her palate from Anglo-Catholics to rank modernists and to some who believe even less.

This tactic has been the standard weapon in the hands of Anglicans ever since the Tractarian Movement. Christopher Hollis, a convert and subsequently the father of Bishop Hollis of Southampton, was confronted with it in the 1920s, when his own father, an Anglican Bishop, tried to dissuade him from going over to Rome. In our time, the same tactic was prominently used by the Archbishop of Canterbury, when the ordination of women in the Church of England was found by some Anglo-Catholics— bishops, priests, and laity—to be the last straw for them. They failed to recall that Newman's chief effort consisted, in a sense, in discrediting any further waiting for another last straw to come.

Those Catholics in England who thought that the doors of the Establishment had sprung wide open to them, had less and less interest in Newman, except in carefully cultivated clichés about him. Insofar as the Establishment stood for worldliness in the guise of polished comportment, Newman could only diminish in significance to Catholics who set the highest spiritual premium on rising on the ladder of social respectability. Meanwhile the obfuscation of what Newman really stood for proceeded by leaps and bounds. A good deal of what was published to celebrate the centenary of his death would have made him turn in his grave.

It would surely be interesting to probe into the studied vagueness of those Catholic dignitaries and theologians who referred to Newman as the inspiration of Vatican II. It is not easy to sum up the inspiration of Trent and Vatican I, although both were emphatically dogmatic and therefore very specific in their messages. Contrary to clichés, Trent was not a counterblast at Protestantism but the final stage of a positive Reform movement within the Church. Vatican I was not meant to be, and was not, a blast at the world. It was meant to be above all a revitalization of dogmatic Catholic faith in Catholics caught in a growing secularization around them and within their ranks.

It is far more difficult to sum up clearly the inspiration of Vatican II, a Council that decidedly did not wish to be dogmatic, and in that sense specific, but aimed to be pastoral. To be sure, both Trent and Vatican I meant to be pastoral as well, but in the sense, and this is especially true of Trent, that only after the truth had been spelled out, could pastoral tasks, including reforms, be confronted.

Exactly the reverse position was taken at Vatican II. It is well to recall that even the Dogmatic Constitution on the Church is primarily a pastoral document. Apart from that everything is "pastoral" or markedly non-doctrinal in the manifold documents of that Council. Tellingly, its sole definitional part, the passage on episcopal collegiality, is not a dogmatic definition but merely an authentic statement of the mind of the Church. In adopting this non-dogmatic, or attenuatedly dogmatic approach, Vatican II unintentionally opened the gates to vagueness, ambiguity, and indecision (all, of course, in the disguise of "pastoral" solutions) that do not cease to take a heavy toll on Catholic life—priestly, religious, and lay. Worse, Vatican II cultivated the non-dogmatic and in that sense vague approach, in a distinctly unbalanced way. Indeed, leading *periti* of Vatican II did not cease criticizing Trent and especially Vatican I as one-sided Councils. They still have to discover Newman's rather dim view of Councils as so many places of infighting, as so many events that have been invariably followed by long phases of crisis within the Church.

With his penetrating eyes Newman might even note today that if Vatican II had much less bitter infighting than the previous Councils, it was possibly because it was the first Council held under the watchful eyes of the media. The latter is particularly effective at putting those under its glare on their best behavior. At any rate, the theological decibels of those who accused Trent and Vatican I of being very one-sided drowned out the voices of those who said that Vatican II had become an intentionally one-sided affair. For indeed there were *periti* (to leave aside bishops, whom only their fellow bishops and the pope should judge) who were hell-bent on turning Vatican II into a one-sided affair.

Paul VI knew whereof he spoke when, shortly after Vatican II, he bitterly deplored those who tried to protestantize the Church from within. By November 1964 he had found that there were Protestantizing traitors even among his own theological councilors. They aimed at nothing less than to lay mines under the very citadel of the Church, papal infallibility, by securing a potentially ambiguous text for episcopal collegiality. Paul VI, who broke down in tears on finding out that some of his own had betrayed him, had no choice but to make crystal clear what the authentic meaning of the text on collegiality was. Newman, of course, would have recalled that this was not the first time that divine Providence protected the See of Rome from being ensnared by the scheming of the Prince of Lies. Pope Paul VI revealed some of the agonies he felt over all this when on an occasion he noted, with an eye on Vatican II, that all Ecumenical Councils have been unbalanced. His words created no serious echo. Or rather those who wrote most and controlled most the direction of the new theology did their best to prevent the words of Paul VI from taking the center stage of theological attention. They did so because otherwise much of the new theology would have been revealed to be studiedly one-sided. This they had to forestall at any price in order to save their skin and reputation and to protect their cherished aims.

Tellingly, some remarks which Cardinal Ratzinger made a dozen or so years after Paul VI unburdened himself in reference to Ecumenical Councils created a far greater echo. No wonder. The Cardinal, in his conversations with the Italian journalist Vittorio Messori, admitted that the Council was greatly mistaken in an all-important pastoral respect. Most Council Fathers and *periti* felt, so Cardinal Ratzinger reminisced, that certain points of belief and morals were so much engraved in Catholic consciousness as to make it unnecessary to emphasize them along with points that the Council Fathers and the *periti* felt it was their timely duty to impress on the minds of the faithful.

Purgatory is mentioned but in passing in the Documents of Vatican II, whereas Hell is passed over entirely. Grace is celebrated, though not with sin as a stark background, as if grace could abound except where sin had proliferated. Original sin is treated with theological kid gloves as if there were nothing seriously wrong with man. While the Documents acknowledge the World's undying antagonism to the Church, this fact, which the Documents characterize as a most realistic condition of the Church in the world, receives a scant five lines out of the twenty-thousand or so that make up the Documents.

Clearly, there was a monumental imbalance here set up in the name of a "balanced" approach. Its justification, that Vatican I and Trent were "lopsided," should seem an egregious error in a dubious balancing act. Such a misjudgment could not help but invite its rebuttal. It came with the radical secularization, first of the affluent world, then of the developing nations. Some underdeveloped nations were also very successful in catching up in the techniques and pleasures of secularization, that is, in the joyful celebration of naturalism, with no restraint whatsoever.

For only those who slighted the stark dogmatic teaching of the Magisterium of Church Fathers, of trustworthy theologians, and, last but not least, of the Saints, could ignore the obvious: Already during Vatican II, the trend toward naturalism was moving ahead apace within the Church, and it turned, shortly afterwards, into a juggernaut. Clearly, when Cardinal Ratzinger said three years ago to another journalist, this time a German, that "to a certain extent we simply did not properly appraise the great trends of the times," he did not make an insignificant admission.[1] For is it possible to think that the Council Fathers were not to some extent shortsighted in appraising those trends? Do not the texts of Vatican II bespeak of a lopsided optimism, at least in the sense that they contain no appropriate presentation of mankind's fallen predicament and of the chain of ongoing historical tragedies implied therein? Did not, say, a Maritain give witness right there and then that such an optimism was misplaced, an evaluation which within a few years amply proved itself by the rapid de-Christianization of public mores throughout the Western world? Did not that admission imply that the *periti* were the weakest in what they took for their *forte*, namely, their ability to read the signs of times? They looked forward to the emergence of a new humanism most sympathetic in many ways to the most cherished cultural objectives of the Church. Such a hope proved itself very hollow when the legalization of rank immoralities made great strides even in such Catholic countries as Ireland and Poland, to say nothing of half a dozen other so-called "Catholic" countries in Europe.

No such vain hopes were part of Newman's reading of the signs of times, both in respect to his own times and to the

---

relatively near future. He, as the subject of an apparently
unshakable British Empire, could hardly foresee World War I,
which as late as 1913 prominent experts in economics thought to
be impossible on the ground that big companies were now
spread across national boundaries and shareholders were an
internationally mixed lot in almost every major business venture.
Much less could he foresee World War II with its genocides, and
the two hundred local wars that had taken place prior to Mao's
Cultural Revolution, which took no fewer victims than each of
the two World Wars had taken. Nor could Newman foresee
television and internet, although he would have been right on
target in stating that like other means these two would become
the channels of incalculable evil, as well as of much good.

The huge losses suffered by the Church, especially in the
affluent world, bear out Newman's cultural pessimism. Whether
he was right or wrong in his views on his own times and on the
decades to come, his cultural pessimism stands in stark contrast
to the optimism of the 1960s that saw him established as the
guiding light of Vatican II. And he was proven right in his
repeated observations that a firm guiding hand was absolutely
indispensable to the Church and that even with such a hand at
the helm a wholesale apostasy was in the making. He was wrong
in taking the view that there was no real need for the definition
of papal infallibility, although he explicitly held it to be a matter
of faith from almost the moment of his conversion on, that is,
twenty or so years before Vatican I. Contrary to his view, it was
that definition that provided the Church with its strongest means
of self-preservation in ever more turbulent times. That dogma
proved itself to be the only means to prevent "consultation" from
turning into a theological and pastoral filibuster, a chief weapon
of some willful groups.

About the turbulence of those times he had grim premoni-
tions. He foresaw a not-too-distant future when only some peaks
would be visible in a deluge of infidelity. As one who saw the
age of the Antichrist coming, he would now shake his head on
finding no reference to the Antichrist in the documents of
Vatican II. As one who took theological schools for the chief
agents in the promotion and unfolding of truth, he would now

be appalled by the anti-papal revolt of so many theological faculties all over the Catholic world. As one who hardly ever was at loss for a word, he would now find no words on learning that the officially approved catechists in this or that large archdiocese can tell Catholics of tender age that there is no such a thing as Purgatory and that the doors of Hell were shut tight by Vatican II. As one who could imagine no greater pain than to sin against purity, he would certainly find the Antichrist's doing in so-called "dignity" masses, going on for years before public outrage forces local Church authorities to bear down on defiant culprits, who, incidentally, have a solemn vow to obey the Pope!

This should not be surprising when ecclesial impunity, indeed great respectability, can accrue to theologians some of whose dicta imply that Hell may be completely empty and that the human soul of Jesus was not in the state of beatific vision during the excruciating agony of his passion. Could such vagaries be tied to a Newman who was hardly ever more acerbic than when he denounced Eusebius for not calling Arius a most dangerous heretic and for treating with sympathy those bishops who sympathized with that heresiarch? Was not Eusebius, who knew the heretics of the past but not those of the present, a strange forerunner of some theologians very active in Vatican II?

Could the celebration of the role of laity by Vatican II invoke a Newman when it led to a heedless campaign to assure to lay-people "leadership" positions in the Church? Did he not most emphatically deny to the laity precisely that leadership which is to speak authoritatively in matters theological,[2] even though he wanted them to be consulted and to be fully articulate? He would today wonder on seeing, three full decades after Vatican II and four centuries after Trent, long instructions come forth from the Vatican about the difference between laity and priests (hierarchy), as if this should not be self-evident and glaringly obvious.

Newman would then be right in registering a strange contrast: whereas the medical profession cannot allow itself the

---

[2] See his letter of Aug. 3, 1870, to F. Rymer, in *Letters and Diaries*, vol. 25, p. 172.

luxury of tampering with such basics as the circulation of the blood, the Church apparently cavorts in the luxury of such tampering and yet does not founder. From this he would rightly infer the presence of some divine force at work in the Church that protects it from the bungling of humans within it. He would then challenge his fellow Catholics to be alive to this superhuman feature of the Church and not to take it for a licence for irresponsible behavior in matters of faith, morals, and discipline under the pretext of an "in depth approach" to inculturation that includes everything except the true cult.

The reader of this collection of essays, published over a period of ten or so years, finds in them a Newman who is a challenge to various fashionable trends in the Church today, but especially to the most dangerous of them all, the trend toward naturalism in the guise of renewal. Newman may have been, and indeed was, mistaken on a number of points, which only such Newmanists would sweep under the rug who try to use him in their strategy, first to "protestantize" the Church, then to "humanize" it by setting up the natural as the measure of the supernatural. But his writings contain no trace of those contortional discourses on the supernatural that have certainly weakened missionary zeal. Why indeed should the Gospel be preached in the arenas of technological wizardry, in the sleek comforts of higher education, and in the torrid zones of moral jungles, if the supernatural is already flourishing among those who have never heard of Jesus Christ and among those who are literally hell-bent on having Him on their own terms?

In this age when the Pope had to urge, on a visit to Lourdes, that Catholics should pray more intently for miracles, Newman's thoughts on miracles may seem an anticipation of that pontifical concern. His thoughts on miracles should seem a devastating challenge to theologians who systematically slight the natural evidence about miracles by overemphasizing the supernatural effects they ought to produce. In this age when science acts as a cornucopia of devices that produce "miraculous" cures of physical and mental ills, Newman's insistence on the truth of miracles, biblical and ecclesiastic, as well as on the prodigious number of the latter, should give pause to some "enlightened" Catholics.

In an age that saw so many Catholics take for a sign of theological progress that Saint Michael and his undoubtedly supernatural hosts were no longer to be invoked after the Mass, there may be found a much needed corrective in Newman's views on angels. Those views were also ecological in the best sense. For a healthy life of body *and* soul, he insisted that Catholics should keep a keen awareness of the presence of angels everywhere, even in the small details of wildlife, which are now worshiped by so many nature fanciers as a substitute for true worship.

In this age of science, when science is being turned into the sole avenue to truth and reality, Newman's excoriation of a science-based education should seem offensive, though very timely. Today even more than in his time, he would look askance at efforts to take scientists as a body for unbiased spokesmen of objective truth. Today, he would lash out as much as he did in his own time at conspicuous gatherings of scientists that sound increasingly like platforms for declarations of secularist dogmas. And just as he turned his back on the British Association for the Advancement of Science from its first meeting in Oxford, in 1833, so he would warn his fellow-Catholics about the anti-supernatural propaganda that blares forth from the big annual gatherings of the American Association for the Advancement of Science and from the pages of magazines that popularize science.

Although he would not tolerate even for a moment the irresponsible supernaturalism of creationists, he would protest against being ranked as one of Darwin's soul-mates. What he told Baron von Hügel about the failure of the Darwinian mechanism of evolution to explain a mere blossom in a rhododendron tree, should refute all those who take Newman for an evolutionist and do so with no stark qualifications. He disagreed with Darwin on precisely the basic issue, the issue of the adequacy or inadequacy of the merely natural. He saw the supernatural at work everywhere, without slighting the role of purely natural forces and agencies. He was no mystic though, in spite of being a saint, a point one does well to ponder nowadays when so many fancy that they are engaged in "contemplation" in the midst of their feverish social and pastoral activities, if not activism.

He knew how to distinguish, as befitted a master of logic, who time and again made feel desperate, at times furious, his ecclesiastical and secular antagonists by advancing conceptual nuances they could grasp but were unable to match. Like many other masters of logic, he could have easily gone astray. In his major philosophical work, the *Grammar of Assent*, he came time and again to the edge of an epistemological abyss, with sheer subjectivism and egocentric personalism at its bottom. If he drew back again and again, as if at the last moment, it was only because the supernatural realities remained his chief guiding lights and inspiration even in the midst of what could appear on his part to be a most naturalistic logic-chopping. One wonders whether such caution was at work with the spokesmen of that most dangerous Trojan horse, Aquikantism (or transcendental Thomism), lately spirited into the Church.

It was his unlimited trust in the supernatural as deposited in the Church that saved him from becoming another Döllinger in connection with debates on the advisability on the definition of papal infallibility. A man of "imperial" or universal intellect, he remained forever an Oxford man, with a distinct touch of insularity. He never fully mastered a major foreign language. He failed to perceive that there were considerations far more weighty in support of defining that dogma than that one against it, namely, that one should not cause further aggravation to former Tractarians who did not follow him to Rome. As one who had such a profound faith in the divine Providence assisting the one in the chair of Peter, he failed to see that the same Providence would certainly prevent the definition of "maximalist" views on infallibility. If he ever lost his theological nerve, it was in 1870. In fact it took an Anglican to make him realize that in his opposition to the definition of the dogma, he had unwittingly taken the Gallican position, for which he had only contempt.

Only Newman's infatuation with Oxonian insularity can explain that someone so conscious of the unique contributions of the Church to human history could be so mistaken in his strategy toward an act of the Church without which, as history was soon to show, the Church would have become as paralyzed as she was at the height of the Gallican crisis. In this age, when Catholics are caught in heedless acts of begging forgiveness for the Church's failures, real and imaginary, it may come as a shock to find Newman roundly rejecting this policy. Newman, who took special delight in evoking the past of the Church as a pattern to follow, spoke from the depths of his mind and from the bottom of his heart when setting forth in several long letters his thematic apologetics of Church history. It was an apologetics with no essential concession to anyone, because the supernatural at work in the Church had to be unfailing if it was supernatural and therefore patently productive in benefits which the World could not match at all.

At the basis of Newman's attachment to the supernatural, which is his chief challenge to Catholics today, there lay his conviction that natural man's fallenness was something empirically most evident. To be sure, Newman was no Puritan, no Calvinist. However emphatic he was on the empirical obviousness of man's fallenness and on its dire particulars, he held that even fallen man could recognize the existence of God and the voice of a conscience aware of an absolute difference between moral evil and good. Newman's supernaturalism was sound because it rested on the natural. The rest was a logic strengthened by the supernatural: If there is God, and obviously there is one, then it follows that divine mercy could not leave man a ruined being. Hence a divine plan of salvation, a plan not offered as a convenience but as a sole means of rescue in the midst of a moral deluge. To seek entry into the Church was for him equivalent to finding the sole ark of Noah, the search for which was a most serious moral obligation.

A convert he was, who all his life had as his chief mission the making of converts. Nothing else can better convey the gist of his challenge in this age of often misguided and mistaken ecumenism and of rampant naturalism. His challenge is the challenge of the supernatural in its full and pristine strength, a supernatural to which he never failed to show a commitment with no reservations whatsoever.

Herein lies his achievement, the achievement of a saint. He was not a saint who practiced virtues "heroically in an unheroic way," whatever such a phrase may mean. Many Newman

fanciers today still have to discover that as a saint he too was a
"peculiar being," as he once characterized saints. Peculiar as this
may sound, he was no mystic, in spite of having practiced the
virtues heroically. At a time when it passes for theological
enlightenment to push for the marriage of priests, Newman
would appear very peculiar for his defense of priestly celibacy.

Nobody can disagree, however, that he was peculiarly good
at articulating, at verbalizing God's appeal to man and man's all
too often fumbling responses to it. Yet he would never have taken
that articulation for an end in itself. He knew with Thomas
Aquinas that all sins consist in taking means for an end. The end
he never put so charmingly and strikingly as when he spoke, in
his last years, of his approaching death as something to which he
looked forward as schoolboys wait eagerly for the moment of
going home for Christmas. Heaven was his home which, he
knew, could be anticipated only supernaturally here below.

Most of us, who are admirers of Newman, fall far short of
having a similar attitude. But all true admirers of his must keep
in focus that supernatural heaven because it was his focus. It was
the motive force, the steady reference point, and ultimate
objective of his vast achievement. To weigh Newman according
to whether he was a liberal or a conservative, a progressive or a
traditionalist is a thoroughly misplaced approach to him, because
he was all this, provided those terms are carefully defined. His
real stature emerges only in the perspective of seeing him as the
giant spokesman of the supernatural. The supernatural was his
focal point where everything came together in his burning zeal
for God's cause on earth. To be his true admirer is to keep that
focal point in view when speaking of what Newman did and
wrote, so as to live up to the challenge of doing justice to him.
For he was one who largely ignored all challenges of a purely
natural sort, however appealing and promising they might be,
but he never shirked any challenge that served the supernatural.

2

A Gentleman and Original Sin

A gentleman Newman was, indeed the epitome of a gentleman. Even in tense theological confrontations he handled his opponents with gentleness, while mercilessly dissecting their views and arguments. Newman had so high a regard for the ideal of a gentleman as to make it the chief objective of a truly catholic university education. Yet he viewed with abhorrence the mere gentleman who set the ideal pattern of social living in the England of his time. The "State's pattern-man,"[1] as Newman called the phenomenon in his *Anglican Difficulties*, embodied, in his searching eyes, the treacherously "gentle" bartering of supernatural virtues and perspectives for their natural mimicry. Newman saw in that barter the penetration into Christian ranks of the program of the Enlightenment: man through his natural powers alone could be genuinely gentle, that is, fully noble or virtuous. But such gentlemen, however virtuous, remained barred from the heavens, the very scope of all supernatural revelation.

Newman first tried to reverse that penetration into the Church of England. This is in part what he meant when in 1833 he bade farewell to Dr Wiseman in Rome with the words, "We have a work to do in England." Of course, he also meant to convey, though gently, his conviction that the work would also

---

[1] *Anglican Difficulties*, p. 250. This and subsequent references to Newman's works are, unless otherwise indicated, to their standard edition (London: Longmans, Green, 1897).

19

be an able reply to what Dr Wiseman stood for. When in the late spring and early summer of 1850, at the urging of Wiseman, by then Archbishop, Newman delivered the twelve lectures known as *Anglican Difficulties*, he knew that the work cut out for him by Providence was far broader than working on the conversion of Anglicans. In fact, at about that time the poet Aubrey de Vere, who had just converted to Catholicism, partly under the impact of those lectures, could rightly sense that Newman "was quite annoyed at having to spend any time on Anglicanism." This observation is particularly significant on account of what immediately precedes and follows it. Newman, so begins de Vere, "anticipates an outburst of infidelity all over the world," and "to withstand it he deems his especial vocation." While such a sense of calling occasionally manifests itself in Newman as "an iron hardness," nevertheless, there is in him also "an exquisite and surpassing sweetness."[2]

By 1850 Newman had known for some time that he had lost "the battle of Oxford." There, at the University, the liberals proved to be so victorious as to feel no constraint in secularizing that venerable relic of medieval Christendom. Still, the most incisive analysis of why that loss was so momumental in proportion came not from Newman but from James Anthony Froude, for whom it was a monumental triumph. It is not so much the fact that Froude, a historian, was a noted figure in the English society that took that triumph for one of its signal achievements. Froude's testimony is priceless because he was the younger brother of Richard Hurrell Froude, who really started that battle, although he died years before it came to its dénouement. Froude the historian, whom his older brother introduced to Newman, wrote therefore as a personal experience the history of the Oxford Movement which he came to deplore thoroughly. But he unerringly put his finger on the crucial issue as he insisted that English society had to turn its back on the Oxford

---

[2] So wrote Aubrey de Vere to Sara Coleridge on November 11, 1850, or half a year after the conclusion of those Lectures. See W. Ward, *Aubrey de Vere: A Memoir based on His Unpublished Diaries and Correspondence* (London: Longmans, Green and Co., 1904), p. 182.

Movement, and on Newman above all, because one had to keep religion untainted by theology. The thought was unbearable that through civilized English society, a paragon of gentlemanly behavior, there should run "an invisible line of separation. If they were to die on the spot as they actually were, some would be saved, the rest would be lost,—the saved to have eternity of happiness, the lost to be with the devils in hell."[3]

In other words, Froude deplored the Oxford Movement, because it had disturbed a religious peace within which, for almost a hundred years by the 1830s, Englishmen as well as their curates had safely downplayed those great alternatives of supernatural dispensation. The peace corresponded among Newman's Anglican contemporaries to a broad loss of man's perception of the theological notion of sin, as distinct from legal transgressions and from peccadillos against refined manners. During much of his Oxford Movement days Newman felt that the Church of England had a fund of supernatural resources that could be re-energized to good effect. He certainly assumed a strong sense of the basics of Christian spirituality on the part of most of those who listened to his sermons at St Mary's. This is why only now and then did he elaborate thematically on man's fallen nature as the very reason for saying anything at all on the justification of the Christian. But when he did, he still shocked not a few, one of them being none other than James Anthony Froude. They were not pleased to be told that, if the Church of England was genuinely a reformed branch of the Catholic Church, its votaries should appreciate the emphasis which the Reformation had placed on the fallenness of man.

Nor were they pleased when reminded of such basics. Here Froude's witness is precious, partly because it leads straight to the gist of this essay. For Froude did not rebel against his association with the Movement upon hearing Newman finish his account of the passion of the Lord and, after a long pause, add "in a low, clear voice of which the faintest vibration was audible

---

[3] J. A. Froude, "The Oxford Counter-Reformation," in *Short Studies on Great Subjects* (New York: Charles Scribner's Sons, 1883), vol. 4, pp. 187-88. A series of six letters, it first appeared in *Good Words* in 1881.

in the farthest corner of St. Mary's, 'Now I bid you recollect that He to whom those things were done was Almighty God'." It was not this dramatic way of making real the mystery of God's death at man's hands that made Froude start rebelling against the supernatural. Froude began to feel at cross purposes with the supernatural on account of another sermon of Newman's. Writing about this from a distance of over four decades, Froude guessed that Newman preached that sermon in 1839, adding that he "had never read it since," although it left an "ineffaceable" impression upon him. The sermon was about two children, one baptized, the other not, but similar in all other respects—personalities, behavior, upbringing. "Yet we were required," Froude continued, "to believe not only that their condition was totally different, but that one was a child of God, and his companion was not."[4]

That Froude ultimately found that difference unbearable anticipated his own ultimate revulsion about the fact that in 1845 he let himself be ordained as a deacon of the Church of England. Only four years later, Froude had to give up his fellowship at Exeter College, because in his third novel *The Nemesis of Faith* he disavowed the Established Church insofar as it retained anything of the supernatural, as theologically understood. In the twelve volumes of his *History of England from the Fall of Wolsey to the Defeat of the Spanish Armada* Froude was to celebrate the English Reformation as a factor that established modern English nationhood mainly by reducing the clergy "from a position of almost supremacy . . . into the servants of the State."[5] In other words, the clergy henceforth were to preach only what was acceptable to a society of gentry greatly enriched by the spoils of the dissolution of the monasteries, a society later enlarged into a much broader society of civil servants, that is, those whose chief dedication was to the State to be served with civility. That State kept up the paraphernalia of the supernatural, while disavowing its theological meaning.

[4] Ibid., p. 187.
[5] J. A. Froude, "Condition and Prospects of Protestantism," ibid., vol. 2, p. 140.

With such views on what Henry VIII had brought about, Froude could but delight in reciting long lists of horrors committed in the name of the Catholic Church and theology. He therefore would have certainly found it grist to his mill had Newman suggested, however indirectly, that there was absolutely no hope of salvation for those who died without baptism. Newman, of course, was even in his Anglican days too much of a Catholic to fall in the trap of a Calvinist understanding of original sin. But for Froude, and the society he signally represented, it was enough to hear from Newman that there was something terribly wrong with man, including the fully polished, though unbaptized part of mankind.

Therefore what Newman said about original sin on relatively few occasions at St Mary's is worth recalling, because once more the nature of the work which he saw cut out for him, will appear identical with the basic objective of the intellectual and theological labors in which he was later engaged in his Catholic days. He himself insisted on that identity when he wrote in the *Apologia* that, from the age of fifteen, dogma was the fundamental principle of his religion: "I know no other religion; I cannot enter into the idea of any other sort of religion; religion, as a mere sentiment, is to me a dream and a mockery. . . . What I held in 1816, I held in 1833, and I hold in 1864. Please God, I shall hold it to the end."[6] What he called dogma was the concrete reality and absolute truth of a supernatural dispensation. It was God's plan to rescue all men and women from the abysmal depths into which they had fallen when their first parents chose to know the good by choosing the evil as well.

Without taking the portrayal of that abyss for the main theme of any of the sermons he preached while still an Anglican, he let his listeners look into its frightening depths whenever it was logical to do so. One such occasion was the topic of baptismal regeneration. This regeneration as something supernaturally real, though the baptismal water remained a plainly natural water, drifted into sharp focus only with the Gorham Judgment of March 1850. Then the Privy Council, or the Crown's theologi-

---

[6] *Apologia*, p. 49.

cal bureau, decided that the Rev. Mr. Gorham could rightfully be presented to a curacy, even though he did not believe in baptismal regeneration. Long before that, Newman noticed that many Anglican clergymen shared Gorham's heterodoxy. Otherwise Newman would not have emphasized time and again the sacramental efficacy of baptismal waters in sermons he delivered in St. Mary's. In doing so, he also had to explain the measure of that efficacy. The measure was no less than the infinite distance from spiritual death to spiritual life.

It was also supremely logical for Newman to use the feast of our Lord's nativity to portray that distance and that efficacy. In his sermon "The State of Innocence," he painted starkly the dark background to that state, the state of sin, inaugurated by Adam's fall. What made that state of sin doubly miserable was the praise which men accord to it: "Yet can anything be more certain than that men do glory in it; glory in their shame, and consider they are advancing in moral excellence, when they are but gaining a knowledge of moral evil?"[7]

The Gospel's "narrow" way they therefore decry "narrow in contumely." The children of men "wish to judge and act for themselves. They think it manly to taste the pleasures of sin; they think it manly to know what sin is before condemning it. They think they are then better judges, when they are not blindly led by others but have taken upon them by their own act the yoke of evil. They think it a fine thing to curse and swear and to revel, and ridicule God's sacred truth, and to profess themselves the devil's scholars."[8] And close on the heels on this there was a footnote, a reference to a sermon by James Anthony Froude's saintly brother.

But just as Newman would have found a sermon on Christmas wanting in completeness had it not contained an instruction about Adam's sin as affecting all of us, he found also the topic of our Lord's suffering a most logical context for the same. His suffering and death were, so Newman stated in a Lenten sermon on "The Incarnate Son, a Sufferer and Sacrifice,"

---

[7] *Parochial and Plain Sermons*, vol. V. p. 110.
[8] Ibid.

our means of reconciliation: "We had need of a reconciliation, for by nature we are outcasts. From that time that Adam fell, all his children have been under a curse. 'In Adam all die,' as St Paul says. So that every one of us is born into this world in a state of *death*; such is our natural life from our very first breath; we are children of wrath, conceived in sin, shapen in iniquity. We are under the bondage of an inborn element of evil, which thwarts and stifles whatever principles remain of truth and goodness in us, directly we attempt to act according to them." More poignantly, it is the state of any newborn baby. "Innocent as he may look, there is, till he is baptized, an evil spirit in his heart, a spirit of evil lying hid, seen of God, unseen by man (as the serpent among the trees of Eden), an evil spirit which from the first is hateful to God, and at length will be his eternal ruin."[9]

Of course, the great majority of those who listened to Newman's preaching at St. Mary's had enough Christian sensitivity to feel something of the drama which is felt when one is reminded not only of the fact that one sins, but also that one's very nature is prone to sin: "Men can without trouble be brought to confess that they sin, i.e., that they commit sins. But they do not like to be told that the race from which they proceed is degenerate. Even the indolent have a pride here." And the truly virtuous did not resent that they too were aimed at in that sermon of Newman's on "Sins of Ignorance and Sins of Weakness."[10]

For only the truly virtuous could understand Newman about a paradoxical feature of spiritual life, which he set forth in the sermon on "Shrinking from Christ's Coming." The more one prayed to see Christ and longed for His coming, the more one felt one's uncleanness and became apprehensive about that coming. Moreover, clean in one sense one could never become: "If by 'clean,' you mean free from that infection of nature, the least drop of which is sufficient to dishonour all your services, clean you never will be till you have paid the debt of sin, and lose that body which Adam has begotten." And now Newman

---

[9] Ibid., vol. VI, 77.
[10] Ibid., vol. I, p. 87.

lifted a bit of the veil of that drama: "Be sure that the longer you live, and the holier you become, you will only perceive that misery more clearly."[11]

Not that Newman would have called in doubt, even as an Anglican, that grace or righteousness was not merely imputed to man but was a gift truly given him in order to be really in him. Only man was never to imagine that it was not a gift, that it was from man himself, and not through God's generosity. Such was the point of his sermon, "Righteousness not of us, but in us." Moreover, he characterized that point as "that great truth which is at "the foundation of all true doctrine as to the way to salvation. All teaching about duty and obedience, about attaining heaven, and about the office of Christ towards us, is hollow and unsubstantial, which is not built *here,* in the doctrine of our original corruption and helplessness; and, in consequence, of original guilt and sin."[12]

At this point one would be tempted to elaborate on some of the dramas triggered by newfangled catechetical instructions and theological discourses that try to be as tight-lipped as possible on that very foundation of all true doctrine about salvation. But let Newman be heard first, in detail, partly because he sounds more and more dramatic in dealing with that foundation. In speaking on "The Law of the Spirit" as contrasted to the law of the flesh, he made a brief allusion to the "peculiar piercing distress which follows upon the commission of sins of impurity." He then conjured up those "indescribable feelings in our nature, to which our first parent alludes" when he tries to hide himself: "Are not these feelings a type of the horror with which the Angels now look, with which we shall look hereafter, upon all transgressions of the Law, or unrighteousness?" Then he elaborated on that horror: "Unrighteousness then is a state of misery, frightful as the murderer's, acute as theirs who follow Belial, and overpowering as Adam's when he fled from God." And in a more abstractly theological vein Newman summed matters up: "Such is our state by nature: the best things we do are displeasing to God in

[11] Ibid., vol. V. pp. 52-53.
[12] Ibid., vol. V. pp. 134-35.

themselves, as savouring of the old Adam, and being works of
the flesh and not spiritual."[13]

In preaching on "Sins of Infirmity" Newman began with, of
all sins, original sin, and again in a manner that was not without
a touch of drama: "How it is that we are born under a curse
which we did not bring upon us, we do not know; it is a mystery."
Of course, he noted that the grace of Baptism took away the guilt
deriving from that curse, but he added that "the infection still
remains." Yes, infection, which is so humiliating to modern man,
bent on hygiene and health above all. Newman characterized
that infection as a "most grievous humiliation" to all those who
strive after perfection. The more they advance, the more they feel
in themselves the Old Adam: tendency to "pride, profaneness,
deceit, unbelief, selfishness, greediness," in sum, the whole
"inheritance of the tree of knowledge of good and evil; sins
which the words of the serpent sowed in the hearts of our first
parents, which sprang up and bore fruit, some thirty-fold, some
sixty, some an hundred, and which have been by carnal descent
transmitted to us."[14] Yes, a tree and a serpent, and not their
mythical shadows, which a more "enlightened" new exegesis,
not yet available to Newman, is now marketing, throwing into
the bargain the dubious overemphasis on original sin as
something purely "negative" and "non-personal," that is,
perhaps not real at all!

For Newman original sin was most real, and he wanted it to
be such in the eyes of all those whom he felt to have been
entrusted to his guidance. "In this world even the best of men,
though they are dead to sin, and have put sin to death, yet have
that dead and corrupt thing within them, though they live to
God; they have still an enemy of God remaining in their hearts,
though they keep it in subjection. This, indeed, is what all men
now have in common, a root of evil in them, a principle of sin,
or what may become such." That it could be resisted by the help
of grace was, of course, true. But still it represented the very
basic point about which all, whatever their status in spiritual life,

---

[13] Ibid., pp. 148-49.
[14] Ibid., p. 212.

needed to be reminded constantly: "This is a point which must be insisted upon for the encouragement of the fearful, for the confutation of the hypocritical, and the abasement of the holy." One wonders how many latter-day homilists drive home this point when preaching, as Newman did, on "Love of Religion, a New Nature."[15] Has not the supernatural meaning of love lost much of its distinctness by the exaltation of late of a love which is mere sensual desire?

Undoubtedly, nothing is more natural than to experience desires of that kind, so much grist to the mills of a new "experimental" theology and spirituality. It, however, has nothing to do with Newman, although its champions love to invoke him in season and out of season. Of course, Newman was a great experimentalist in theology. He could describe, as few moderns can, with gripping concreteness what happens in the Christian soul, and also in the non-Christian soul, for that matter. He offered the best of "experimental" theology in his sermon, "Inward Witness to the Truth of the Gospel," and especially in the section where he portrayed the spiritual growth of a child, "under God's blessing, profiting by a teacher's guidance." Such a child would gradually perceive "that there is much in him which ought not to be in him. His own natural sense of right and wrong tells him that peevishness, sullenness, deceit, and self-will, are tempers and principles of which he has cause to be ashamed, and he feels that these bad tempers and principles are in his heart. As he grows older, he will understand this more and more." And what is it that such a child would finally understand? Nothing less than that "he will learn from *experience* the doctrine of original sin, before he knows the actual name of it" (emphasis added). Lucky child, indeed, but perhaps not so nowadays when various fashionable catechetical instructions aim at making him unlearn what his very experience teaches him.

Happily for the purposes of this essay, it is Newman himself who characterizes all this as "the strong language of the Homilies," meaning in part his parochial and plain sermons. He offers that characterization in his first major theological work, *Lectures*

---

[15] Ibid., vol. VII, p. 186.

on Justification. The context is his explaining the problem: "How can we, children of Adam, be said *really and truly* to be righteous, in a sense distinct from the *imputation* of righteousness?"[16] By emphasizing the words *really and truly,* Newman, still an Anglican, amply revealed his latently robust Catholic convictions. This should be a guarantee, if one was needed, that "the strong language" of his Homilies also reflected a genuinely Catholic spirit. No less interesting is the fact that he did not refer to any of the homilies discussed above. He quoted very strong, indeed harsh phrases from other sermons of his, such as that we are "firebrands of hell," and but a "lump of sin." Apart from the harshness of such phrases, they show the naturalness with which he returned in most varied contexts to the erstwhile wounding by Adam's sin of our human nature. One such context was the Feast of Nativity. Christmas for Newman was not a celebration of life as if life did not carry the sting of spiritual death.

As a Catholic, he did not refrain from recalling the abysmal depths into which original sin let man fall. But words even stronger than "abysmal" may be in order to convey what he meant to evoke in speaking of original sin. Take, for instance, the sermon he preached in early 1851 on disease as the type of sin. Already the fact that he spoke of sin as the ultimate cause of our bodily infirmities would rub the wrong way many modern Catholics who, in cozying up to the world, take health for the supreme good to be secured at almost any price. And he did not refrain from resorting to irony when he pointed out that "men would forget sin, but they cannot," obviously because sickness ultimately catches up with them and all too often much sooner than they expect. And it is then that "false views of religion fail." Why? Because "a bright careless religion" (he obviously had in mind a "carefree" religion) "does [well] in the sunshine," that is, as long as one has money and health, but "not in the shade." This is why Christ, always the supreme realist, "spoke to the heart" as He connected sickness with sin: "He comes to do that

---

[16] *Lectures on Justification,* pp. 88-89.

which false religions and infidelity *ignore*—to cure sin,"[17] whenever he cures the body.

All this would confound "the positive" homiletics inspired by much of latter-day theology and spirituality. Sheer revulsion would, however, greet Newman's tracing out the bottom line of his bluntly old-fashioned discourse. For the bottom line is nothing less than original sin. Moreover, that original sin, which in the "new" theology is all too often sublimated into Kantian abstractions, is described by Newman in words that send shivers down the spine: "When man fell, the grace which covered his soul and body was like a *skin* torn off and leaving him raw."[18] It was he, not his editors, who put emphasis on that word. More frighteningly to our greenhouse spiritualities, he warned himself that he should "enlarge" on the literally bloody metaphor of a flayed body. Had he lived in America, he might have compared original sin to the condition of one who had been scalped. At any rate, Newman's "bloody" metaphor is all the more significant, because, in line with the theological parlance, he could have compared the situation to a man stripped of all his garments. In January, when Newman preached that sermon, this relatively gentle metaphor would have reminded his audience that they were sitting in an unheated church. But the metaphor he used made them feel far worse. However, Newman knew that he was still speaking at a time when Catholics sitting in the pews did not mind being reminded, now and then, of harsh realities, including their spiritual kind.

Ten years later, in 1861, in preaching thematically on the state of original sin, Newman once more used a simile with eerie instructivenes for our times. When the seal of the Gospel is being put by some on the art of growing rich through investment portfolios, only deep-seated uneasiness can greet Newman's words: "And as a spendthrift involves all his descendants, so here," that is, in the state of original sin. For a society obsessed with the idea that everybody should get a university education

---

[17] *Sermon Notes by John Henry Cardinal Newman. 1849-1878* (London: Longmans, Green and Company, 1913), p. 57.
[18] Ibid.

as the means to wealth and culture, Newman's other simile should sound equally disconcerting: "Take the case of a person born to wealth, etc., cultivated mind, etc., banished to a desert island." No more popular in some Catholic circles today would be Newman's listing of human nature's three wounds effected by original sin: sloth, selfishness, sensuality. Then Newman reminds himself that he should describe sloth: "that deadness, blindness of soul, dislike of prayer, disgust at religion, liking to ridicule it. Dislike of ruling our mind and heart etc., etc."[19] Those *et ceteras* will mean much to anyone familiar with Froude's recollection of Newman's preaching at St Mary's: "He seemed to be addressing the most secret consciousness of each of us—as the eyes of a portrait appear to look at every person in a room." [20]

In view of all this, Newman could have just as well stated about original sin in the *Apologia* what he stated there about dogma as the lifeblood of religion as he always understood it. For by dogma he meant the truth of revealed religion, which in turn rested on God's infinite mercy toward fallen man. Tellingly, his most penetrating analysis of the place of the doctrine of original sin in the theological understanding of existence, individual and social, is in the *Apologia*. The context, no less tellingly, is the general answer to Mr Kingsley, whom he rightly took for the "theological" champion of the ideal of the "State's pattern-man," that is the mere gentleman, thriving on the progress of civilization. But Newman's was not a mind to be fooled by appearances of cultural glitter, not even by the glittering glory of the British Empire, then at its historic height. The true situation appeared to him an utterly dismal picture. He painted that picture in a long paragraph of remarks as concise as they are cuttingly graphic. And since copies of the *Apologia* are everywhere, let only Newman's own vignette of that picture, or, really, that vision, be quoted here: "All this is a vision to dizzy and appal; and inflicts upon the mind the sense of a profound mystery, which is absolutely beyond human solution."[21]

[19] Ibid., p. 175.
[20] J. A. Froude, *Short Studies on Great Subjects,* vol. 4, p. 187.
[21] *Apologia*, p. 242.

Beyond *human* solution, to be sure, that is, a solution without any reference to God. But once God is included, it is possible to argue about *that* world, as Newman did: "*If* there be a God, *since* there is a God, the human race is implicated in some terrible aboriginal calamity. It is out of joint with the purpose of its Creator." To call original sin "some terrible aboriginal calamity" was hardly an advance encouragement of some recent smooth theologizing in anthropology. The latter received an immediate advance rebuff for etherealizing the reality of mankind's being "out of joint with its Creator" in what Newman declared in the next breath: "This is a fact, a fact as true as the fact of its [the human race's] existence; and thus the doctrine of what is theologically called original sin becomes to me almost as certain as that the world exists, and as the existence of God."[22]

In a philosophical climate created by Kant's dismissal of all reasoning about the existence of God and about the world as a a universe, simply abhorrent should appear Newman's nutshell epistemology. For, as if to rub vinegar into wounds, Newman asserts not only that in speaking of God and universe man's mind is fully reliable, but throws discourse about original sin into the bargain. Worse, at least for those basking in that climate, Newman then goes on speaking about man's mind as it operates when subject to original sin. He does this in order to suggest the magnitude of the opposition of the human mind to religious truth. In other words, he speaks not of man's "right reason, but of reason as it acts in fact and concretely in fallen man."[23] The action is an irresistible gravitating towards the abysmal depths of scepticism and unbelief.

In order not to be misunderstood, Newman pointed out that "even the unaided reason, when correctly exercised, leads to a belief in God, in the immortality of the soul, and in a future retribution." He was no fideist; he held that "truth is the real object of our reason, and that, if it does not attain to truth, either the premiss or the process is in fault." But he also held that the tendency of fallen man's reason "is towards simple unbelief in

[22] Ibid., pp. 242-43.
[23] Ibid., p. 243.

matters of religion." The tendency acted like a deluge, with no breakwater against it, or at least the means set up to stem the tide proved to be patently inadequate. This was the truth everywhere in what Newman might have called the most developed, the most affluent, the most progressive parts of the world of his time, that is, England, France, and Germany. They represented the "European mind." But insofar as these breakwaters were constructed in separation from the Catholic Church, they proved to be utterly ineffectual "to arrest the fierce wilful human nature in its onward course,"[24] be it the nature, one may add, of the European or of the American mind.

Newman listed three of those breakwaters. First came Protestant state religions, established three hundred years earlier, which soon began to show cracks and crevices through which "the enemy" poured in. Then in the 1830s came the emphasis on universal education. And finally in the 1850s came the scientific progress as a means of putting an end to wars. Recalling all these vain hopes as the 21st century—with its internets, space probes, stealth bombers as well as appalling crime rates—is dawning on us, one cannot help sensing the perennial validity of Newman's question: "Will any one venture to say that there is any thing any where on this earth, which will afford a fulcrum for us, whereby to keep the earth from moving onwards?"[25]

By "earth" he meant, of course, mankind. By "move" a steady, indeed accelerated trend for the worse. Were he alive today, he would recall a truth already brought out by "experience" long before his days. Against that almost runaway course or secularism, it is not enough to wave the Bible, as done by Fundamentalists, Evangelicals and their naive Catholic admirers. "Experience," he warned, "proves surely that the Bible does not answer a purpose, for which it was never intended." Newman admitted that the Bible may on occasion be the means of individual conversions, but it is just a book, however revealed, and therefore constitutes no exception to a truth about all books: "A book, after all, cannot make a stand against the wild living

[24] Ibid., p. 244.
[25] Ibid.

intellect of man." What Newman meant was that a mere printed text is no match for the wild dynamics of a living mind. The latter is always prone to interpret, that is, to turn and twist whatever text it looks at. And once more the ever "experimental" Newman referred to what was unfolding under his and his contemporaries' eyes: "In this day it [the Bible] begins to testify, as regards its own structure and contents, to the power of that universal solvent, which is so successfully acting upon religious establishments."[26] He meant the impact of Higher Criticism, which by today has reached very low levels indeed as far as respect for truth is concerned.

Newman saw only one effective breakwater, the infallible Catholic Church as embodied not in inert texts but in an authority which is forever alive. He rested the need for such an authority upon the wisdom of the Creator, who had chosen "to introduce a power into the world, invested with the prerogative of infallibility in religious matters." This had to be the case if the Creator was "to preserve religion in the world and, to restrain that freedom of thought, which, of course, in itself is one of the greatest of our natural gifts, and to rescue it from from its own suicidal excesses." Moreover, since these excesses—so many witnesses to that "terrible aboriginal calamity"—were indeed suicidal (today they are, at the worst, called deconstructionism), that living authority had to be "happily adapted . . . for smiting hard and throwing back the immense energy of the aggressive intellect." That authority had to be an ongoing "emphatic protest against the existing state of mankind," a state caused by the fact that "man rebelled against his Maker."[27]

Against that rebel, against his moral rebellion, that living authority or the Catholic Church had to protest day in and day out: "The Church must denounce rebellion as of all possible evils the greatest. She must have no terms with it; if she would be true to her Master, she must ban and anathemize it."[28] This is why, Newman elaborated a little later, that living authority "observes

[26] Ibid., pp. 244-45.
[27] Ibid., p. 245.
[28] Ibid., p. 246.

no half-measures, no economical reserve, no delicacy of prudence." It is a power which, "viewed in its fulness, is as tremendous as the giant evil which has called for it." Such was the
beginning of a long paragraph which ended with a reference to a
"supereminent prodigious power sent upon earth to encounter
and master a giant evil."[29] The power was the Catholic Church,
with infallible credentials, because "of the intensity of the evil
which has possession of mankind."[30] Original sin was in turn
the "giant evil," partly because it paraded as virtue consummate
displayed by consummate gentlemen, who, unfortunately, were
but gentlemen.

For the author of the *Apologia* did not for a moment forget
why he had to write that masterpiece that culminated in an
impassioned discourse on original sin and an infallible Church.
He had just been accused of having countenanced lying as part
of the armour with which he and his fellow priests kept defending the Catholic Church. The charge was that Catholics were
insincere in denouncing the civilized society of gentlemen as
being in the power of evil and without any chance of salvation
insofar as it was the embodiment of mere natural virtues and
nothing higher. Newman, however, turned the tables on that
society by suggesting that its parading as the paragon of not only
civic but also domestic virtue was bordering on plain hypocrisy,
the worst kind of lie.

Time has once more justified Newman. For not even a fig
leaf can be put nowadays on the sexual hypocrisy of Victorian
society. To be sure, Newman defended lying, though not in
defense of the Catholic Church. He defended "the white lies"
habitually committed by any "lazy, ragged, filthy, story-telling,
beggar woman, if chaste, sober, cheerful, and religious"[31] as
opposed to the "lies" of that hypocrisy just mentioned. Lies,

---

[29] Ibid., p. 250.
[30] Ibid., p. 247.
[31] Ibid., pp. 248-49. Newman referred, of course, to a statement in his
Lectures on *Anglican Difficulties*, that made not only theological but also
literary history, insofar as it entered the *Oxford Dictionary of Quotations*, most
likely as a hostile reminder of his "true" mien.

Newman argued, could be mere random acts, not really coming from the heart. It was otherwise with society's condoning the habit of looking at women and lusting after them. For any such look called for our Lord's emphatic condemnation as being nothing short of an act of adultery. And what if Newman lived today and saw that society of gentlemen celebrating alternate lifestyles while praising civic virtue?

Today Newman would be infinitely more justified in referring to that divine condemnation and to other biblical texts in order to conclude as he did: "On the strength of these texts I have surely as much right to believe in these doctrines as to believe in the doctrine of original sin, or that there is a supernatural revelation, or that a Divine Person suffered, or that punishment is eternal."[32] It was a conclusion which showed how the dogmas of the Church form an inseparable whole, a seamless garment indeed. But he never thought it prudent to start weaving that garment by taking some modern social problem, such as nuclear disarmament, to justify his procedure. He always looked for the first step where alone it could be located: in man's fallen nature that revealed its utter misery long before the invention of the first catapult.

Compared with the impassioned witness which Newman brought in the *Apologia* on behalf of the reality of man's awful aboriginal calamity, rather pale may appear his strong words on the same subject in *The Grammar of Assent*. He was obliged to touch on it simply because there he dealt with natural religion. After all, the same natural religion was the background against which he portrayed the devastating effects of original sin in the *Apologia*.

He once more appealed to experience before saying anything further. "Experience enables us to ascertain the moral constitution of man, and thereby presage his future from the present." The inference to the future on the basis of experimental observation performed in the present was all the more "scientific," because it left no room for wishful thinking. First, there was the fact that

---

[32] *Apologia*, p. 249.

none of man's acquisitions can follow him beyond the grave. Second, there was man's habitual resistance to his moral sense of what is right. This resistance "is even by itself a misery," but, in addition, man carries it "about him, however he is, though no divine retribution followed upon it." Third, man "cannot change his nature and his habits by wishing, but is simply himself and what he now is, wherever he is, as long as he continues to be, . . . and that the longer he lives, the more difficult he is to change." Fully knowing that his readers, no less than he, were such beings so difficult to change, he did not leave it to them to draw the conclusion. He knew that man is prone to shut his eyes to the obvious. So he raised the question, a question so full of his customary realism: "How can we meet these not irrational anticipations, except by shutting our eyes, turning away from them, and saying that we have no call, no right, to think of them at present, or to make ourselves miserable about what is not certain, and may be not true?"[33]

But, again, the natural misery of man, his natural sense of guilt was to be fully understood in the light of the supernatural. He held that sense of guilt to be the very foundation of religion, natural as well as revealed: "Without this sense there is for man, as he is, no genuine religion. Otherwise it [religion] is but counterfeit and hollow; and that is the reason why this so-called religion of civilization and philosophy is so great a mockery."[34] Consequently, revealed religion, as embodied in the Catholic Church, made sense only insofar as it was taken for a unique healing power that had to be constantly applied: "It [the Church] has with it that gift of staunching and healing the one deep wound of human nature, which avails more for its success than a full encyclopedia of scientific knowledge and a whole library of controversy, and therefore it must last while human nature lasts. It is a living truth that never grows old."[35]

Other references by Newman to original sin may be dealt with briefly. In the *Development* he spoke of original sin as "an

---

[33] *Grammar of Assent*, p. 311.
[34] Ibid.
[35] Ibid., p. 376.

instance of a doctrine held back for a time by circumstances, yet in the event forcing its way into its normal shape, and at length authoritatively fixed in it, that is, of a doctrine held implicitly, then asserting itself and at length fully developed."[36] To be sure, this succinct conclusion of a brief discussion is not without significance for some new theological trends about original sin. More of this shortly.

Another of Newman's discussions of original sin is in the context of his defense of Mary's immaculate conception against Pusey. Today, when mainline Protestant Churches show no concern for original sin, and often not even for sin itself unless it is a sin against "political correctness," Newman's starting point may strike the average reader as almost outlandish. For he states nothing less than that while for Catholics original sin is something *negative*, a deprivation of supernatural grace, for Protestants it is something *positive*, that is, a "radical change of nature." Therefore they "fancy that we ascribe a different nature from ours to the Blessed Virgin, different from that of her parents, and from that of fallen Adam. We hold nothing of this kind." By nature, Newman, of course, meant that supernatural status of grace to which the first parents were raised in their very formation. While Mary, being a child of Adam, could not earn that status of grace, she was granted it "from the very first moment of existence, and therefore she never came under the original curse, which consisted in the loss of it [the state of grace]."[37]

The manner in which Newman explains matters to Pusey is not so much argumentative as meditative. Such is a saintly soul's attitude in the presence of original sin, this most human of all supernatural predicaments. Newman would have been perhaps argumentative on the awesome mystery of that sin, had he not often meditated on its effects, one of which is man's natural gravitating towards abysmal moral depths: "As sure as a stone falls down to the earth if it be let go, so surely my heart and spirit fall down hopelessly if they are let go by Thee. . . . How

---

[36] *Development*, p. 127.
[37] *Anglican Difficulties*, vol. 2, pp. 48-49.

strange it is, but how true, that all my natural tendencies are towards sloth, towards excess, towards neglect of religion, towards neglect of prayer, towards love of the world, not towards love of Thee, or love of sanctity, or love of self-governance." And once more he refers to experimental evidence: "My God, I have had experience enough what a dreadful bondage sin is. . . . In time the old Adam within me gets so strong, that I become a mere slave. . . . I bitterly lament my bondage, but I cannot undo it. O what a tyranny is sin! It is a heavy weight which cripples me—and what will be the end of it?"[38] The only answer to that agonizing question was prayer, ever renewed prayer, for the grace of perseverance.

All the more so as the religious climate in society at large was steadily worsening. Such was at least Newman's most considered view, which grew more and more robust in him. He was in his seventy-sixth year when he referred to a foreboding of his that had kept him in its grip for fifty years: "I have all that time thought that a time of widespread infidelity was coming, and through all those years the waters have been rising as a deluge." Looking ahead beyond his life, he saw faith confined "to the tops of the mountains" sticking out "like islands in the waste of waters." He saw Protestant countries in danger of sinking into the sea of scepticism, though he also felt that "great actions and successes must be achieved by the Catholic leaders, great wisdom as well as courage must be given them from on high, if Holy Church is to be kept safe from this awful calamity."[39]

It would tempting to evaluate the last hundred years or so of Church history, and especially the last thirty years, in the light of Newman's foreboding. Yet, even a well documented analysis would not necessarily achieve its aim. For history, and here Newman would agree with Chesterton even with regard to Church history, is "so rich and complicated that you can make out a case for any course of improvement or retrogression."[40] Not

---

[38] *Meditations and Devotions*, pp. 258-59.
[39] Letter of Jan. 6, 1877, to Mrs Maskell. In *Letters and Diaries*, vol. 28, p. 156.
[40] G. K. Chesterton, *All Things Considered* (New York: John Lane, 1909), p. 221.

that either Newman or Chesterton would have hinted that history does not witness to truth. But its data can be twisted by "the wild living intellect" of man, who can be most insincere with his own innermost facts. Newman would have endorsed Chesterton's rebuttal of H. G. Wells' dismissal of the idea of Fall: Had Mr Wells "begun with the human soul—that is, if he had begun on himself—he would have found original sin almost the first thing to be believed in."[41]

In brief, original sin is that supreme negative with countless positively verifiable effects. It is the most experimentally true of all dogmas, because each of us experiences its effects a hundred times every day. It is also easy to experience that the same dogma is resisted by the world at large. Worse, the resistance translates itself into a haughty attitude that no counter-arguments are to be taken seriously, as if man's fallen nature had been disproved once and for all and Rousseau's fantasies about noble savages were facts valid for all times, including these modern times of countless ignobly civilized savages.

Newman knew full well that haughty attitude, especially strong in the worlds of academia, of publishing, and of public affairs. He could talk quietly about the progress of unbelief, but only up to a point. As he once elaborated on that progress in the Oratory's common room, he noted that there would be a time when the world at large would take it for granted that Christianity had been disproved. He foresaw—a most accurate prediction, indeed—that those who believed in supernatural revelation would neither be listened to nor reasoned with. Arguments of believers would be brushed aside, so Newman remarked, with the claim that since revelation "has been disproved, we cannot disprove it again." These last words of Newman's were remembered precisely because in uttering them he put "a tone of anger and impatience into his voice." So are we informed by that great guardian of Newman's spirit and thought in the Oratory, Father Henry Tristram, who himself heard it from someone present.[42]

---

[41] G. K. Chesterton, *Heretics* (New York: John Lane, 1911), p. 79.
[42] H. Tristram, *The Living Thoughts of Cardinal Newman* (New York: David McKay, 1946). p. xi.

That tone of anger and impatience made well-deserved ripples precisely because Newman was a gentleman's gentleman. As such he could be expected to keep his composure in the most irritating contexts. Clearly, there had to be some profound justification for going counter not only to gentlemanly standards but also to the Apostle's injunction that all anger be put aside (Col 3:8). Newman could take for justification the anger in our Lord's eyes when He himself was resisted as being of no consequence, indeed as being the very opposite to truth (Mk 3:5). Or Newman perhaps thought of the anger to which our Lord yielded on seeing the merchants in the Temple suffocate the sacred with the secular.

A painful, an almost choking sense of anger may not therefore be too great a vice on our part in reaction to a most dubious tactic employed in recent years with respect to original sin. Undoubtedly, it is most praiseworthy to present such a harsh truth as original sin and its consequences with all the gentleness possible. After all, if it is true that man is greatly weakened in his moral perceptions and comportment, he should be approached with all the gentleness due to the sick and feeble. But it would be the greatest disservice to that same sick and feeble man to make him think that he is in a state of health for all practical purposes.

Thus, there is much justification for using a very moderate tone in presenting the harsh doctrine of original sin. Being a most loyal son of the Church, Newman quite possibly would use today a tone different from the one that characterizes some of his accounts of original sin. As a gentleman he would proceed particularly gently in times when the texts of Vatican II and of the New Catechism impose a gentle approach. But he would find full justification in those texts for emphasizing that the sickness and feebleness in question are most real. It was that harsh doctrine that prompted Newman to forego work in the center of attention in glittering London, for exactly the same work to be done in the comparatively peripheral Birmingham, simply because there too souls were to be saved. But would souls have needed to be saved either in Birmingham or anywhere, had they not inherited from Adam a sinful state?

That sinful state of theirs was not their natural state but a loss of a supernatural state to which they had been raised in Adam in the first place. Mere human nature as such was not given an actual course in history. Of course, the fact that human nature was raised immediately to a supernatural status, the state of grace, proves that the supernatural is the "natural" completion of sheer human nature. This was the gist of the hallowed phrase, "*gratia non destruit sed elevat naturam*," a phrase fully understood long before the idea of nature's receptivity to the supernatural was pushed, as in some "new" theologies, to that limit where no line of demarcation between the natural and the supernatural stands out any longer.

It was in that studiedly nebulous soil that newfangled theological celebrations of "nature" or "life" took root. What grew out of there casts an ever deeper shadow on a clear perception of the faith's very foundation, or belief with no ifs, ands, or buts in the dogma of original sin. For without that belief being firmly planted in one's mind, one's faith is bound to become unstable. Joyful appreciation of what is "positive" in salvation gains genuine momentum only in the measure in which one keeps in mind the extent of the deprivation which grace is meant to replace. A weakened awareness of that deprivation can only foster insensivity to the fearsome consequences of original sin. Then ultimately *rigor mortis*, taken for youthful life, sets in on the spiritual level.

Perhaps, after decades of at times wild celebrations of life, Catholic theology may need some somber actuaries, in addition to wise physicians. Not that the counting up of the many who have died spiritually for having failed to distinguish between life and its ersatz packaged in "progressive" theological parlance were of itself the paramount purpose. The real purpose of such a somber stocktaking would be to open the eyes to the fact that the Church remains alive because God keeps creating children of Abraham from a soil where the "new" theology sees only stony barrenness. What Newman said on original sin may be that much needed eye-opener.

3

Miracles

To take up the topic of Newman and miracles is all the more intriguing as Newman himself was a sort of a miracle. Newman's life and thought draw interest at an accelerated rate that is astonishing. Around 1933, or the centenary of the inception of the Oxford Movement, about ten thousand studies saw print that, in part at least, had Newman for their subject. Twelve years later the centenary of his conversion did not, partly because of war conditions, increase in the same measure the bibliography on Newman, but interest in him was even more intense. An explosive increase of the Newman bibliography was occasioned by the centenary of his death. Between these two centenaries came Vatican II, which many called Newman's Council. Or as one of the leading Council Fathers, Cardinal Gracias of Bombay, reminisced: "Representatives of the Hierarchy from all over the world, theologians, philosophers, faithful from everywhere, and from all ranks, see in Newman a guide in their sincere search for the truth."[1]

"All Councils have been one-sided," said Paul VI in one of his somberly pensive moments and with an oblique reference to Vatican II. The one-sidedness of Vatican II received a memorable airing in the interview which Cardinal Ratzinger gave to the Italian journalist Vittorio Messori in 1984. There only such monumental instances were mentioned as the absence in the

---

[1] See "The Friends of Cardinal Newman," *The Examiner* 128 (May 21, 1977), p. 278.

documents of Vatican II of any significant reference to Purgatory, matched by a total silence on Hell. Among the less startling instances one could mention the passing reference to miracles in those documents.[2] While this hardly reflects Newman's keen interest in miracles, it reveals the attitude of not a few *periti*, which is also displayed by a similar lack of interest in miracles on the part of an increasing number of Newmanites. A far cry indeed from the role which the reality of miracles played in the spiritual and intellectual contests Newman fought with himself and with others. Those contests had one overriding objective, namely, to ascertain the presence of the early Church, bursting with the vitality of supernatural deeds and comportment, somewhere in modern Christianity.

Relatively short statements of Newman's on miracles turn up here and there in the forty or so volumes of his collected works. The fact that one volume is entirely taken up by two long essays of his on miracles makes any slighting of his ideas on miracles rather strange. Indeed it suggests not so much an oversight as some strong motivations that are hardly in keeping with the spirit of Newman. Thematic disagreement with Newman's dicta on miracles (and even the slighting of them) gives away their critics' incomprehension of Newman perhaps more effectively than anything else.

In fact, precisely those students of Newman, whose principal interest lay in tracing out his spiritual development as theologically distinct from and superior to its psychological overtones, should have seen much food for thought in one of Newman's reminiscences of the year 1826-27, of which his *Essay on Miracles* was the chief literary product: "I felt," he wrote, "eagerly, but not very logically, High Church."[3] No wonder. A year or so earlier, there came a decisive turning point in his theological thinking. He was seized with "the idea of the Christian Church, as a divine appointment, and as a substantive body, independent of the

---

[2] The Dogmatic Constitution of the Church, #5, where Jesus' words are quoted that his casting out of devils signals the arrival of the Kingdom of God.

[3] In a letter of January 26, 1867, where Newman refers to the long vacation of 1827. See *Letters and Diaries*, vol. 23, p. 38.

State, and endowed with rights, prerogatives, and powers of its own."[4] He might have just as well said tersely, that he had been seized with the idea of the supernatural as institutionalized in the Church.

However, this new perspective, riveted on the supernatural, took a long time in coming to its fullness. But it was in full view when seventeen years after the publication of the *Essay on Miracles*, or simply *Essay*, Newman came out (in the momentous year of 1843) with an essay three times as long, again on miracles. Unlike the *Essay on Miracles*, which was commissioned for the *Encyclopaedia Metropolitana*, a work suitable for anyone with a vague interest in something concretely divine in the Gospel and the Church, the *Essay on the Miracles Recorded in the Ecclesiastical History*, or simply *Ecclesiastical Miracles*, could please only the Tractarians. Only they looked foward to the translation into English of a part of Fleury's *Histoire de l'Eglise* that dealt with the early Church. The early Church, the Church of the Fathers, was an ideal cherished by the Tractarians precisely because that Church was tangibly brimming with the supernatural. The translation was graced with an introduction containing Newman's *Ecclesiastical Miracles*, which ran over two hundred pages.[5] *Ecclesiastical Miracles* signaled a crucial step in Newman's secession from the Anglican Church as an entity incapable of including genuine Catholicism, synonymous with an enthusiastic espousal of the concretely supernatural.

For that reason alone the *Ecclesiastical Miracles* should have attracted the close attention of all those who focused much of their work on Newman's spiritual and intellectual journey. The fact that it failed to do so may reveal motivations rather similar to the ones that resulted in the omission of not a few distinctly Catholic topics in the documents of Vatican II. The addition of the phrase, "for what I have failed to do," in the new *Confiteor* of the new liturgy as decreed by Vatican II, is not without its irony

---

[4] *John Henry Newman. Autobiographical Writings*, ed. H. Tristram (London: Oxford University Press, 1956), p. 69.

[5] *The Ecclesiastical History of M. l'abbé Fleury: Translated with notes, and An essay on the miracles of the period* (Oxford: J. H. Parker, 1842-44), where pp. xi-ccxv carried Newman's essay.

even in respect to the cultivation of Newman's thought, to say nothing of other and at times even more important respects.

The *Essay on Miracles* was written with an eye on Hume and Gibbon, and was greatly indebted to what Newman could learn from standard Anglican rebuttals of rationalist arguments against miracles.[6] Those Anglican apologists, however, agreed with Hume and Gibbon that non-biblical miracles were not worth considering, a point which Newman fully shared at that time. In the *Essay on Miracles* Newman does not spare biting remarks on the miracles performed in the early Church and has only contempt for miracles of the post-Patristic Church. Seventeen years later he was fully aware of the fact such a distinction between biblical miracles and ecclesiastical miracles implied the adoption of the standards of Hume and Gibbon. Indeed in 1843, as will be seen, he spoke of various Anglican defenders of biblical miracles who, at the same time, rejected post-biblical miracles as so many unwitting allies of Hume and Gibbon.

Already in the *Essay on Miracles* Newman defended biblical miracles against Hume and Gibbon in a way that put him in a class subtly different from Anglican apologists of miracles. Not that these did not note that biblical miracles had a moral purpose

---

[6] Given the fact that Newman's references, though accurate, are exceedingly scanty, a full listing of authors and works may seem appropriate: G. Campbell's *A Dissertation on Miracles* (London: [s.n.], 1834); J. Douglas, *The Criterion, or, Rules by which true Miracles recorded in the New Testament are Distinguished from the Spurious Miracles of Pagans and Papists* (Colchester: [s.n.], 1824). H. Farmer, *A Dissertation on Miracles: Designed to shew, that they are Arguments of a Divine Interposition, and Absolute Proofs of the Mission and Doctrine of a Prophet* (Edinburgh: 1798); J. Hey, *Lectures in Divinity* (Cambridge: Printed by John Burges, Printer in the University, 1796-1798). C. Middleton, *A Free inquiry into the Miraculous Powers, which are Supposed to Have Subsisted in the Christian Church, from the Earliest Ages through Several Successive Centuries: by which is Shewn, that We Have no Sufficient Reason to Believe, upon the Authority of the Primitive Fathers, that Any Such Powers was Continued to the Church, after the Days of the Apostles* (Dublin: 1749); last but not least, S. Vince, *The Credibility of Christianity Vindicated in Answer to Mr. Hume's Objections: in Two Discourses Preached before the University of Cambridge* (Cambridge: J. Burges, 1799). The Rev. Samuel Vince (1749-1821) was also a theoretical physicist, well known for his works in celestial mechanics. Authorities for Newman in 1826, Douglas and Middleton become the target of his sharp criticism by 1843.

and perspective. But Newman made that point emphatically. According to him unless one viewed biblical miracles within the framework of a biblical revelation that had a moral purpose, they were deprived of their basic meaning. This is not to suggest that Newman did not take biblical miracles for real interferences with the ordinary, regular course of nature. He was no minimizer in this respect, a point that many modern Catholic re-interpreters of the physical nature of biblical miracles as so many moral "signs" should well ponder.[7]

But he rightly emphasized that in addition to the physical world, there was a moral universe, a universe no less objective than the physical. It was the universe of moral conscience, the universe of a keen awareness of the difference between virtue and sin, a universe pivoted on an infinitely supreme moral Lawgiver and final Judge, a universe with an ultimate phase of eternal reward and punishment. Biblical miracles were physical because only as such could they effectively draw sinful, fallen man's attention to a plan of salvation which God has set on a plane much higher than the level of mere physical interaction and mere natural life.

Already in the first chapter of the *Essay on Miracles* Newman could not have made any clearer the moral purpose of miracles:

> Hence beside banishing ideas of Fate and Necessity, Miracles have a tendency to rouse conscience, to awaken to a sense of responsibility, to remind of duty, and to direct attention to those marks of divine government already contained in the ordinary course of events (p. 12).[8]

Let it be noted right here, that what Newman calls "moral" throughout the *Essay on Miracles* intimately relates to that morality which is biblical salvation history. Biblical miracles, Jewish and Christian, therefore

> must be considered as immediate effects of Divine Power beyond the action of nature, for an important moral end; and

---

[7] Examples are L. Monden, *Signs and Wonders: A Study of the Miraculous Elements in Religion* (New York: Desclée, 1966), p. 51, and the article "Miracle" in *Sacramentum Mundi.*

[8] This and subsequent page numbers refer to the text of the *Essay on Miracles* as given in the Longmans edition of Newman's collected works.

are in consequence accounted for by producing, not a physical but a final cause (p. 18).

Newman's chief objection to all objectors to miracles aims therefore at their studied "forgetfulness of moral laws." They "consider Religion as founded in the mere weakness or eccentricity of the intellect, not in actual intimations of a Divine government as contained in the moral world." The weakness in question consists, according to those objectors, in insensitivity to the invariable processes of nature. But, as Newman argues, the moral universe too has invariable laws, which it takes even greater intellectual insensitivity to ignore or to slight than to be unimpressed by the regularity of nature. Biblical miracles have a morality which is a superstructure on what is known from nature "of His Providence and Moral Attributes" (pp. 20-21 and 26).

If the miracles of the Old Testament were performed by the Prophets, it is only because Prophets were God's spokesmen of His moral plan for man. If therefore worthy miracles should be distinguished from the unworthy ones, it is again on the ground of whether they serve a distinctly high moral purpose or not. Hence the rejection of the miracles of the Apocrypha as mere satisfaction of idle curiosity. Hence Newman's branding some miracles of the early Church, of the Roman breviary, and of Rabbinical tradition as so many cheap stories. The high moral connotation of biblical miracles makes Newman state that "Miracles and inspiration go together" (p. 34).

Inspiration on behalf of salvation history is, of course, an eminently moral process. Any weakening of this aspect of Biblical miracles would end, Newman aptly notes, "in pruning away the Christian system, till little is left for the Miracles to attest" (p. 41). And he rightly referred to the Socinian trend, a form of deism with Christian hues. Those belonging to the Broad Church could but feel stung to the quick. Indeed, three quarters of a century later, one of their number, as will be seen, produced the most biting, though utterly hollow criticism ever of the *Essay on Miracles* as well as of *Ecclesiastical Miracles*.

Emphasis on inspiration, like anything else, cuts both ways. It forced Newman to lay down principles which he had to turn upside down seventeen years later. One of them was the rule that once enough miraculous interventions had taken place, there was no need for further ones. Therefore miracles, however close to New Testament times, and however well attested by the virtue of witnesses, had to appear gravely suspect. "Popish" miracles quickly got Newman's axe. He had to say that miracles of the primitive Church greatly differed "in manner, design, and attendant circumstances, from those recorded in Scripture" (p. 42).

This put him in a difficult position because exorcisms were very frequent in the early Church. To remain consistent, Newman had to characterize the New Testament stories about demoniacs as not really miraculous. He overlooked that the cure of demoniacs bespoke most directly of the moral purpose which miracles meant to serve above all. Without trying to whittle down the importance of physical miracles, with which he began the *Essay on Miracles,* he concluded it by stating that physical miracles constituted a principal, though only one class of the various proofs "on which the cause of Revealed Religion rests." In tune with this, his final remark in the *Essay on Miracles* was a listing of the markedly moral ones among the miraculous proofs of the Gospel, such as "the character of Christ, the morality of the Gospel, the wisdom of its doctrines, displaying at once knowledge of the human heart, and skill in engaging its affection" (p. 94). Here was an uncanny anticipation of the idea which found its pregnant expression in Newman's choosing Saint Francis de Sales' words, *cor ad cor loquitur,* for his coat of arms as a Cardinal of the Roman Catholic Church.

This is not the place to survey, however briefly, the steps that brought Newman ever closer to the Catholic Church during the seventeeen years that separate his two essays on miracles. In that process, the year 1843 was crucial. Newman's Catholic interpretation of the Thirty-Nine Articles was roundly disavowed by the Oxford Colleges, by the bishop of Oxford, and by the Church of England at large. Compared with Tract 90, the *Ecclesiastical Miracles* had to appear unworthy of attention. In fact, Newman spoke of it in a disparaging tone when he finished writing it at the end of July 1842. "It is not much of a thing," he wrote to a fellow Tractarian, although he had spent months writing it, especially the historical part, which he thought would sell the book.[9] The Tractarians themselves, who were behind the publication of Fleury's *Ecclesiastical History*, had too big a problem on hand with Tract 90 and with its grave consequences for some of them, to worry about *Ecclesiastical Miracles*, with which Newman introduced that translation.

Yet Newman's engagement in the topic of miracles should have appeared enormously significant as to the drift of his thinking, the final destination of which was not yet a foregone conclusion in early 1841. Miracles stood for the supernatural, and indeed nothing stood for the supernatural so palpably as miracles did. He came to see the early Church as reverberating with the supernatural. It was therefore utterly logical and imperative for him to demonstrate that the miracles of the early Church were no less genuine than were the miracles recounted in the New Testament and that miracles had to remain ever present in the Church if it was a genuine continuation of the Church established by Christ himself.

Looked at in this light, *Ecclesiastical Miracles* is far more significant, theologically speaking, than Tract 90. In fact, Tract 90 will forever remain a futile exercise in theological reasoning, except for those who still see something viable in the Church of England as a form of Catholicism. *Ecclesiastical Miracles* has a lasting instructiveness, and a particularly strong one for these post-Vatican II times. *Ecclesiastical Miracles* began indeed on a note similar to the general thrust of Tract 90, namely that the Church of England could be given a Catholic interpretation. Newman clearly forced matters by claiming that the policy of restricting miracles to New Testament times was a temporary deterioration of theology among Anglican divines. He specified the "last century" (the period 1730-1830 would certainly fit the bill) as the time during which the validity of post-New Testament miracles was not viewed as "an open question," but rather viewed "in a light, which he [Newman] believes to be both false in itself and dangerous altogether to Revealed Religion" (p. 97).[10]

---

[9] For these details, see I. Ker, *John Henry Newman. A Biography* (Oxford University Press, 1990), pp. 248-49.

[10] This and subsequent page numbers refer to the text of *Ecclesiastical Miracles*

Why? Because such a light deprives of visibility that very supernatural which gives to the history of Religion, or Christian religion, "a necessarily theological cast" (pp. 97-98). In the same breath Newman avowed "the arduousness" of the task of writing such an essay, but he also made it clear that he was not apologizing. Here too, as later in 1864, when he penned his *Apologia*, he did not apologize. He was never the kind of theologian, of which there are today aplenty, who is begging on his knees the pardon of the secular world, and especially of his colleagues in secular academia, for being a Christian. In fact he was blunt right at the start: "There was no Age of Miracles, after which miracles ceased" (p. 100).

But even harsher words were yet in store. After noting that nobody has so far succeeded in specifying the line which separates the Age of Miracles from subsequent ages no less full of miracles, he threw down the gauntlet of his sharp logic. Referring to a notable Anglican defender of that imaginary line of demarcation, he stated flatly: "He acts towards the miracles of the Church, as Hume towards the miracles of the Scripture." Almost immediately after, Newman laid down a precept which is one of the best he ever penned, but also perhaps the most ignored: "Let us not be religious by halves" (pp. 110-112). This may be a bitter pill for some Newmanists to take, but the only pill that can cure them of that myopia of theirs which was very much in view when the centenary of his death was celebrated a few years ago. If their sin against the light can be characterized, it may be their studied readiness to be Newmanites by halves. In that venture they merely reveal their tragically incomplete Catholic and Christian convictions. In both cases it is their half-hearted espousal of the supernatural which is at play.

So much in a nutshell about what Newman said about the antecedent probability of ecclesiastical miracles. By far the longest part of *Ecclesiastical Miracles* dealt with the character of ecclesiastical miracles. Are they varied? So are the Scripture miracles. As a man of his time, when Bishop Butler's arguments based on the analogy between the natural and the supernatural realms were

as given in the Longmans edition of Newman's collected works.

still widely appreciated (and Newman certainly cherished them), he argued two points. In the first he defended the variety of ecclesiastical miracles with a reference to the wealth of variety in the animal kingdom. In the second, he argued that the greatest difference among ecclesiastical miracles is puny compared with ordinary differences among animals. It was, of course, a teasing *ad hominem* argument on Newman's part to write:

> There is far greater difference between the appearance of a horse or an eagle and a monkey, than between the most august of the Divine manifestations in Scripture and the meanest and most fanciful of those legends which we are accustomed without further examination to cast aside (p. 151).

But there was more to this argument than its apparent facetiousness. Newman quoted paragraph after paragraph from Hume's "Essay on Miracles," all of them emphasizing the uniformity of nature. He suggested that those who rejected ecclesiastical miracles because of their alleged difference from Scriptural miracles, towed the line set by the "skeptic [Hume] who . . . denies that the First Cause can act supernaturally at all, because in Nature he can act but naturally." He charged them with a "happy inconsistency" insofar as they "continue to believe the Scripture record, while they reject the records of the Church" (p. 157).

Well, something or somebody must have opened Newman's eyes. His reading of the miracles of the Old and New Testament had hardly anything in common with the way he had formerly recounted them in the *Essay on Miracles*. He now saw the Old Testament miracles as being of any of three classes: one class was formed by judicial or retributive miracles, wrought on a large field; another he described as miracles of mercy; and in between the two, chronologically as well, miracles "more or less of a romantic and poetical cast" (p. 166). But where the shackles fell most dramatically from his eyes concerned the demoniacs and their exorcisms. He now even spotted instances of the use of relics in the Bible. In the resurrection of the man whose body was touched by the bones of Elisha (2 Kings 23:11), he saw a perfect anticipation of so called ecclesiastical legends. If one admitted the

former, he argued, one had little reason not to consider the latter
seriously: "Their credibility turning first on whether they are
expected at all, and next whether they are avouched on sufficient evidence" (p. 169).

Then he came to the very essential inference to be drawn,
namely the identity of the prophetical and ecclesiastical office.
Clearly, Newman was way beyond his former narrow interpretation of the prophetical office of the Church as the mainstay of the
Via Media. Ecclesiastical miracles did not differ more from the
prophetical miracles than these differed from the ones in the
Books of the Law. For those, Newman wrote,

> who admit the Catholic doctrines as enunciated in the Creed,
> and commented upon by the Fathers, the subsequent expan-
> sion and variation of *supernatural* agency in the Church,
> instead of suggesting difficulties, will seem to be in corre-
> spondence, as they are contemporaneous, with the develop-
> ments and additions in dogmatic statements which have
> occurred between the Apostolic and the *present* age, and
> which are but a result and evidence of *spiritual* life (p. 171).

Newman might very well have put the emphasis on those three
italicized words because they were the essence of what he was
arguing about miracles in a broader ecclesiological context. Those
three words anticipated the thrust and conclusion of the *Development*, to be written within a year or so, and they sum up the
reason why he chose the Roman Catholic Church. Those three
words serve also as a badly needed corrective to the moving and
often quoted comment which Dean Church, Newman's close
friend, made on his conversion. According to Dean Church,
Newman left Canterbury for Rome because only in the latter did
he find the devotion and sacrifice that characterized the early
Church. Dean Church would have better served Newman had he
spoken not of devotion and self-sacrifice but simply of the
supernatural of which the kind of devotion and self-sacrifice he
held high were patent manifestations. Then he would have
touched that strictly theological note which alone interested
Newman, because it alone was germane to the question of
whether there was a God-given duty, valid for any and all, to

comply in full with God's supernatural dispensation. To speak of anything else was mere rhetorical flourish.

Indeed it was against that flourish, beautiful yet purely natural, that Newman warned as he opened the concluding part of his *Ecclesiastical Miracles* dealing with the state of the argument among Anglican writers on miracles around 1843. He found them wanting in the supernatural. First he spoke of a state of mind within which the Church figured in an uncannily deistic form. Within that picture the Church was "little more than a creed, or doctrine, introduced into the world once and for all, and then left to itself . . . unattended by any special Divine Presence or any immediately *supernatural* gift" (emphasis added). Yet, if one considered that such a presence in question was nothing less than the one inaugurated by the Incarnation, the conclusion was inescapable, and Newman drew it with relish: "We shall feel that no miracle can be great after it, nothing strange or marvellous, nothing beyond expectation" (pp. 184-85).

Hence there was only one alternative: to "disbelieve the divinity of the Church" (yes, these are Newman's very words, the words of an Anglican groping his way towards Rome) and do our best "to deny that the facts attested are miraculous, even admitting them to be true." For, if the Church is just another society of men, then it is only logical to attribute all miracles to purely natural agencies. But "if the Church be possessed of supernatural powers, it is not unnatural to refer to these the facts reported." In other words, "our view of the evidence will practically be decided by our view of theology" (p. 186). Instead of "theology," he could have just as well used the phrase "the supernatural."

In the rest of *Ecclesiastical Miracles,* Newman offered a magnificently theological and therefore supernatural recital of ecclesiastical miracles. But he prefaced that recital with pithy theological arguments: if one truly believed that the bodies of the saints were truly so many temples of the Holiest, and were to rise on the last day in full glory, it was hardly logical to frown on the use of their relics against evil spirits. In general:

> Where there is an admission of Catholic doctrines, there no prejudice will exist against Ecclesiastical Miracles, while those

who disbelieve among us the existence of the hidden Power, will eagerly avail themselves of every plea for explaining away its open manifestations (p. 188).

The "among us" then referred to a strictly Anglican ambiance. Today it may very well be applicable to various Catholic ambiances as well. Those caught there seem to forget that the Fathers of Vatican II, rightly or wrongly, did not speak of miracles (or of Purgatory and Hell) because they felt that such doctrines were too well embedded in Catholic consciences to need further emphasis. In such a policy, clearly misguided in retrospect, one can find a chief reason for the religious, theological illiteracy of so many Catholics today. Some of them were indeed taught (and in catechetical courses at that) to reach theological conclusions about the supernatural before they could read a single book on theology or any other serious book at all.

Those who taught them in this vein will have much to account for. For as Newman insisted, quoting the words of Saint Irenaeus (often spoken of as *the* theologian of Vatican II),

> *it is not possible to tell the number* of gifts which the Church throughout the world has received from God in the Name of Christ Jesus, who was crucified under Pontius Pilate, and exercises day by day for the benefit of the nations, neither seducing nor taking money of any (pp. 224-25).

Instead of explaining away what is unexplainable by human reason, those "teachers" should reflect on some truly prophetic words of Newman from the very last page of *Ecclesiastical Miracles*. While one could argue that some of the facts of once fantastically great miracles are not well known to us today, it would be utterly wrong to ignore that "the Fathers wrote for their contemporaries, not for modern notions and theories, for distant countries, for a degenerate people and a disunited Church" (p. 226). Only an Englishman could be entitled to write so bitingly about his own.

No less biting, though a bit humorous, was the remark which Newman made in the context of nine lectures delivered in Birmingham in the summer of 1851. Since those lectures, known subsequently as *The Present Position of Catholics in England*, were

addressed to the Brothers of the Oratory, Protestant Englishmen
were not to hear immediately that, according to Newman, "Tea
and toast, port wine, roast beef, goose at Michaelmas, these are
their great principles" (p. 296).[11] The remark was from the Eighth
Lecture in which Newman took miracles as a chief illustration of
his broader theme, namely the great difference between the first
principles assumed by Protestants and by Catholics. Imposition
of one's first principles on others Newman called bigotry, and he
made Protestants guilty on that score. They would never look
even for a moment into the possible merits of the first principles
assumed by Catholics. "Protestants, then, if any man alive, are,
on their own showing, bigots, if they set up their First Principles
as standards of all truth." English goods were not to be valued
by French measures. "Prove your First Principles and, if you
cannot, learn philosophic moderation" (pp. 293-94).

     With respect to miracles, Newman was far from disputing
the Protestant view that "the Catholic Church, from east to west,
from north to south, is, according to our conceptions, hung with
miracles." In fact, no Protestant could have given a more vivid
catalogue of Catholic relics than Newman did. After a breathless
page and a half he stopped:

> I need not continue the catalogue; here what one party urges,
> the other admits; they join issue over the fact; that fact is the
> claim of miracles on the part of the Catholic Church; it is the
> Protestants' charge, and it is our glory (p. 301).

Newman was not to be bogged down into arguing that, say, St.
Philip Neri's miracles were very credible. He limited himself to
portraying the role which respective First Principles played in the
dispute. The Protestant's "First Principle *blocks* belief" in ecclesiastical miracles, because according to that Principle what God has
wrought once he would not do again. On the other hand,
Newman continued, diminish as one may the evidence on behalf
of a miraculous application of a relic, as long as there remains
some evidence on its behalf, "you would not altogether wean the

---

[11] This and subsequent numbers in the text refer to *Present Position of
Catholics in England* in the Longmans edition of Newman's collected works.

Catholic's mind from belief in it; for his First Principle *encourages* such belief" (p. 302). He himself emphasized those two words.

Not only did Newman feel encouraged but he made a profession of faith in miracles that is still most encouraging to read:

> I firmly believe that portions of the True Cross are at Rome and elsewhere, that the Crib of Bethlehem is at Rome, and the bodies of St. Peter and St. Paul also. I believe that at Rome too lies St. Stephen, that St. Matthew lies at Salerno, and St. Andrew at Amalfi. . . . I firmly believe that saints in their lifetime have before now raised the dead to life, crossed the sea without vessels, multiplied grain and bread, cured incurable diseases, and superseded the operation of the laws of the universe in a multitude of ways (pp. 311-12).

One wonders whether of Newman's many endorsements of ecclesiastical miracles, there would be a single one, that would put more on the spot the present-day minimizing approach in Catholic theology to miracles.

Moreover, just as in *Ecclesiastical Miracles*, in that Eighth Lecture too, he set up the genuineness of one's belief in the Incarnation as the litmus test for his readiness to believe in any and all miracles.

> Catholics . . . hold the mystery of the Incarnation; and the Incarnation is the most stupendous event which ever can take place on earth; and after it and henceforth, I do not see how we can scruple at any miracle on the mere ground of its being unlikely to happen. No miracle can be so great as that which took place in the Holy House of Nazareth; it is indefinitely more difficult to believe than all the miracles of the Breviary, of the Martyrology, of Saints' lives, of legends, of local traditions, put together. . . . If, through divine grace, we once are able to accept the solemn truth that the Supreme Being was born of a mortal woman, what is there to be imagined which can offend us on the ground of its marvellousness (p. 307).

No "progressive" Catholic theologian would feel comfortable with Newman's argument that if one admits the miracle of Incarnation, the most inconceivable of all miracles, then it makes no sense to be squeamish about miracles of far less magnitude. Whether such Catholic theologians would perceive the connection between the resurgence of Arianism in Catholic theology, is another matter. At times the process is rather covert, such as when the great dogmatic declarations of Nicea and Chalcedon are taken for a mere beginning in fathoming the mystery of Incarnation. At times the process is all too obvious, as in the case of Hans Küng, who precisely because of this was deprived of his status as a Catholic theologian. The same type of Catholic theologian would be even more willing to oppose openly the First Principle formulated by Newman: "When God begins [working miracles], he goes on" (p. 306). The newfangled theologizing in terms of existentialism and phenomenology has certainly prepared the way for a distrust in the principle of continuity. For this too Newman had a prophetic warning. It would be dishonest, he wrote, to expect a Protestant to hold Catholic Principles, and it would be no less dishonest to expect Catholics to think and act in terms of Protestant First Principles: "though we should be partners to a fraud, if we thought like Protestants, we surely are not because we think like Catholics" (p. 311).

The broader British public was first alerted to the content of those lectures through a letter that appeared in the *Times*. This aroused Dr Samuel Hinds, Bishop of Norwich, who in a public meeting denounced Newman for raising ecclesiastical miracles to the level of Scripture miracles, or rather for lowering the latter to the level of the former.

The ensuing correspondence between Hinds and Newman has one point worth recalling.[12] Hinds could hardly be proud to be told by Newman that he had already treated the question of ecclesiastical miracles at great length in 1843. He sent a copy to Hinds. In his letters to Hinds, Newman restricted himself to clearing up some definitional misunderstandings. He did not touch on the thrust of that Eighth Lecture which is of capital importance for understanding Newman's approach to and

---

[12] The principal pieces of that correspondence are reprinted at the end of the Longmans edition of the *Present Position of Catholics in England*.

understanding of miracles, especially as connected with the relics of martyrs and saints.

In fact, Newman did not seem to think much of his essays on miracles even when Kingsley's attack forced him to speak of, among other things, his views on miracles. It was, of course, logical that in Appendix 5 of the *Apologia* Newman should quote at length from that Eighth Lecture, because Kingsley had identified the Catholic approach to miracles as credulity. Yet one cannot help being puzzled by the fact that Newman did not refer to at least the second and longer essay of his on miracles when he dealt at great length in the *Apologia* on his spiritual development during the years immediately preceding his conversion.

From what has already been quoted here from *Ecclesiastical Miracles* it should be clear that he expressed in that work convictions that he must have known to be incompatible with the official Anglican reaction to Tract 90. In fact he spoke in this vein in his letters to Pusey and Hope written in the summer of 1843. It was about that time that the series *Lives of the Saints*, in which he had an active part, sharpened his divergence from the Church of England. No wonder. Those lives, including the lives of British saints, were full of miracles.

Ecclesiastical Miracles provides Newman's clearest public testimony about his having genuinely Catholic convictions on a crucial issue at least two years before his conversion. That Newman had those two essays on miracles reprinted as a single volume in 1870 is not without significance of its own.[13] It proves, if further proof were needed, that his opposition to the definition of papal infallibility did not stem on his part from a lack, as was the case with some others, of genuine belief in the supernatural. He knew that the supernatural, as anchored in the Incarnation, had its most strenuous defenders in those who occupied the chair of Peter. He knew that Peter was established as the Rock, so that he and his successors might stand with rocklike solidity on behalf of Jesus' divinity, the source of all miracles in the Church through all ages.[14]

---

[13] *Two Essays on Scripture Miracles and on Ecclesiastical Miracles* (London: Basil Montague Pickering, 1870).

[14] See on this connection ch. 6, "Jesus of the Rock," in the third enlarged

Critics of Newman's defense of miracles invariably failed to see that their real differences with Newman on this point went much deeper than technical questions of logic or historical documentation. T. H. Huxley certainly displayed this failure when at the age of seventy-four he took up the cudgels against Newman's defense of miracles. Newman was by then eighty-nine and had for some time ceased to engage in any controversy. At any rate, he could have merely said in reply that his and Huxley's first principles were poles apart. In his "Agnosticism and Christianity," of which about a third was devoted to Newman,[15] Huxley could have hardly been less emphatic in stating his view that anything supernatural, even the idea of a personal God, was a sheer abomination to a scientifically trained mind. What a science, what a training, what a mind!

Huxley's picking on this or that biblical and ecclesiastical miracle is best left aside. A surgeon turned biologist, he should have gone to Lourdes, which he dismissed with a flourish, if he was really interested in facts that baffled not a few eminent colleagues of his. Only a dozen years later, a young French surgeon went there and saw something take place under his very eyes which remains perhaps the best attested sudden cure of what had been diagnosed by a dozen doctors as a lethal condition.[16] Huxley could not have questioned young Carrel's grim empiricism, nor his achievements on which much of 20th-century surgery is based and which won for Carrel the Nobel Prize in 1912.

But did empirical science have anything to do with Huxley's insistence on the "Nazarenism" of James, Peter and John, for which Jesus was a mere man? Scientists in their old days are apt to wax philosophical, all too often to their own discomfiture. They invariably achieve this unhappy result when they wax theological. Only the theologian in Huxley could be agitated over

edition of my *And on this Rock: The Witness of One Land and Two Covenants* (Front Royal, VA: Christendom Press, 1997).

[15] The article, first published in *The Nineteenth Century* (May, 1889) was reissued in Huxley's *Science and the Christian Tradition*.

[16] For details, see my introduction to Carrel's *Voyage to Lourdes* (Fraser MI.: Real View Books, 1994).

the pernicious influence of Tractarianism within the Church of England, which he wanted free of that evil. Did he suggest thereby that the Church of England had hitherto exuded so little of the supernatural as not be an offense to his radical naturalism? Why should someone like Huxley have discussed theology in general and miracles in particular, when the only certainty for him was the inverse square law?[17]

Similar considerations are in order about the book-length criticism of Newman's *Ecclesiastical Miracles*, which the educator and philologist E. A. Abbott published a year after Newman's death, under the title, *Philomythus*.[18] There was little point in picking holes in Newman's histories of some miracles if one's view of Christ was the one set forth in Sir John Robert Seeley's *Ecce Homo* (1865), a purely humanistic account of Jesus as one who never worked a miracle, which Newman did not spare of appropriate comments right there and then.[19] Already Abbott's first shot at Newman made it plain that no serious argument was to be expected from him. Clearly, Abbott made a mountain out of a molehill in reporting the still Anglican Newman's remark that Wiseman was an "unscrupulous controversialist." This matched Abbott's account of the Newman-Kingsley controversy as a mere sham as far as Newman's argumentation was concerned!

Then came the Abbé Bremond's *Mystery of Newman*, which undoubtedly is the most accomplished mystification of Newman's person and thought. The foregoing numerous samples of Newman's views on miracles should at least indicate the

[17] Such was the gist of Huxley's refusal to accept Kingsley's overtures that, following the tragic death of his seven-year-old son, he should consider the hope of immortality.

[18] E. A. Abbott's *Philomythus: an Antidote against Credulity: A Discussion on Cardinal Newman's Essay on Ecclesiastical Miracles* (1891) is a 300-page-long book, which came out in two editions within a few months, in evidence of the "educated" public's interest, not so much in serious argumentation as in verbal sparring.

[19] Since Seeley said nothing on Jesus' miracles, Newman made no mention of them in his review of *Ecce Homo* in *The Month* (June 1866), reprinted as the last chapter in *Discussions and Arguments*. Newman's concluding remark, "do not attempt to halve a spiritual unit" (p. 398), echoes a dictum of his quoted above.

enormity of Bremond's self-deception. Nothing is indeed so misleading as his claim that in perusing those extraordinary stories Newman "forces himself, and with great difficulty, to believe in them." Newman's faith, Bremond continues, does not rest on miracles; Newman's faith "tries to stretch itself so as to include them, and only succeeds with difficulty." Bremond ignored the question of whether Newman accepted the miracle of Incarnation, of which he spoke perhaps nowhere more movingly than in the *Ecclesiastical Miracles*, on a purely subjective basis. Nor did Bremond explain how so much credulity could flourish within a Newman whom he also called "the least credulous of men."[20] To crown the comedy, Bremond expected the science of psychology to clear up the uncertainties of theology. Less hazardous would it be to entrust a cabbage patch to goats.

Surely Newman was a most sensitive man, with fully extended intuitive antennas to detect any sign from the supernatural. As such he was wont to read the direct acting of Providence into sundry coincidences. He had a predilection for the number seven and for its tenfold multiples.[21] But he had an even more sustained fondness for logic and clear arguments. Most importantly, he was ready to give up everything for truth, a feature which none of his critics, whether writing about miracles or anything else, could boast of.

He was ready to sacrifice everything natural, convinced as he was of the incomparably higher value of the supernatural as mediated by the Church. Herein lies his perennial challenge. Those latter-day Newmanists, who celebrate him as the prophet of *aggiornamento* but at times fail to say a single word about Newman's sustained attention to miracles during the crucial year of 1843, hardly do justice to that challenge.[22] An additional

[20] H. Bremond, *The Mystery of Newman*, with an introduction by G. Tyrrell, tr. H. C. Corrance (London: Williams and Norgate, 1907), p. 104.

[21] For details, see W. Ward, *The Life of John Henry Cardinal Newman* (New York: Longmans Green & Co., 1912), vol. 2, pp. 342-44.

[22] Examples are C. Hollis, *Newman and the Modern World* (Garden City, N.Y. Doubleday, 1968); M. Trevor, *Newman: The Pillar of the Cloud* (London: Macmillan, 1962); and also her *Prophets and Guardians: Renewal and Tradition in the Church* (Garden City, N.Y.: Doubleday, 1969). Clearly there is far more

challenge they have to face is the publication of his *Letters and Diaries*. The material they contain will for many years keep Newmanites busy, and rightly so, because Newman looked upon correspondence as being more expressive of the person than published writings. Certainly, in respect to miracles Newman's letters contain statements that will prove bitter pills to swallow for those who try to set him up as a model of "civilized" theologians not "overzealous" about the supernatural.

Take, for instance, his reply to Henry Wilberforce, not yet a Catholic, who asked him whether he believed that Saint Rose at the age of three months practiced mortification on her fingers. Newman's first remark was that he would not, of course, believe such stories in the manner in which he held that even a touch of deliberate doubt about the Incarnation was a serious sin. But he noted that the very fact of Incarnation, which implies that "our Lord's human mind received from His Godhead as perfect a knowledge of all things as it has now," introduced "a new idea, a new (if not law, yet) order of things." Therefore stories like the one reported about the infant Saint Rose must be looked upon in a supernaturally channelled perspective of a new whole, anchored in the Immaculate Conception of Mary, who, "though she *grew* in all graces, yet had a consciousness and active intellect from the moment of her conception."

What happened to Saint Rose may have been a participation, on a lower level, "for what I know, of the same gift." That it might have happened, that one could not be sure that it did not, that one was to venerate it if it did happen, that the mere chance of its having happened was an object of veneration—all this, Newman argued, "is part of a whole, one out of a number of sacred facts which belong to a saint, and to be viewed as such." Therefore, although one did not have to accept it categorically, nevertheless one was to adore "God who is so wonderful in His Saints." He allowed that this view may seem unnatural to Wilberforce, but not to him, because, as he put it by emphasizing

in Newman's two discussions of miracles than that the second anticipates some of the logical methods he was to use in the *Grammar of Assent* as I. Ker would have it in his *John Henry Newman* (Oxford: University Press, 1990), see p. 28.

it graphically too, A SAINT IS A PECULIAR BEING.[23] Certainly, if we may add, to those who are not saints. That saints did not appear peculiar to Newman is a vote on behalf of his canonization. Compared with all this, quite "innocent" from the progressive theological perspective should seem Newman's urging the still Anglican T. W. Allies to visit all the places in Italy where a miracle similar to the blood of Saint Januarius takes place.[24] Without the slightest qualification Newman reported about the same time a miraculous cure that took place in Birmingham through the instrumentality of a relic of Saint Philip Neri. A dying factory girl, a convert who had no taste for miracles, "heard a voice within her say 'Dust and ashes, get up and walk'." And she did. Two months later Newman reported another very similar incident.[25]

Newman's dicta on miracles are a sharp challenge, for instance, to those who expect Newman's canonization to take place without miracles having been performed through his intercession, because this would be "the really English way." Yet, unless Catholics in England and elsewhere storm Heaven for miracles, that canonization will not be forthcoming. This may perhaps please their progressive kind, but this is not the kind of progress Newman would have ever countenanced. Advocates of that progress might invite his stricture, quoted above, about "a degenerate people and a disunited Church." Newman would have fully endorsed John Paul II, who, on the occasion of his first visit to Lourdes, noted a decline in the number of miracles there and urged Catholics to pray more fervently for miracles to happen.

Catholics who under the pressure of *aggiornamento* pretend, for instance, that they are not seriously committed even when they are, may find themselves challenged in Newman's various statements quoted in this essay. Those among them who refer to a sermon of his where he apparently discounted miracles should at least not overlook plain chronology. The sermon, "Miracles no Remedy for Unbelief," was preached by Newman in 1839, four

[23] *Letters and Diaries*, vol. 13, pp, 3-4.
[24] Ibid., p. 216.
[25] Ibid., p. 330.

full years before 1843. Most importantly, Newman kept saying in 1843 that miracles were a rich nourishment for the believer. He would indeed have given a lesson in elementary logic to anyone oblivious to the enormous difference between those two propositions, one concerning unbelievers, the other believers.

The supernatural in recent Catholic theology is treated according to a dubious procedure: the advocacy of the supernatural is couched in copious references to the natural, with insufficient attention to the possibility that one may have on hand merely the advocacy of the natural couched in vague hints about the supernatural. The dangers which this poses to Catholicism are to be met head on. Few means may prepare one so effectively to face those dangers as a meditative perusal of Newman's essays on miracles, especially the one on the miracles still performed within the ever-living Church. Such is the gist of the challenge which Newman sets forth in those essays. Only if that challenge of his is taken seriously will Newman be a genuine guide in the search not simply for truth, but for Truth writ large.

4

Angels, Brutes, and the Light of Faith

"We have more real knowledge about the Angels than about the brutes." Such a statement, obscurantist at first look, would not be worth considering had it not been penned and preached by John Henry Newman. The statement is in fact his nutshell summary of the sermon, "The Invisible World," which he preached in 1837, at the very height of his intellectual and moral leadership of the Oxford Movement.[1] The sermon antedates by less than two decades his lectures on the idea of a university which was catholic, or truly universal in its purview precisely because it was unabashedly Catholic. In those lectures Newman called that purview the privilege of an "imperial intellect," an epithet rightly applicable to the powers and sincerity of his mind.[2]

Obviously, one cannot assume one thing about Newman as he set up that strange disproportion between the respective measures of our knowledge of angels and of brutes. We cannot assume that Newman ignored the vast fund of knowledge about animals that was on hand in 1837, two decades or so before the first edition of Darwin's *Origin of Species* sold out within a few

---

[1] The sermon is part (pp. 200-213) of the fourth volume of Newman's *Parochial and Plain Sermons*, first published in 1838, and reprinted many times afterwards. References are to the edition by Longmans, Green and Co (London, 1899). For Newman's statement, see pp. 205-06.

[2] *The Idea of a University* (8th ed.; London: Longmans, Green and Co., 1888), p. 461. In his modesty, Newman took that epithet for a succinct characterization of a true university.

hours. Nor can one assume that Newman would have deliberately slighted the numerous editions, not only in the French
original but also in English translation, of the many volumes of
Buffon's *Histoire naturelle* bursting with data on the realm of the
brutes. It is also most unlikely that Newman had not heard of
Cuvier who, as if by magic, had reconstructed, from small bones,
entire skeletons not only of still living species but also of long
extinct ones.

None of this can be assumed on the part of one who was
elected fellow of Oriel largely on the strength of his mathematics
and who for some years still took a keen interest in various
branches of the natural sciences.[3] His astounding claim that we
know more about angels than about brutes poses therefore a
challenge worth exploring. And all the more so as he meant that
claim to serve for a startling backdrop to a no less startling
proposition to which he assigned an even greater degree of
reality: "We are then in a world of spirits, as well as in a world of
sense, and we hold communion with it, and take part in it,
though we are not conscious of doing so."[4]

In 1837 Newman was just entering a crucial phase of his
theological development. For the next three years he tried to
work out the idea of a Via Media between Romanism and
Protestantism. That idea was to serve as the theological capstone
of the Tractarian Movement (or Oxford Movement) which he had
been spearheading since 1833. By 1840 or so Newman began to
suspect that the Via Media existed only on paper and was a
version of that private judgment which invariably invited the
reduction of the supernatural to a glorified version of the natural.

That the restoration of the sense of the supernatural, and
nothing else, was the chief motivation of the Oxford Movement,
Newman set forth in twelve lectures in 1850 for the benefit of
those fellow Tractarians who had failed to follow him into the
Catholic Church. These lectures, which he himself liked to call
Anglican Difficulties, remain Newman's truly prophetic work, far
surpassing in prophetic power what he offered about the

[3.]See Chapter 11 on Newman and science in this book.
[4.]*Parochial and Plain Sermons*, vol. 4, p. 205.

Prophetic Office of the Church as part of his elaborating the idea of a Via Media.

The book should seem particularly prophetic in view of the latest manifestations of the logic that forces the Church of England to renounce the supernatural ever more palpably. Women's ordination in that Church exposes now in full the pathetic nature of what Newman, right at the outset of his *Anglican Difficulties,* called a "mimic Catholicism". The same logic of naturalism which conferred a pseudo-supernatural halo on feminism through that ordination, recently prompted the Archbishop of York to speak of the "biology of the soul"[5] and reduce its survival after death to its continued existence in the mind of God. His Grace carefully skirted the question of whether the self created by God was strictly spiritual or just a manifestation of bodily processes. He equally ignored whether the same theologically coated naturalistic reasoning—"the continuity of the self is rooted in the faithfulness of God towards what he has created"—would not also reduce those pure spirits called angels to beings that exist only in the mind of God.

All this would have deeply shocked the Anglican Newman. For him the souls of the departed were no less real than were the angels, including the guardian angel of each and every soul, whether still in the body or already separated from it. With an eye on the Bible he said in that sermon: "No Christian is so humble but he has Angels to attend him." With an eye on the Bible he spoke of angels as "our fellow workers."[6] With an eye on the Bible he spoke with assurance about the angels' nature, destiny, and function, however mysterious to us. But no more mysterious, he added, than that multitude of beasts, "so various in their natures, so strange and wild in their shapes, living on the earth without ascertainable object."[7] Obviously Newman did not wish to dispute Buffon or Cuvier or any of the great naturalists of the eighteenth and early nineteenth centuries. He merely wanted to drive home that all our vast knowledge about animals

---

[5] See *The Times* (London), Nov. 8, 1994, p. 4.
[6] "The Invisible World," p. 204.
[7] Ibid., p. 206.

leaves us in utter ignorance about the really important questions about them, whereas to similar questions about the angels we have been given clear answers in Revelation. Then he quoted verse after verse from the letters of St Paul and St Peter to show that true Christian life is lived in the presence of angels. He exposed the vanity of men who lord it over others and over the earth whereas, in truth, this earth "has other lords beside them, and is the scene of a higher conflict than they are capable of conceiving. It contains Christ's little ones whom they despise, and His angels whom they disbelieve; and these at length shall take possession of it and be manifested."[8]

Newman then turned one's duty to care for Nature (the environment, one would say today) into a chapter on angelology. It was springtide when he preached on the "invisible world." The bursting into blossoms of a dormant nature was for him not a topic for its own sake, although no present-day ecologist could have spoken with greater tenderness about something as little as a single petal. In the inevitable rejuvenation of nature he saw the pledge of the eventual turning of nature into a world hidden to physical eyes but not to the eyes of faith: "A world of Saints and Angels, a glorious world, the palace of God, the mountains of the Lord of Hosts, the heavenly Jerusalem, the throne of God and Christ."[9]

He was ready to stand up for that vision of a world replete with angels and governed by them. The sermon he preached on the Feast of Saint Michael, in 1834, may send shivers down the spine of all moderns imbued with the idea that nature obeys laws and nothing else. Whatever strictures some dark ages deserved for attributing too much to angels, it was not too much, Newman claimed, to attribute to angels all the world's motions, local and cosmic: "The sin of what is called an educated age, such as our own, is just the reverse: to account slightly of them [angels], or not at all; to ascribe all we see around us, not to their agency, but to certain assumed laws of nature. This, I say, is likely to be our sin, in proportion as we are initiated into the

8. Ibid., p. 208.
9. Ibid., p. 210.

learning of this world." And he singled out "chemistry, geology and the like" as putting us in "the danger of resting on things seen, and forgetting unseen things, and our ignorance about them."[10]

Clearly, Newman was not one of those ready to smile at medieval Christian versions of Ptolemaic astronomy, where angelic powers were credited with the motion of celestial bodies. He would have immensely rejoiced had he known what was to be unearthed only a decade or so after his death. I mean the full facts about that epoch-making moment in the history of science when Buridan, around 1350, postulated inertial motion for celestial bodies. For Buridan was not a forerunner of Voltaire in claiming that the material world runs like a clockwork mechanism, utterly left to itself after being once wound up and let go. Cherish as he did the image of the world as a clockwork, Buridan pointedly noted that bodies once created remain in existence only through that divine power which theologians had long ago called conservation, as distinct from creation. By dispensing with motor intelligences (angels), Buridan merely kept physics distinct from metaphysics and theology, the only way to safeguard the activity of angels in the physical world, an activity in which he believed no less firmly than Newman did.

It is that distinction which undergirds Newman's apparent slightings of science in that sermon on Saint Michael and his hosts. He had very clear notions about the limits of scientific laws. They were good for prediction, for a vast range of practical uses, but they had nothing to say about what physical things and processes were and why they stayed in existence at all. The world not only had to be created but also to be sustained as well as kept in motion. In that latter work, God relied on his angels, so Newman declared: "Every breath of air, and ray of light and heat, every beautiful prospect, is, as it were, the skirts of their garments, the waving of the robes of those whose faces see God in heaven." Newman was so serious on this point that he asked whether it was not "as philosophical . . . to refer the movements

10."The Powers of Nature," *Parochial and Plain Sermons*, vol. 2, p. 359.

of the natural world to them, as to attempt to explain them by certain theories of science."[11]

Once more he affirmed the great usefulness of the methods of science but only within strict confines. He knew that those laws do not "explain." They merely coordinate data. Anyone ready to ascribe relevance to scientific laws outside these confines ran the risk, according to Newman, of becoming "a poor weak worm and miserable sinner," not merely by putting nature in the place of God but also by slighting "the agency of the thousands and ten thousands of His unseen Servants." Scientific discourse on nature has to be a religious discourse "as in the hearings of the great Servants of God, with the sort of diffidence which we always feel when speaking before the learned and wise of our own mortal race, as poor beginners in intellectual knowledge, as well as in moral attainments."[12]

A rough and rude approach toward nature, indeed the useless destruction of a single petal, did, in Newman's eyes, to the robes of angels what such treatment would do to the hem of the garments of one's fellow men. Anticipating the charge that all this smacked of rank exaggeration, he asked whether one was to assume that Scriptures spoke of angels for nothing and not for very practical purposes. And, though still a dozen years away from his conversion to the Catholic Church, he revealed something of his instinctive Catholicism when he disposed of the polity, typically Protestant, that called for the abandonment of a practice just because it could be carried to an extreme: "The abuse of a thing does not supersede the use of it." In calling this "the principle of our Church,"[13] he spoke, yet unbeknownst to himself, as a Catholic who is resolved not to engage in the Protestant error of throwing the baby out with the bathwater, whether that water is really dirty or is merely imagined to be such.

Veneration of the angels had to be acted out in daily lives lest "we make the contemplation of them a mere feeling, and a

[11] Ibid. p. 362.
[12] Ibid., p. 365.
[13] Ibid.

sort of luxury of the imagination." He wanted an angelology that went far beyond mere phrases, however soaring. Or as he put it at the very end of his sermon: "Many a man can write and talk beautifully about them [angels], who is not at all better or nearer heaven for all his excellent words."[14]

The so-called new Catholic theology contains many examples of a discourse on angels which is not even beautiful, theologically that is, whatever the rhetorical gloss. A very recent instance is the article, "Angels," in *The New Dictionary of Catholic Spirituality*.[15] Its thrust is the very opposite of Newman's priceless principle that "the abuse of a thing does not supersede the use of it," apart from the tendentious overblowing of the extent of the abuse.

Newman had well in advance discredited the further claim in that article that patristic angelology is largely a neoplatonist graft on biblical parlance. Long before the ultra-Platonist Pseudo-Dionysius came up with his esoteric choirs of angels, there was enough Platonism in the Alexandrian School of theologians, who, with Athanasius in the lead, were Newman's chief theological masters. Yet they taught Newman, so he stated in the *Apologia*, a biblically realistic view of angels. He learned from them to revere the angels "not only as the ministers employed by the Creator in the Jewish and Christian dispensations, as we find on the face of Scripture, but as carrying on, as Scripture implies, the Economy of the Visible World." Then he referred to his sermon of 1832, on Saint Michael.[16]

For Newman, a professed respect for a truly christological angelology called for including at least a brief reference to Christ's stern warning about scandalizing those little ones whose angels constantly see the face of God (Mt 18:10). But there is not a reference in that article in *The New Dictionary* (whose author purports to restore the central character of Christ's mediation) to the dozen or so cases when in the New Testament our Lord's mediation is in turn mediated through angels, from his concep-

---

[14.]Ibid., p. 367.
[15.]Edited by M. Downey (Collegeville, MN.: The Liturgical Press, 1993), pp. 38-41.
[16.]*Apologia pro vita sua*, ch. 2.

tion to his resurrection and beyond. Much less is it recommended there that a good Christian should invoke the intercession of angels, and in particular, of his guardian angel.

The mediation which Newman most intently hoped to obtain from his own guardian angel is described in *The Dream of Gerontius*. For the soul of Gerontius is his own, carried by his guardian angel past the howling choirs of devils towards the throne of God. Of course, only that poem's esthetic beauty, enhanced by Elgar's music, appeals to most moderns. Its vividly concrete theological content is alien to most, who are delighted to hear the Archbishop of York declare that "hell is not regarded as a serious option these days."[17] Newman would say that hell, heaven, angels and devils form one indivisible whole on the landscape of the supernatural.

And this is what Newman asserted in a series of four sermons he preached on angels on four consecutive Sundays in September 1860. Those sermons exist only in outline,[18] but they fully evidence the continuity between the attention which Newman the Anglican paid to the reality of the supernatural world of angels and devils and the firmness with which he preached about that reality as a Catholic. The fourth of those sermons is about guardian angels, not only of individual souls but of entire celestial bodies as well. In fact, the outline of that sermon includes a reference to his sermon preached in 1832 on Saint Michael and his celestial hosts.

The first of those sermon outlines echoes in a nutshell his claim that we know much more about angels than about the brutes and indeed about the entire physical world. For only after sketching the marvels of angelic knowledge—"Their knowledge most comprehensive . . . whereas the greatest philosophers with pains knew a little"—did Newman conclude: "Many wonderful things in this world, but an angel more wonderful than all. If a creature so wonderful, what the Creator?"

[17.]*The Times* (London), November 8, 1994, p. 4.

[18.]*Sermon Notes of John Henry Cardinal Newman. 1849-1878*, edited by the Fathers of the Oratory (London: Longmans, Green and Co.: 1913), pp. 160-67.

But, as always, Newman was much more interested in the fate of individuals than in the cultural fate or progress of mankind. For individuals alone could be saved for eternal life. The "imperial intellect" fearlessly stated in his *Idea of a University* that "in the province of physiology and moral philosophy, our race's progress and perfectibility is a dream, because Revelation contradicts it, whatever may be plausibly argued on its behalf by scientific inquirers."[19] In quoting this passage, the editors of those sermon outlines added: "In other words, the history of man on this planet is to end in Antichrist and the triumph of wickedness."[20]

This comment was most warranted as far as Newman's thinking about angels and his sermon notes are concerned. For in that outline he speaks also of the Guardian Angels to whom Judas and the Antichrist himself are confided. Once more Newman is consistent. The one who gave consistency as the hallmark of saints merely gives here too a glimpse of the saint he was.

It is this saintly Newman, saintly to the hilt in his theology in general and his angelology in particular, who poses the great stumbling block to the juggernaut of theological and spiritual liberalism. The various coachmen (and more lately coachwomen too) of that juggernaut have heavily banked on the trick of expropriating Newman to themselves. They are the ones to set up Newman as the guiding spirit of Vatican II, by which they all too often mean their Vatican III if not IV.

In view of the foregoing it should be easy to imagine what Newman's reaction would be to the fact, largely unnoticed, that the prolific texts of Vatican II contain not a single passage worth mentioning about angels, guardian or other. Perhaps, in a strange consistency with this, those texts include no significant mention of hell and devils either.

One cannot help recalling Cardinal Ratzinger's undoubtedly most sincere plea in the Messori report that the Council Fathers felt that such and similar items were too well engraved in the

---

[19.]*The Idea of a University,* p. 273.
[20.]*Sermon Notes,* p. 341.

minds of the faithful to need renewed emphasis. This plea was offered ten years ago, at a time when it was all too clear that hardly anything specific was by then engraved on the minds of younger Catholics raised on new booklets of instruction. Their compilers all too often avoided even the word "catechism" while busily promoting shops that sell colored crayons.

This omission, however well-intentioned, of points of faith from the catechetical instruction has created gaping holes in Catholic consciousness. All too many Catholics, especially in the developed world, have been treated to woefully little about angels. There have been some new treatises on angels about whose authors Newman's words, already quoted, may not be altogether inapplicable: "many a man can write and talk beautifully about them [angels], who is not at all better or nearer heaven for all his excellent words." For the beautiful style and novel approach all too often go hand in hand with that theological pride which sees too much dirty bathwater around the baby handed down by a tradition, in which such authors are reluctant to see Tradition writ large.

The spiritual desert thus created will not automatically be rejuvenated by the publication of the *New Catechism*. Its genuine espousal of supernatural reality is already the target of reinterpretations by liberals. Once more they prove that the hallmark of liberalism is a deep-seated intolerance of the supernatural. Spokesmen of theological liberalism will try to obliterate from Catholic memory anything that concretely brings back to the mind the true real world, the supernatural. Very few among those who graduated from American and European seminaries during the last thirty years have the habit of reciting the prayer which was still on the lips (and in Latin at that) of their forebears half a century ago: "Angel of God, my guardian dear, to whom His love commits me here, ever this day be at my side, to light and guard, to rule and guide."

Yet in this short prayer more sound theology is contained and conveyed than in "theological investigations" about angels that were inspired, in part, by the writings of that Immanuel Kant who once wrote of himself: "I am an Archangel!" and went on to state repeatedly: "I am God!"[21] The archetype for this self-enrichment was none other than Lucifer. If one looks for the source of the pride, of the self-sufficiency, of the naturalism that heavily mark much of the so-called new theology, one merely has to look in the direction of the camp that still breeds Aquikantists. They are the barren offspring of the shotgun wedding engineered by "enlightened" theological faculties between Aquinas and Kant.

Aquikantists were overjoyed when the invocation of Saint Michael after mass was dropped as a first step toward the new liturgy. Of course, the mass had been said for almost nineteen-hundred years without closing it with the request that Saint Michael be our protection against the wickedness and snares of the devil. But never was and never would the Kingdom of the supernatural, that is, the Church, be spared the onslaughts of the Evil One. Nor would that Church ever succeed in resisting the hordes of the Evil One and all their craftiness without the assistance of the heavenly host.

With a craftiness unexcelled, the Evil One knows how to fill the place of genuine goods with their counterfeits. The present craze for angels is a symptom of such a treacherous transaction. It would indeed be a huge mistake to see too readily in that craze a craving for the truly supernatural, of which angels are the classic touchstone of truth, to slightly rephrase Maritain's felicitous remark. That craze will not be cured and that craving will not be satiated by theologians who liberally drag their feet when it comes to delivering that priceless commodity called the supernatural. In doing so they promise a cure with placebos.

Much of the cure would be on hand if a sincere attention were given to Newman's claim that through the light of faith the realm of angels looms far more real than all the flora and fauna around us. Newman's clarity of perception is all the more needed because it has become a theological fad to believe that in saving the environment we will have saved our very souls. It may be that the angels whom Newman saw with the eyes of faith

[21]For documentation and details, see my Gifford Lectures, *The Road of Science and the Ways to God* (Chicago: University of Chicago Press, 1978), pp. 125 and 381, and my *Angels, Apes and Men* (La Salle, IL.: Sherwood Sugden, 1983), pp. 30-34.

everywhere, and whose chief duty is to sing God's glory, can weep not only about souls but also about Nature. But today Newman would insist (as a part of his challenge to his fellow Catholics) that if angels weep, they weep above all for the countless souls caught in a crisis that has not been seen in the Church for a long time.

5

Convert and Converts:
An Existential Ecclesiology

Newman emerges more and more as possibly the most prominent convert in all post-Reformation time. Now that the Church
has officially recognized the heroic character of his virtues, it is
not daring to say that his conversion was truly a heroic act in the
moral sense. The heroic measure of his mind's involvement in his
conversion could be seen from the moment when, a month or so
after his conversion, his *Development of Christian Doctrine* came off
the press. Almost twenty years later, his *Apologia pro vita sua*
made clear to any and all the utter honesty of each of his steps
toward what he called the One True Fold.

Those two immortal books made public record Newman's
claim that he would not have left the Church of England for any
reason other than that he could not see in it the One True Fold,
or the God-ordained haven of salvation. He had already made
this claim privately in the twenty or so letters he had written on
October 8, 1845. It was the eve of his being received into that
very Fold. Among the recipients were Faber, Manning, Pusey,
Church, Woodgate, Allies, and Dodsworth. Each of these found
in the letter written to him the phrase, "One True Fold." Biographers of Newman at times do not even make a generic reference
to this facet of those letters.[1]

---

[1] Not even such a reference can be found in the two pages (pp. 316-17)
which I. Ker devoted to that all-important day in his *John Henry Newman: A*

At least one of those letters, the one Newman wrote to Church, eventually dean of St Paul's in London, should have struck any careful biographer of Newman as a document of more than momentary interest. In witness to their deep friendship, Newman addressed Church as *charissime*. He would never forget that Church as Provost had vetoed the proposal that the University of Oxford censure Tract 90. Only in that letter to Church did Newman give details about Father Dominic, "a simple, holy man, and withal gifted with remarkable powers. He does not know of my intention, but I mean to ask of him admission into the One Fold of Christ."[2] A month later Newman wrote to Church: "There are several things I want to say to you, if you will give me half an hour some day."[3]

Nothing would have been easier for Church than to walk a good half hour from Oxford to Littlemore or to ask him for a meeting somewhere in Oxford. Church did not communicate again with Newman until after the publication of the *Apologia*, when their erstwhile friendship came alive again, although their respective ways of conceiving of the One True Fold remained very different. In fact, Church rebutted Newman's reply to Pusey's *Irenicon* (1865) on the ground that the union of Churches demands that the Roman, the Greek, and the Anglican Church should alike admit to falling short of being the One True Fold![4] Such was the basic premise of the branch theory so dear to all Tractarians. The principal function of the theory was to gloss over the crucial point. Church himself was engaged in that doubtful art when he claimed, shortly after Newman's death, that Newman had become a Catholic because only the Church of Rome preserved in full strength the spirit of "devotion and sacrifice" of the Church of the Apostles.[5] To say this was simply

Biography (Oxford: Oxford University Press, 1990).

[2] *The Letters and Diaries of John Henry Newman* (Oxford: Oxford University Press, 1965—), vol. 11, p. 6. Subsequently referred to as *Letters and Diaries*.

[3] November 5, 1845, ibid., p. 24.

[4] Church did so in *The Times*, March 31, 1886. Reprinted in R. W. Church, *Occasional Papers* (London: Macmillan, 1897), vol. 2, pp. 398-440.

[5] "Cardinal Newman's Course," *The Guardian*, Aug. 13, 1890, in *Occasional Papers*, vol. 2, pp. 470-78.

to evade, by falling back on phenomenology (devotion and sacrifice), the evidence of objective truth (the One True Fold).

Indeed, on reading those letters written on that most momentous day, which decades later prompted Gladstone to write that the Church of England still had not realized the true measure of the loss it suffered by Newman's conversion, it is impossible not to sense the obvious: Newman revealed the innermost recesses of his powerful mind by repeating that he was about to be received "into the One True Fold." On October 9, 1845, when he was received, he assured his own sister Jemima (Mrs John Mozley) that "if I thought that any other body but that which I recognize to be Catholic were to be recognized by the Saviour of the world, I would not have left that body."[6] Five days later he wrote to her that it would have been a betrayal of Truth (writ large) had he kept from others his most considered conviction that the Church of Rome was the Catholic Church. He told her that he could not live with a conscience guilty of dissimulation, with the guilt that he had deprived others of the Truth: "What a doom would have been mine, if I had kept the Truth a secret in my bosom, and when I knew which the One Church was, and which was not part of the One Church, I had suffered friends and strangers to die in an ignorance from which I might have relieved them."[7] He knew which was the pain to be dreaded more: the temporal pain he would feel because he had to pain others, or the eternal pain he would eventually suffer by choosing not to pain them and thereby not to inspire others to convert as he did.

Details of the guidance he gave to prospective converts constitute what may be called Newman's existential ecclesiology. Not that he ever considered theology as something that can be severed from one's very spiritual existence and destiny. But the vital relevance of theology to life, or rather to a decision about eternal life, comes through with a particular force in the concern which Newman felt for the eternal salvation of others. He was naturally most closely connected with those who like himself

---

[6] *Letters and Diaries*, vol. 11, p. 14.
[7] Ibid., p. 16.

tried to see through that facade behind which the Church of England appeared as a mere tool of a secularist Establishment. Far more difficult was it both for Newman and other Tractarians to extricate themselves from their belief that, whatever its defects, the Church of England was Catholic and that it was both possible and legitimate to live a genuinely Catholic spiritual life within it.

For Newman it caused agonizing pain to perceive that the belief in question was but a splendid illusion and that therefore one had to recognize in Rome the only True Fold, no matter what the price. Such was the gist of the instructions he gave to those Anglo-Catholics who, prompted greatly by his example, felt more and more a pull towards Rome. Here too the gist can hardly give more than an inkling of the details. These, strangely enough, have not yet attracted appropriate study. This is all the more surprising because the letters that contain his guidance to prospective converts, have now been available in print for more than thirty years. I mean volumes XI-XIV of the *Letters and Diaries* that cover the time from Newman's conversion in October 1845 to the end of 1851, when his attention was largely retained by the Achilli trial and by the burdens he incurred with his having been charged, as its first Rector, with the organization of a Catholic University in Dublin.

Those volumes appeared in the early 1960s, a time of ecumenical euphoria. Within that atmosphere it would have been jarring to come forth with a study of the letters which Newman wrote to prospective converts between October 1845 and December 1851. Jarring (and unpopular) it certainly would have been, though very much to the liking of Newman, precisely because, as the author of *Development*, he held that although the formulation of truth develops, its content does not change by being further unfolded. The Church of Athanasius and Ambrose was that of the Apostles, and both those saints, he claimed, would recognize today only in the Church of Rome the Church of the Apostles. Union with Rome meant therefore compliance with the very will and command of Christ.

Books, including the book called the Bible, Newman was wont to argue, are unsure guides. About letters, including his own, he would have said the same, and even more forcefully.

But about letters he emphatically said that an author is far more present in his letters than in his books. Moreover, he considered letters as so many facts. Biographers (and theologians, one may add) may forever varnish their subject, but "contemporary letters are facts" and all the more so because, Newman added, "the true life of man is in his letters." This view, he said, "has ever been a hobby of mine."[8] He did not call this a hobby in order to detract from its value. After all, when he wrote this in 1863 he knew that he had crucial pieces of his correspondence ready to be used as soon as there arose the proper opportunity to defend the sincerity of his entire spiritual development leading to his conversion. The opportunity came within less than a year and led to his writing his most famous book, the *Apologia pro vita sua.*

Surely the life of a writer comes through more immediately in letters, which are hardly ever written with the concern that they will eventually appear in print, even if only after one's death. Letters reveal spontaneity, directness, informality, and even an added measure of frankness. Newman, for one, would never criticize ecclesiastical authorities in public, even when he was sorely pained by some of their policies. We know how deeply offended he was when, during Vatican I, a letter of his written in great confidence to Bishop Ullathorne in Rome suddenly appeared in *The Times,* because somebody had abused of Ullathorne's trust.

Most importantly, the letters Newman wrote to prospective converts give, as was noted above, a priceless insight into what may best be called Newman's existential ecclesiology. This is not to suggest that he was ever bogged down in that newfangled theological pastime which is to draft "models" of the Church, so many offerings in an "existential" smorgasbord of ecclesiology. And whatever the temptation of pandering to the fashion of the moment, nothing is more dangerously tempting for a theologian than to discount truths when applying them on the internal forum. In fact this dangerous deviation has become a theological

---

[8] This statement of Newman's from his letter (May 18, 1863) to his sister, Mrs. John Mozley, first first saw print in *Letters and Correspondence of John Henry Newman during his Life in the English Church,* ed. Anne Mozley (London: Longmans, Green and Co., 1890), vol. 1, p. 1.

virtue widely practiced in rank disregard of the relentless instructions issued by the Magisterium. There is not a trace of this dissimulation, hidden or open, in Newman's dealing with converts, for whom the question of converting was existential often in the dramatic sense of the word.

Of course, his own heroic resignation from his living and from his Oriel Fellowship made it in a sense impossible for him to bargain with truth even in strictest privacy. But he kept spelling out the full truth to prospective converts not so much because he did not want to contradict himself, but because only the truth deserved to be obeyed in full, and the truth was riveted on the Church. This sums up his existential ecclesiology, which he articulated nowhere more concretely than in his letters to prospective converts.

To focus on volumes IX - XIV of his *Letters* is all the more advisable because the great wave of conversions was ebbing away a year or so after Newman delivered in the late Spring and early Summer of 1850 a series of twelve lectures, known as *Difficulties of Anglicans*. He addressed them to Anglo-Catholics, so many Tractarians, in the hope that they would act on their principles and join the Catholic Church. With that task accomplished, he himself said to Aubrey de Vere that he now felt it to be burden to be occupied with the Church of England.

Newman's attention turned to the project of working out a set of reasonings (it ultimately came out as the *Grammar of Assent*) to help those who were at best nominal Anglicans, though still with some eagerness to find God, but who were more often than not the victims of an increasingly skeptical mentality. Converts who were to come from these ranks were hardly ever bothered with the branch theory. For them Newman had to show that it was most reasonable to believe that there was a Revelation. Once this had been dealt with, the need for a Church as an authentic and unfailing interpreter of Revelation readily appeared.

Prospective converts from among the Tractarians needed a different set of considerations. Newman had to impress on them the logic that the voice of Jesus Christ could not be echoed by Churches contradicting one another. Newman could be patient and understanding, but he never failed to point out in one way or another that unless one saw the voice of Jesus Christ in the teaching of the Church of Rome, it made no sense to transfer one's allegiance to it. By the same token it was one's God-given duty to complete one's path to Rome.

In those letters Newman refers time and again to his own motives and experiences as a convert. Ten days after his reception he told a correspondent that although the Catholicity of the Church of Rome had broken "suddenly and clearly" on his mind six years earlier, he dreaded to allow it lest it should prove a delusion. This dread stayed with him until the very last month: "I do not mean to say that every one who comes to the same views with myself must be as long about it. Mine was a peculiar case. But I can easily understand that in many minds a conviction will be the work of time."[9]

A month after his conversion he gave a priceless résumé of that slow maturing of his conviction. He spoke of the principal tenets on behalf of the Church of England. The first was the view that Antiquity, not the actual Church, was the oracle of truth. According to the second, apostolic succession was a sufficient guarantee of sacramental grace, and therefore the latter did not require actual union with the Christian Church throughout the world. About these tenets he said: "From the time I began to suspect their unsoundness, I ceased to put them forward—when I was fairly sure of their unsoundness, I have given up my Living. When I was fully confident that the Church of Rome was the only true Church, I joined it." Further, since only Bishop Bull's theology,[10] a theology distinctly hostile to Rome, provided a firm base for the Anglican position, no one could remain a member of the Church of England without opposing Rome, unless, of course, one was willing to have it both ways. He was to say this many times yet to Anglo-Catholics.

He considered their case a most difficult one because Anglo-Catholicism represented the most accomplished and yet at the

---

[9] *Letters and Diaries*, vol. 11, p. 18.

[10] George Bull (1634-1710), bishop of St. David, was the author of *Defensio fidei nicaenae* (1685), a work reprinted in Oxford in 1838, and again in 1851, as part of of the Library of Anglo-Catholic Theology.

same time the most devious mimicry of true Catholicism. For this reason alone he had to be very patient. He knew from his own case how difficult it had been for him to distinguish the imitation from the real. But though patient, he made it clear that conversion was not a matter of personal fulfillment but a matter of fulfilling one's duty to belong to the One True Fold. He never waxed "pastoral" in order to have an excuse for not reminding any and all of that duty.

One of those whom he kept reminding, though never in a hurtful way, was none other than the Pusey whom Anglo-Catholics considered to be their supreme oracle. A month after his conversion Newman walked through Prior Park in Oxford and met Pusey, who was already reading the freshly printed *Development*. Pusey, visibly strained by the encounter, voiced his dismay on finding that two other converts, Faber and Oakeley, had started "proselytizing." Writing to Dalgairns the next day, Newman reported that Pusey expected them to act like vine-dressers who had merely "transferred to another part of the vineyard."[11] Newman would not hesitate a moment about what to say to those Anglican bishops (and to some Roman Catholics) who nowadays write off the conversions of hundreds of Anglican clergymen as a move from one section to another in the same housing development.

Pusey could not have been more wrong in his view of what Newman the convert stood for. He kept seeing in Newman a mind similar to his, one who was always finding in theological hairsplitting an excuse for evading the obvious, including the obvious duty of making the move. Newman, however, seized every opportunity to insist on that duty whenever he found someone searching for the One True Fold.

One such person in Newman's estimate was the Marquise de Salvo, a cousin of Manning and the wife of a Sicilian nobleman, to whom he wrote on December 18, 1845: "I earnestly exhort you to join the Catholic Church. It is necessary for your salvation, considering your present state of mind." As to the pain the Marquise felt she would thereby inflict on her relations, Newman

---

[11] *Letters and Diaries*, vol. 11, p. 56.

quickly removed it from the psychological domain: "God will support you under every trial He puts upon you—and you will have the strength of the whole Church and of all saints who ever lived."[12]

The same letter is also precious because it is there that Newman first refers to rumors that were to haunt him for many decades to come, namely, that he and his companions had come to regret having joined the Catholic Church: "This is said of every one in turn—and in every case which I am acquainted with most falsely—There is but one feeling of joy and happiness among those persons with whom I am acquainted who have become Catholics."[13]

And what was the source of that joy? He explained it a month later to Miss Giberne, a recent convert who found all her friends turning their backs on her. Newman first reminded her that he himself had lost many more friends than anyone else. To be sure he came over with a handful of friends. But they were new friends. They were undergraduates when they first met him in Oxford. None of those who had studied there with him twenty years earlier and had formed deep ties of friendship with him followed him to Littlemore. But whether the friends were old or new, the real issue was that there in Littlemore he was with "Catholic hopes and beliefs—Catholic objects."[14]

A month later, already at Oscott, Newman reproached Pusey for resisting the evidence of truth. In defense of the apparent harshness of his words, Newman said this: "Excuse this freedom, and do not let me pain you. I am in a house, in which Christ is always present as He was to His disciples, and where one can go in from time to time through the day to gain strength from Him. Perhaps this thought makes me bold and urgent."[15] A month later in a letter to Mrs Bowden, Newman spoke of precisely this gain in becoming a Catholic. But the real point Newman made was that in becoming a Catholic, neither he nor his friends expected

[12] Ibid., p. 71.

[13] Ibid.

[14] Jan. 28, 1846, ibid., p. 102. Miss Giberne, who greatly helped Newman in the Achilli trial, later became a nun in France.

[15] Ibid., p. 128.

to find that real gain. He explained himself by recalling that in 1833 he had visited various churches in Italy and found it a soothing experience, but nothing deeper. He did not dare then to fancy "the extreme, ineffable comfort of being in the same house with Him who cured the sick and taught his disciples, . . . but now after tasting of the awful delight of worshipping God in His Temple, how unspeakably cold is the idea of a Temple without that Divine Presence!" And he begged pardon had he sounded as if he were proselytizing. In his defense he could refer only to his closeness to the Bowdens: "While there are few persons to whom I could say what I have said, I cannot keep from saying it where I can say it."[16]

He said this on March 1. In the first days of July, Newman was present at Mrs Bowden's reception into the Church in London. The way Newman handled the anxieties of her brother-in-law, not yet a Catholic, is usually a part of Newman biographies. Newmanists still have to exploit that gem of a letter which Newman wrote on the day of Mrs Bowden's reception into the Church to a first cousin of hers Mr Manuel Johnson, who, as an undergraduate, had first been introduced to him in Oxford in 1834. The Tractarians often met at Johnson's house, and it was there that Newman spent his last days in Oxford. Newman knew that Johnson would be deeply pained by his cousin's conversion, and so he expressed his firm hope that the joy found by Mrs Bowden would eventually be shared by all those dear to her. This prospect could be realized by their eventual coming together in the Catholic Church: "And then the lingering, prolonged, repeated, wearing distress which they undergo in their successive losses, will be recompensed to themselves and to us by their regaining all at once all that has gone from them. And thus, my dear Johnson, the Catholic Church will be the true type of heaven to all of us—for it will bring together all in one all those who die off from the world. . . ."[17] No, Newman was not to hint, even as a gesture of consolation, that the Catholic Church somehow was not really the One True Fold.

[16] Ibid., p. 131.
[17] Ibid., p. 197.

In August 1847 Newman visited with Pusey. What he said to Pusey can easily be guessed. Then on September 1, he left for Rome. The first stage of his ministering to prospective converts was over. It lasted but ten months, too short a period to allow Newman to speak at length about the experience of being a convert to Catholicism. He came back from Rome not as a lay convert but a priest charged with the task of establishing the Oratory of St Philip in England. The counsels and precepts he urged on prospective converts remained the same as those he had voiced during that ten-month period, but now he voiced them as that official representative of the One True Fold which every priest is or should be. Furthermore, as the years went by, he could with ever greater credibility refer to his own experience as a convert.

All this is amply shown by the very first letter he addressed, following his return from Rome, to a prospective convert. The recipient of that letter, dated February 10, 1848, was the Rev. Anthony John Hanmer, who first met Newman in 1839 and took orders the following year. Newman already in December 1845 had advised Hanmer on two points. One concerned a difficulty, the wish to clear up all particular problems and make too much of extreme cases in Church history, a concern typical of some Anglican inquirers after truth. The other was more pastoral. Newman told Hanmer that the genuineness of feeling a call to the true Church did not consist so much in its vividness as in its continuance. He asked Hanmer to test whether that feeling would still be on hand six or so months later. Also the elimination of doubts was not ultimately a function of reason, "an uncertain guide," but of grace. As to himself, Newman wrote this: "I am so convinced of the truth of the Catholic Church that I am pained about persons who are external to it in a way in which I was not before."[18]

Now in February 1848 Newman pointed out to Hanmer that only a Catholic could understand what the Church and the sacraments were for him, because only a child could understand what it meant to have a father and a mother. For Newman this was

---

[18] Dec. 11, 1845, ibid., vol. 11, p. 60. Hanmer died in 1907 at the age of 92.

not a pious dictum but an experience which he hastened to convey in a theologically existential form: "From the time I became a Catholic, the shadow of a misgiving has not crossed my mind that I was not doing God's will in becoming one."

No, Newman was not to talk of his own fulfillment, but of his having done the will of God. He could further reassure Hanmer that all the other converts who had come over to Rome were similarly free of doubts, because, like him, they had joined the Church "in the spirit of a child to a Mother—not to criticize anything, but to accept—and if we have had no trials of faith, it doubtless is, by natural consequence, a reward, (I hope I may say so without boasting,) of our having come to the Church in this spirit." To have this spirit in coming to the Church was the only way of coming to it. Nothing would be more miserable than a mere outward conformity or reservation: "God is not wanting to us, and hard as faith is, and above reason, yet He who made the Church to speak, makes us, if we earnestly pray for the gift, to hear and accept."[19]

That letter to Hanmer also contains the anticipation of an inscription which Newman eventually wanted to have on his tombstone: *ex umbris et imaginibus in veritatem.* Newman did not mean something abstract by those words, and not even the transition from the earthly shadows of eternal verities to their full contemplation in heaven. He meant by that phrase the transition from that shadowy church, the Church of England, to the Church of truth, the Church of Rome: Conversion, he wrote, "is coming out of shadows into truth—into that which is beyond mistake a real religion—not a mere opinion such that you have no confidence that your next door neighbour holds it too, but an external objective substantive creed and worship. The thought of Anglicanism with nothing fixed or settled, with Bishops contradicting Bishops within, and the whole world [the Catholic Church] against it without, is something so dreary and wretched, that I cannot speak of it without the chance of offence to those who still hold it."[20]

[19] Letter of February 10, 1848, ibid., vol. 11, p. 168.
[20] Ibid.

Almost two years later, Hanmer was still struggling with his difficulties. Newman could only feel sorry for him. He referred to many others who had already "seized and are enjoying the high calling offered to them," while he, Hanmer, was still "wasting precious years in vanity. Having myself been called to the Church late in life, when my best days were gone, I feel for those who persevere in losing what cannot be recalled." Newman brushed aside an argument of Hanmer's about a non-infallible Pope and an infallible Church with devastating simplicity, dismissing Hanmer and the gallican Bossuet by the same stroke: "Bossuet would not have felt the force of this argument."

For Newman the argument with "overbearing force" was that "were St Athanasius and St Ambrose in London now, they would go to worship, not to St Paul's Cathedral, but to Warwick Street or Moor Field." Not that Newman thought his reading of church history could be communicated to others. But he pointed out the difference between a Catholic Church "vibrant with altars, tombs, pilgrimages, processions, rites, relics, medals etc.; whereas I hardly see a trace of the Church of the Fathers, as a *living*, *acting* being, in the Anglican communion." It was useless to argue, Newman went on, that either this or that was not necessary to the Church. All these items, he wrote, "*make up* together a great note of the Church. The Church was to be one and the same from Christ's first coming to His second. The modern Roman communion is unmistakably like the Church of the Fathers; and this great argument is confirmed by finding that the Church of England is unmistakably unlike it." The case of an Anglican trying to escape into the Greek Church was, Newman wrote, a mere absurdity. He called Hanmer's attention to the fact that whereas a Catholic could logically debate theological nuances concerning papal infallibility as a means of perfecting his knowledge, the same was "foreign to the position of an inquirer into the truth of Catholicism."[21] Finally, he asked Hanmer to come from Tiverton in Devon to Birmingham and have a conversation with him. Hanmer was received into the Church a month later.

---

[21] November 18, 1849, ibid., vol. 13, pp. 295-96.

In mid-June 1848, Newman pointed out to the Marquise de Salvo that no specific Marian devotion was strictly obligatory, but that he himself had found great spiritual pleasure in reciting the Rosary: "to my own feelings nothing is more delightful than the contemplation of the Mysteries of the Incarnation, under the invocation, so to call it, of her who was the human instrument of it—so that she who ministered to the Gracious Dispensation itself, should minister also to our adoring thought of it." He also told her that a new convert has to make conscious efforts "to *make* distinct acts of faith, love etc. when it all comes quite as a matter of course and without effort to one who has been a Catholic from birth." He concluded by saying that a short reply was better than a long but delayed one, and assured her of his readiness to answer any question he could "or [do] any thing I can do for you."[22] Such was a convert-priest's pastoral solicitude for another convert.

About the same time, Newman received an anxious letter from Henry Bourne, who converted in 1845 and wanted to know whether it was true that Newman was dissatisfied as a Catholic. "I can only say, if it is necessary to say it," Newman wrote in reply, "that from the moment I became a Catholic, I never had, through God's grace, a single doubt or misgiving in my mind that I did wrong in becoming one. I have not had any feeling whatever but one of joy and gratitude that God called me out of an insecure state into one which is sure and safe, out of the war of tongues into a realm of peace and assurance." Had he said only that much, the phrase— "out of the war of tongues"—would have made it one of the best characterizations ever of certain aspects of theologizing that deserve only the kind of criticism which Swift handed out in his *The Battle of the Books*.

Newman would not have been the convert he was had he not added the note, which many recent Catholic ecclesiologists would not strike at any price: "I shrink to contemplate the guilt I should have incurred, and the account which at the last day would have lain against me, had I not become a Catholic—and it pierces me to the heart to think that so many excellent persons

---

[22] June 11, 1848, ibid., vol. 11, pp. 217-18.

should still be kept in bondage in the Church of England, or should, among the many good points they have, want the great grace of *faith*, to trust God and follow His leading." Newman could surpass even that, as if it had not been superlative in its expressiveness: "This is my state of mind, and I would it could be brought home to all and every one, who, in default of real arguments for remaining Anglicans, amuse themselves with dreams and fancies."[23] One wonders if some Catholic members of ARCIC (Anglican Roman Catholic Interfaith Commission) have any inkling of these words of Newman's.

One of Mr Bourne's sons was the future Cardinal Bourne. He read that letter aloud as part of the sermon he gave at the opening of the Newman Memorial Church at the Birmingham Oratory, on October 9, 1906. The day was the anniversary of Newman's conversion to the Catholic Church. Similar testimonies were heard at the celebration of the hundredth anniversary of Newman's conversion, but hardly any at the centenary of his death. *Tempora mutantur et nos mutamur in illis,* but is this a genuine development of dogma as Newman held it?

Three days later, on June 16, 1848, Newman assured Mrs William Froude about his being in good health, indeed feeling better than ever. No longer did he have the pressing anxieties that had been his lot for so many years, but it was not in his power to delete from his face the trace of them: "At least I feel it an effort to brighten up. . . those sad long years of anxiety have stamped themselves on my face—and now that they are at an end, yet I cannot change what has become a physical effect." But the sadness of his facial features was not to be taken for a sign of something similar inside of him: "I will add that the Hand of God is most wonderfully over me, that I am full of blessing and privileges, that I never had even the temptation for an instant to feel a misgiving about the great step I took in 1845." The other side of this related to those still outside: "The hollowness of High Churchism (or whatever it is called) is to me so very clear that it surprises me, (not that persons should not see it at once,) but that any should not see it at last, and, alas I must add that I do

---

[23] Ibid., p. 218.

not think it safe for anyone who does see it, not to act on his conviction of it at once."[24]

It was not until ten years later that Mrs Froude and her children became Catholics. She was to become one of those converts whose husband would not follow her. A predicament both painful and puzzling, as Mr Froude, a naval engineer, was more than anyone else in Newman's mind when he wrote the *Grammar of Assent*. Puzzling it was not, however, for Newman, all too aware of the supreme role of grace in any act of conversion. For even if Newman could satisfy his desire to be near Mrs Froude and talk with her, he felt he would still need "great grace to know what to say to you." At least he could point out something all-important. It was not enough to know that the Church of England failed as a Church. To come to the true Church could not be done on such grounds, because this would still leave one in the world which is full of troubles and failing: "You must come to the Church, not to avoid it [the world], but to save your soul. If this is the motive, all is right—you cannot be disappointed—but the other motive is dangerous."

One impression he certainly did not wish to leave, namely that he had tried "to disguise that Catholicism is a different religion from Anglicanism—you must come to learn that religion which the Apostles introduced and which was in the world long before the Reformation was dreamed of—but a religion not so easy and natural to you, or congenial, because you have been bred up in another from your youth." One can only guess what Mrs Froude thought of Newman telling her that he was thinking of her that very same morning as he was saying mass: "Oh that you were safe in the True Fold!—I think you will be one day. You will then have the blessedness of seeing God face to face. You will have the blessedness of finding, when you enter a [Catholic] Church, a Treasure Unutterable—the presence of the Eternal Word Incarnate—the Wisdom of the Father who, even when He had done His work, would not leave us, but rejoices still to humble Himself by abiding in mean places on earth for

---

[24] *Letters and Diaries*, vol. 12, p. 223.

our sakes, while He reigns not the less on the right hand of God."[25]

Ten or so days later, another letter of Newman's was sent to Mrs Froude, a letter no less inexhaustible in its instructiveness. There Newman first told her, "my most dear Sister or Daughter as you choose to let me call you," about his own greatest concern prior to his conversion. Events brought out, Newman told her, that not a few of those who hung on to his words of assurance about the soundness of the Anglo-Catholic position would pass into skepticism once they learned that he now considered that position a mere delusion. The very fact that so few of them followed him into the Catholic Church proved that there was "really no medium between scepticism and Catholicism." A symptom of the scepticism into which many Anglo-Catholics were sliding was the fact that while they "still profess to believe [they] secretly doubt."

And why? because they do not think that they have the obligation to submit to Truth. Applying this to Mrs Froude's predicament, he told her that the real question she should ask herself was simply this: "Have I a conviction that I ought to accept the (Roman) Catholic Faith as God's word?, if not at least, 'do I tend to such a conviction' or 'am I near upon it'?" And he asked her to respond to this question: "Now can you, my dear Mrs Froude, say this, that, directly you feel sure you ought to believe the Catholic Faith, you will begin making efforts to control your mind into belief?" Newman was not willing to go along with the objection—I *cannot* believe. The question to be answered was whether one felt that one *ought* to believe. And here Newman, this great champion of grace, often charged with rank Methodism, turned the tables on Anglo-Catholics. "Is it not plain that many of Dr Pusey's followers are at this very time exerting an act of *will, commanding* their minds, . . . *because* Dr Pusey believes? . . . Do you think that they could not in like manner, *if they pleased*, believe what the Catholic Church teaches?"[26]

[25] June 16, 1848, vol. 12, pp. 223-24.
[26] Ibid., p. 228.

What was then to be done? One was to make acts of will that all too often are the starting points of faith. Faith may not come suddenly, and in a startling manner, "but in reality faith is always so begun, so sustained, so increased. This, and this only, makes martyrs." One was not, however, to begin with what one might end with. Newman advised Mrs Froude to read *Paradisus animae* (a Greek Orthodox book of devotions, just translated into English), not in order to nourish her piety, but to help her to "*make acts* of faith, hope, charity, contrition etc daily."[27]

As one may expect, Mrs Froude found most painful Newman's reference to scepticism as the only alternative to Rome. In his reply Newman urged her "to cultivate that great virtue, faith, which I acknowledge may be possessed in the Anglican Church; which, knowing your earnestness and sincerity, I will believe that you possess in it, if you tell me so." But this did not save Mrs Froude from having to face up to the question of whether one had the duty to believe and whether it was possible to believe without believing in a creed. Catholics had clear statements in which they believed. As an Anglican, Newman said in his next to final remark, "you should either have in your hand your whole Creed, or be able to ascertain any point of it when necessary."[28] His last remark was a promise that she would be remembered daily in his mass.

No exchange of letters took place between the two until about a year later when, on July 14th, Newman felt, as he put it, tempted to write. The day was the 16th anniversary of the beginning of the Oxford Movement, in which the Froudes were heavily involved. Having known her from days even antedating that beginning, Newman expressed his fear that she might fall back into the kind of religiously coated agnosticism from which the Oxford Movement had rescued her. But he had an even greater fear. As one who had become familiar with the true object of faith, he felt that Mrs Froude seemed to be, by her reluctance to become a Catholic, taking the risk of losing "a state of mind which cannot live except in its Object! Alas, how many

[27] Ibid., p. 229.
[28] Ibid., pp. 232-33.

instances do we see around us of a wrecked and ruined faith! Of those who either deliberately, or at least virtually, have preferred scepticism to Rome! Surely faith is the gift of God, as it was in St Paul's day, and the divine election is as wonderful now as then."

Newman must have lived up to his promise to remember Mrs Froude daily in the mass. Otherwise his next remark would not have referred to the awesome responsibility of those for whom the masses were being said. In no other letters written by Newman to prospective converts do we come across the following frightful alternative: "What passionate efforts have I witnessed after the conversion of individuals. What multitudes of Masses were said for Pusey! I have heard those who said that they *would* have him. I have never liked this way of talking, and have never given in to it. I believe that it is an awful thing to say Mass for a conversion, for it may bring down a judgement on the person whom you offer it for, if it does not convert him. I have fancied I have seen this. No, the election is with God; we can but co-operate with him—and we must submit to His decision. . . . Yet is it dreadful to have to give up the hopes of those one has loved so much, and has worked with."[29] Two brief letters of Newman's to Mrs Froude from 1851 contain no reference to her spiritual state. The year 1859, when she would become a Catholic, was still eight full years away. Newman kept praying.

One should only touch upon a long letter which Newman wrote about that time to E. J. Phipps, who acted as an intermediary between another Anglican clergyman G. Dawson and Newman. It is not clear to what extent Mr Dawson considered conversion. Instead of conversion, Dawson seems to have looked forward to the eventual union or fusion of Rome and Canterbury. Newman firmly stated his conviction that there could be no such fusion because the two were two different religions. The difference between the two was not that "one believes a little more and the other a little less." Newman listed a large number of points of crucial difference, including the question of intention in administering the sacraments, and above all that of ordination: "It is a dream then to think of uniting the two religions; I speak from

[29] July 14, 1849, ibid., vol. 12, p. 219.

experience of both. And, in finding this to be the case, I am recording no disappointment on my part. I joined the Catholic Church to save my soul; I said so at the time. No inferior motive would have drawn me from the Anglican. . . . Never for an instant have I had since [then] any misgiving I was right in doing so—never any misgiving that the Catholic religion was the religion of the Apostles." His final remark had for its target Anglican presumptions about what Catholicism really was or rather the readiness to take any group of Catholics for Catholicism. Newman warned that it would be just as easy "to make the philosophy of Epictetus or Plotinus like Catholicism, as you can identify with Catholicism any form of Anglicanism that ever existed though in only half a dozen minds."[30]

One Anglican with an acute mind able to make a case for his Church and also with a great hunger for truth was T. W. Allies. In 1848 he was still three years away from becoming a convert at great personal sacrifice. Newman's letters to him dealt with intellectual points, precisely because he was fully aware of the mental powers of Allies, whom he found bogged down in an elementary fallacy in logic. Newman formulated it in a way that could not have been simpler or more telling: "Say the Catholic Church *is not*, that it has broken up,—this I can understand:—I don't understand saying that there is a Church, and one Church, and yet acting as if there were none or many. This is dreaming surely. . . . When I think of your position and that of others, I assure you, it frightens me."[31]

Allies meanwhile kept drifting toward the Church. Early in 1849 his book of reminiscences of his travels through Italy and France in 1845, 1847 and 1848, caused a furor. Samuel Wilberforce, bishop of Oxford, almost prosecuted Allies for promoting Catholic dogmas. Allies sent a copy of the book to Newman and

[30] July 3, 1848, ibid., vol. 12, pp. 234-36.
[31] Sept. 6, 1848, ibid., p. 260. Allies (1813-1903) was possibly the most brilliant among those who converted through Newman's help. Newman chose him to serve as professor of Church history at the new Catholic University in Dublin. Later Allies found a secure post as the director of Catholic education in England. Newman was to speak of Allies' two-volume *Per crucem ad lucem. The Result of a Life* (1879) as the best portrayal of the Catholic position.

suggested that Newman had spoken contemptuously of the Church of England. Newman's reply came swiftly and with a theological incisiveness. He stated once more that he had left the Church of England only because of his conviction that "salvation was not to be found in it." It was therefore logical for him "to wish others to leave it." Nay, much more. "The position of those who leave it in the only way in which I think it justifiable to leave it, is necessarily one of *hostility* towards it. To leave it merely as a branch of the Catholic Church for another which I liked better, would have been to desert without reason the post where Providence put me. It is impossible then but that a convert, if justifiable in the grounds of his conversion, must be an enemy of the Communion he has left, and more intensely so than a *foreigner* who knows nothing about that Communion at all."[32]

A further consequence of that logic was the sense of anxiety in the convert for those whom he had left behind, on seeing them sink further "into a state in which there is no hope." Then Newman explained this hopelessness by referring to those who put themselves forward as "teachers of a system which they cannot trace to any set of men, or any doctor before themselves; who give up history, documents, theological authors, and maintain that it is *blasphemy against* the Holy Ghost to deny the signs of Catholicism and divine acceptance, as a *fact*, in the existing bearing and action of their communion." Newman's final words were prophetic: "But of such as you, my dear Allies, I will ever augur better things and hope against hope, and believe the day will come when (excuse me) you will confess that you have been in a dream; and meanwhile I will not cease to say Mass for you and all who stand where you stand on the 10th day of every month, unless something very particular occurs."[33] And he excused himself for having spoken so freely.

Newman therefore could be blunt, in a letter to Henry Bittleston, another hesitating Anglican clergyman, about Allies' great effort, *The Church of England cleared from the Charge of Schism*

---

[32] Letter of February 20, 1849, ibid., vol. 13, p. 59.
[33] Ibid., p. 60.

(1846). He described it as full of "apparently incontrovertible arguments" which his admirers would eventually find to be "ashes in their mouths."[34] Outspokenness once more proved to be the right medicine. Four days after Bittleston read that letter, he was received in the Birmingham Oratory. By then Allies was writing his *The Royal Supremacy viewed in reference to the two Spiritual Powers of Order and Jurisdiction* (1850). It carried on its front page the question of St Athanasius, "When did a judgment of the Church receive its validity from the Emperor?" Clearly, Allies' argument were turning ashes in his mouth too, as predicted by Newman, who knew that plain words were not alien to the Christian spirit. This is a point still to be appreciated by some latter-day Catholic ecumenists, who abhor nothing more than the prospect of making converts.

The four long letters Newman wrote to Catherine Ward between October 12 and December 18, 1848, are certainly a testimony to Newman's readiness to explain patiently the details about history and dogma to one hardly an expert in them. Once more Newman counted it no loss of time or energy to come to the help of anyone in whom he saw a sincere inquirer after truth. Catherine Ward became a Catholic and a most devout one, in July 1849.

Newman's fourth letter to her from 1848 has a conclusion that deserves to be quoted in full, because there he considers the case of a Catholic converting to Protestantism. Without mincing words, Newman states as his most considered view that behind all such conversions there lies some criminality, some moral failure, to be revealed on Judgment day. But long before that, one may see an unfailing pattern unfold: "Look too at the sequel of their history—they turn *from* the Church, but they turn to *nothing*. When was there a seceder from the Church who remained in *one* state of mind? They have no peace." Then after recalling the sad fate of Blanco White, he concludes: "What a contrast to the satisfaction of mind which the convert to Catholicity experiences!"[35]

---

[34] November 19, 1849, ibid., vol. 12, p. 297.
[35] Letter of December 19, 1848, ibid., pp. 378-79.

But before she converted, Mrs Ward needed another nod
from Newman. The nod was rather blunt. Newman the logician
found little merit in the illogicality with which she went back on
her earlier agreement with him, that the Church must have one
policy or else its unity is illusory. Now she tried to shift the
dispute to miracles. She received a firm lesson from Newman:
"So you give up what I certainly think was your, as well as my
view of this proposition, because others (viz [some Anglican]
controversialists) dissent from it; and you wish a new proof, one
from miracles, because what for four months has passed between
us is not of an Anglican character. Is it not so, my dear Madam?
and are you not in the way to be of those who *ever* seek and
therefore never find? Alas I can believe how wayward the mind
may be under the fearful pressure of perplexities in faith; but
how many there are in the Anglican Church who would leap for
joy to attain that intellectual conviction which you have possessed."

Newman's patience was running out, though not his good
will. "Let me not seem harsh—but I have no heart, as I have no
call, to enter upon a fresh discussion, which when completed
may be simply put aside without better reason than the allega-
tion that some third persons for whose judgment you have no
great opinion do not see the force of our common concordant
conclusion. I have mentioned your name in my daily Memento,
since I first told you I should do, and shall continue it, though
with less cheerful feelings."[36] Three years later Newman was able
to register the victory of grace in Mrs Ward's soul and to write to
her: "I congratulate you with all my heart on your reception into
the Catholic Church, and pray, and am sure, you will enjoy to
the full those blessings which there alone are to be found."[37]

A few months later, in June 1851, Newman wrote what may
be his most incisive letter ever written to a prospective convert.
She was Mrs Lucy Agnes Phillips, the widow of an evangelical
clergyman who had died in 1847. Newman began by noting that
he had put her (without disclosing her name) "on our private

---

[36] March 5, 1849, ibid., vol. 13, pp. 74-75.
[37] Feb. 14, 1851, ibid., vol. 14, p. 211.

prayer list." Then he assured her that she was absolutely right in thinking that "the Catholic Church claims absolute submission to her in matters of faith—Unless you believe her doctrines, as the word of God revealed to you through her, you can gain no good by professing to be a Catholic—you are not one really."[38] Of course, the Catholic Church puts forward most worthy proofs on behalf of her claims, but as in other cases of intellectual persuasion, it is not necessary to clear up all problems prior to coming to the conclusion that the case has indeed been proven.

Newman in particular mentioned the great notes of the Church as so many assurances that the guidance of the Church was most reliable because it was a visible, concrete, living guide, something far superior to anything written, be it the Bible itself: "How ignorant we are! do we not *want* a guide? Is the structure of Scripture such as to answer the purposes of a guide? How can a bare letter, written 2000 years ago, though inspired, *guide* an individual now? Every thing has its use—God uses it according to its use—Is it the use of a written Word to answer doctrinal questions starting up to the end of time? as little surely, as it is the use of a spade to saw with, or a plough to reap with."[39] Three months later Mrs Phillips entered the Church, went abroad to prevent that her two children be brought up as Protestants, trained herself as a nurse in France, returned to Birmingham, and died on March 3, 1857, as she was setting up a hospital near the Oratory.

From the end of 1851 there is a brief letter of Newman's to a woman whose name is not known. Perhaps her anonymity qualifies that brief letter to be one which countless anonymous souls, who have ever looked and still look for guidance from Newman, may take as something written to them: "Of course, my only answer to you can be that the Catholic Church is the true fold of Christ, and that it is your duty to submit to it. You cannot do this without God's grace, and therefore you ought to pray Him continually for it. All is well if God is on our side."[40]

---

[38] June 5, 1851, ibid., vol. 14, p. 292.
[39] Ibid., p. 293.
[40] November 12, 1851, ibid., vol. 14, p. 423.

To Viscount Feilding, still a new convert in November 1850, he wrote: "Be of good cheer my dear Lord, the first months of a convert's life, though filled with joy of their own, have a pain and a dreariness of their own too. We feel the latter when nature overcomes grace—the former when grace triumphs over nature. But no one made a sacrifice without effect. God does not forget what we do for Him—and whatever trouble you may have now, it will be repaid to you a hundred fold."[41] Later, as one of the founders of the *Universe* and honorary president of the Peter Pence Association, the Viscount could very well see a prophetic touch in Newman's words to him.

In July 31, 1851, Newman assured Robert B. Seeley, a publisher and a zealous evangelical, that he had not yet met a single Catholic priest "who doubted or disbelieved." As for himself: "I assure you solemnly that I have not had a single doubt of the truth of the Catholic religion and its doctrine ever since I became a Catholic. And I have an intense certainty that the case is the same with my friends about me, who have joined the Church with me."[42] A friend James Hope, a prominent lawyer, was still to join. Newman offered prayer and assurance: "For myself, I say it from my heart, I have not had a single doubt, or temptation to doubt, ever since I became a Catholic."[43] This was on November 20, 1850. Six months later Hope joined the Church. Once more an existentially unimpeachable ecclesiology did more than a thousand learned pages on it.

Newman's same letter to Hope also shows the extent to which the man is in his letters. Newman longed for peace, but he knew that others looked to him to have their own peace. So the struggle for souls had to go on: "My great temptation is to be *at peace*, and let things go on as they will, and not trouble myself with others." He could not help smiling on reading Hope's suggestion that he should list and expose the difficulties which beset Anglicans. Well, Newman had just published his twelve

---

[41] November 15, 1850, ibid., vol. 14, p. 130.

[42] Ibid., vol. 14, p. 323. Seeley believed that there were many Catholic priests in England similar to the plainly unbelieving Blanco White, an apostate.

[43] Ibid., vol. 14, p. 134.

lectures *Anglican Difficulties,* the greatest clarion call ever to Anglo-Catholics to be logical and convert.[44] What was the point of writing on the same theme endlessly? Indeed Newman himself said it in the same letter: "Surely, enough has been written—all the writing in the world would not destroy the necessity of faith—if all were made clear to reason, where would be the exercise of faith?"[45]

It is indeed most unlikely that arguments proved to be the final factor that brought William Maskell into the Church on June 22, 1850. In all likelihood Maskell was present at all those lectures that were coming to a close by then. In fact, in the lectures there were few formal arguments. To anyone present, and by far the largest number of them were Anglo-Catholics, the lectures sounded rather like a clarion call, indeed the impassioned call of a shepherd of souls to some sheep still hesitating to enter the sheepfold. Early that year Newman assured Maskell that he would burn his letter after having written a reply to it. Newman, of course, knew full well that Maskell, as a theologian for the bishop of Exeter, held to strictly Catholic views concerning baptismal regeneration in connection with the Gorham case. Not only Maskell but many other prominent Anglo-Catholics, including Pusey, threatened secession from the Church of England were it to acquiesce in the Crown's decision that a clergyman who does not hold baptism to be necessary for salvation can still function as a parish priest.

Newman told Maskell that given his "present state of mind" he had no right to keep his living and go soldiering for the Church of England. Moreover he laid it down that "*whenever* the conviction comes to you, that the Church of Rome is *the* Church, you ought to act upon it at once. It may be a work of time to arrive at that conviction, but when attained, it demands prompt obedience." Compared with this point, Newman held as wholly secondary Maskell's experience "about a veil being lifted from his eyes," as if arguments had suddenly vanished. Speaking for

---

[44] This thrust of the book is possibly the chief cause for the studied oblivion into which it has fallen, as argued in my introduction to it, reproduced here as chapter 6.

[45] *Letters and Diaries,* vol. 14, p. 134.

himself, Newman could not recall any such sudden mental or spiritual experience. With him it had been a slow process to form a "clear belief that the Church of England was no part of the Catholic body."[46] For he would not have dreamed of leaving the Church of England for anything less than such a clear belief.

On both points Maskell knew that Newman once more gave only those counsels which he had already fully obeyed. He gave up his living once he knew he could not soldier for the Church of England. He asked with great swiftness to be received into the Church once those doubts as to where the True Fold was had left him. God did not fail to do his part. Unknown to Newman, the saintly Passionist (and now a saint) Father Dominic was going through Oxford. Once more, and all of a sudden, everything was converging for those ready to heed the call to convert into the One True Fold. This was also part of Newman's existential ecclesiology. It is existential because it touches concretely and specifically on the living person and his duty to obey objective realities and norms set by God. Those who specialize in stretching the boundaries of ecclesiology to suit almost any personal whim and fancy had better stop appealing to Newman. His ecclesiology is not about a motley plurality of personal preferences, not about "alternate" models of the Church among which one can pick and choose, but about the real actual One True Fold. Otherwise he would not have converted and would not have urged, implored, and, when necessary, even warned others to follow him. Conversion and converts meant for Newman converging on Rome.

Newman's ecclesiology as directed at converts and at making converts, especially from among those who kept deluding themselves about being Catholics outside the Catholic Church, was also a saintly theologian's ecclesiology. His heroic practice of virtues implied a heroic disciplining of the intellect, the intellect of a great logician. Discipline of the mind means consistency, the kind of virtue about which Newman wrote in

---

[46] January 7, 1850, ibid., vol. 14, pp. 372-73.

March 1846 to a prospective convert that he had "ever made it the mark of a Saint."[47]

More than a quarter of a century later Newman still told converts that only if they held the Church of Rome to be the One True Fold, should they join it. He also told them that once they had that conviction, they must promptly make the move. One such convert was the wife of an Anglican clergyman. Newman wrote to her that if she held that "the Church we call Catholic is the one true fold of Christ," she must make the move, regardless of the acute personal pains it might entail. On the same day Newman addressed, in a separate letter to her husband who did everything to dissuade her, the following question: "O, my dear Sir, will it be a thought welcome on a death bed to recollect that you have hindered her? Excuse me if I seem rude."[48] True, existential Catholic ecclesiology must in fact include statements that will appear rude in the measure in which they reflect truths leading to the only life that counts in the long run, life eternal.

[47] Letter of July 4, 1846 to Henry Wilberforce, ibid., vol. 11, p. 191.
[48] Letters of July 23, 1873, to the Rev. and Mrs Alfred Newdigate, ibid., vol. 26, p. 341.

6

Anglo-Catholics

During the last century or two the Church of England dealt more than one blow to a small segment of its communicants known as Anglo-Catholics. Among those blows the most shattering was the latest, the decision to ordain women. As a result, one Anglo-Catholic after another cried out, "This is not a Church!" and, with a cabinet minister and some members of Parliament among them, they turned their steps toward Rome. They saw no further point in clinging to their image of a Church of England as one of the main branches of the Church Catholic, a legitimate continuation of the great communion of the Church Fathers and through them of the Church of the Apostles.

Devotees of that image have sought support for it in the Decree on Ecumenism issued by Vatican II. There the Anglican Communion is singled out as occupying a "special place" among those communions formed at the Reformation in which "some Catholic traditions and institutions continue to exist." But that Decree contains no trace whatever of the idea that the Catholic Church consists of three branches—Roman, Orthodox, and Anglican. Blinded by the glitter of their long-cherished image of the Church Catholic, Anglo-Catholics have for too long failed to take a distinct pattern at its face value: Time and again, at crucial junctures, the Church of England acted in a decisively Protestant way. All those acts could but compromise the Catholic significance of splendid liturgical apparel and of a Prayerbook at subtle variance with the very Protestant Thirty-nine Articles.

One of those fateful actions took place in early March 1850 and helped Newman to shape the thrust of the Lectures that have become known as *Anglican Difficulties*.[1] Only ten or so years earlier, Newman still tried to justify the Anglo-Catholic image of the Church of England as a Via Media between Protestantism and Romanism. These Lectures are his most sustained effort to show that image to be a mere mirage. More than anyone else he had the qualification to expose the blinding force of that mirage, to help Anglo-Catholics close their eyes to it and join the Church of Rome as the only framework of true Catholicism.

In March 1850, Britain was only a year away from the opening of the Great Exhibition, with its sweeping display of the industrial and economic preeminence of the Empire. Victorian respect for public morality gave an added aura to the Established Church as a trustworthy promoter of happiness on earth as well as in heaven. But in the first days of March 1850 no one with a serious interest in the Catholic character of the Established Church doubted that a most serious disclaimer to it could emerge at any moment. An already two-year-old dispute between Dr. Henry Phillpotts, bishop of Exeter, and the Rev. G. C. Gorham was about to be decided by the Judicial Committee of the Queen's Privy Council, the highest forum for Church affairs.

Set up in 1833, the Committee had the final word in ecclesiastical disputes that did not imply doctrine. In October 1847, Bishop Phillpotts ruled that Mr. Gorham, a nominee of the Crown to the vicarage of Brampford Speke, was not to be installed because he held that the administration of baptism did not impart spiritual regeneration, or sanctifying grace. Two and a half years later, on March 7, 1850, to be exact, the Judicial Committee ordered the Bishop to install Mr. Gorham. The Committee took the view that in a matter in which the Established Church had no clear doctrine, a candidate could not be forced to subscribe to one or another of its interpretations.

---

[1] Quotations made in this chapter from *Anglican Difficulties* will be referred to the Longmans edition, which is much more available than the entirely reset text, published by Real View Books in 1994, to which this chapter served as an Introduction. Here the text of that Introduction is given with references.

Once the ruling had been made, caution was counseled even by the few bishops in favor of the Catholic truth about baptism as a means of imparting sanctifying grace. They let the protest against the Privy Council's ruling be taken up by a small group of high-ranking clergymen, prestigious theologians, and leading laymen—all well known for their Catholic views. Their protest, issued on March 19, could not have been more serious as it spelled out some fateful spiritual implications for the Established Church were it to acquiesce in the Gorham Judgment.

Among the signers of the protest were Archdeacons Henry Manning and Robert Wilberforce, as well as James Hope, the most persuasive legal mind in the House of Lords. Other signers of the protest included John Keble, the renowned spiritual inspiration of the Oxford Movement, and Edward Pusey, the chief Tractarian beside Newman and indeed the author of a major Tract defending baptismal regeneration. The protest stated nothing less than that through its acquiescence in the Gorham Judgment the Church of England would become "formally separated from the Catholic body, and could no more assure to its members the grace of the Sacraments and the Remission of Sins."[2] What could be more fatal for a Church allegedly Catholic?

For all that, Dr. Phillpotts installed Mr. Gorham and provided him with funds to rebuild his parish church. Pusey and Keble began to urge acquiescence by calling it "caution" and "patience."[3] They now bemoaned that the bishop of Exeter had not in the first place tried patience, which might have won over Mr. Gorham to the Catholic view on baptism. Pusey and Keble organized no protest when later that year the bishops, with the archbishops of Canterbury and York in the lead, formally rallied behind the Gorham Judgment. Once more an ecclesiastical camouflage was given to the proverbial national virtue of pragmatism. This made even more pressing for some Anglo-Catholics the alternative: Was the Established Church a branch of

---

[2] This was the seventh of nine points, all of which are fully given in E. S. Purcell, *Life of Cardinal Manning* (New York: Macmillan and Co., 1896), vol. 1, pp. 532-33.

[3] Ibid., p. 540.

the *Catholic* Church, or a Protestant entity, if not mere putty in the hands of the Nation?

Three of the signatories—Manning, Wilberforce, and Hope—decided that the second alternative was the case. They therefore had no choice but to conclude that the Church of England was not Catholic. Before they did so and directed their steps towards Rome, they attended twelve lectures delivered by John Henry Newman in London in May and June 1850.

Few things could have presented to Newman a better opportunity than the fearful alternative posed by the Gorham Judgment. But nobody could yet foresee this when in the fall of 1849 Father Faber of the London Oratory conveyed to Newman the wish of Bishop Wiseman that he should deliver a set of lectures on Anglicanism. Faber thought that the lectures might take the form of Lenten sermons in the chapel of the London Oratory, at that time still on King William Street. Newman demurred. Anglicanism appeared to him a topic unsuited for sermons aimed at a proposition or practical resolution. He could not dream that before long many Anglo-Catholics would suddenly feel the pressing need to face up to that alternative and look to him for light and encouragement to muster resolve. He certainly did not want to start a polemic, or a "little war," as he put it to Faber. At the same time Bishop Wiseman's wish that he should lecture (or preach) was a command to him. But on what topic?

He begged friends for help. From J. M. Capes, editor of *The Rambler*, came two suggestions. One would have been to expand on the chief shortcomings of the Catholic Church as set forth a year earlier by the Italian theologian Antonio Rosmini, in a controversial book which appeared some thirty years later in English as *The Five Wounds of the Holy Church*. Newman felt that the topic demanded a mastery of Church history he did not possess. The other, "Faith and Reason," appeared to him to be a purely intellectual subject and one not leading to concrete applications as sermons should: "I cannot write a Sermon . . . without a *proposition*."[4]

[4] *The Letters and Diaries of John Henry Newman* (various editors; Oxford:

A month later Newman still felt very uneasy for want of a topic with which he could deeply identify. He was most disinclined to deliver grand sermons: "Oratory is not my forte; I must have *matter* in what I deliver, if it is to be worth any thing."[5] In early January 1850 Faber tried to come to the rescue by suggesting two topics, "persecution" and "the influence of opinions in producing character." Newman replied: "I have *thought* of persecution, but was *afraid* of it."[6] The want of a proper topic already made him think of postponing the lectures to the weeks following Easter. He felt he needed time for a most important and most personal reason: "I *dare* not come up," he wrote on January 6 to Faber, "and preach poor lectures—I must do my best, if possible. There are too many eagerly on the lookout to prove that Catholicism hampers me etc."[7]

Three full months later, in early April, he felt he was still nowhere in spite of the Gorham Judgment. "It struck me," he wrote to Faber, "whether there was any way in which I could turn the present Anglican crisis to account—for I fear interfering in a quarrel—it might do more harm than good." He thought that the sermons should not be given because otherwise St. Philip Neri would have already helped him find a topic: "I am extremely desirous of doing something in London, but if I ought, St Philip would enable me."[8]

St. Philip came through after all, by making him, so it seems, understand that many Anglo-Catholics might need the help he alone could give. Newman seems to have been suddenly seized by a purpose, a proposition that would call for an application. He would propose to Anglo-Catholics, and on a grand public scale, that if they were to be faithful to their principles they had to turn to Rome without delay. He was not to preach on Anglicanism as such, but on Anglo-Catholicism and mainly to Anglo-Catholics. He was to preach a "mission" undoubtedly dearest to him.

University Press, 1865-), vol. 13, p. 344.
    [5] Ibid., p. 352.
    [6] Ibid., p. 367.
    [7] Ibid., p. 382.
    [8] Ibid., p. 460.

In identifying with the proposition, Newman, as he stated in the last Lecture, had to overcome his reluctance to give a glimpse to the public of his own spiritual odyssey, which could be a pattern for Anglo-Catholics. Thus, a decade-and-a-half before the *Apologia*, the printed page carried in Newman's own words the outline of the reasonings that made him discover in the Church of Rome the very Church founded by Jesus Christ. And in contrast to the *Apologia*, the odyssey here had for its background a systematic exposure of the non-Catholicity of the Anglican Church, as well as Newman's most sustained discussion of the four Notes of the true Church.

Newman once more entered upon a major intellectual venture with the dynamics characteristic of him. In late April, Newman told Faber that the first lecture could be announced for May 9 and promised to send him in a day or two all the information necessary to print the entire program of "Twelve Lectures on Certain Difficulties Felt by Anglicans in Submitting to the Catholic Church." He could now worry about incidentals such as the length of each lecture (if they were to last an hour each, he should fill 30 octavo letter press pages—he wrote to Faber); a curtain before the main altar (he voiced his fear to Faber at the chance of being occasionally satirical in the proximity of the Tabernacle); the litany to be recited in the Lady Chapel, etc. Last but not least, he worried about the effect of the sermons: "I am perplexed—either some of them will be most impressively dull— or they will be too much on the other tack."[9] And just a week before the delivery of the first lecture he learned from Faber about a teasing remark of Bishop Wiseman's on the lectures to be delivered. Upset, the ever-sensitive Newman complained to Faber: "I am writing them intellectually against the grain more than I ever recollect doing any thing—and now you bother me by putting an additional fetter on."[10]

Rarely was a remark of Newman's more misconstrued by Newmanists who feel ashamed of this book of his. They seem to think that by 1850 Newman had grown oblivious to what he had

[9] April 28, 1850, ibid., p. 468.
[10] May 2, 1850, ibid., p. 470.

taught to be a viable and, indeed, an impregnable position as he concluded, in April 1839, his essay on "Prospects of the Anglican Church" with a taunt to the Roman Church: "Do they not thus recognize in us their real and most formidable opponents?"[11] Within a year or so that solid position began to loom before his eyes like a mirage, a mere fairy tale, and with most pressing consequences for him. The theological reasons for this he almost immediately provided in the *Development*. It was not until 1864 that he disclosed in the *Apologia* the personal or spiritual parameters those reasons entailed for him.

The third, or ecclesial aspect of what Newman had suddenly perceived was, of course, a mere sequel, however important, to the other two. Had it not been for the Gorham Judgment and its challenge to Anglo-Catholics, Newman might have never elaborated on that third aspect. But then he realized that precisely that aspect had to be portrayed on a vast scale for the benefit of those who even after the Gorham Judgment still dreamed that they could be truly Catholic while remaining Anglicans. To be awakened they had to be confronted with an honest-to-goodnesss portrayal of what the National Church was, and no one could provide this shock treatment even remotely as well as Newman could. The result is a masterpiece as Newmanian as those two other works and just as indispensable for forming an adequate picture of the man and his mind.

The perusal of the last Lecture can refute the suggestion that by "writing against the grain" Newman was not writing according to the deepest of his convictions, intellectual and moral. He certainly wrote the lectures under great pressure of time. After four lectures on May 9-10 and 16-17 (consecutive Thursdays and Fridays) there came a pause of two weeks. Again, there were no lectures on June 27-28, with the last two lectures being delivered on July 4-5. In some cases Newman did not finish writing a lecture until almost the moment of delivery.

From mid-January until July 1850 he had no time for his diary and very little time for his always voluminous correspondence. The Lectures had to be ready for the benefit of those

---

[11] *Essays Critical and Historical*, vol. 1, p. 307.

willing to consider two main points: 1. Since the Oxford Movement's sole and legitimate business was about communion with Rome, those of the Movement had to take the full measure of the non-Catholicity of the Anglican Church (Lectures 1-7). 2. Defects of Rome posed no real barriers on the road to it as the One, Holy, Catholic, and Apostolic Church (Lectures 8-12).

The Movement, Newman argued in Lecture 1, took this tendency toward Rome because it alone represented what the National Church had forfeited in order to satisfy the increasingly secularized national mind. The National Church readily subscribed to the societal claim that "the English people is sufficient for itself." The same Church also held that the question, "May not the free-born, self-dependent, animal mind of the Englishman choose his religion for himself?" was to be answered in the affirmative. Consequently, Newman could cite one article after an another article of the Creed and show that their meaning was increasingly diluted within the National Church (and already in the Thirty-nine Articles) in order to please the national sentiment. Anglo-Catholics merely threw themselves "into the arms of the age" (including the politically comforting arms of Downing Street) by trying to remain within the National Church.

In the next three Lectures, Newman set forth his profound conviction that the Oxford Movement had, from its inception on, an identity, a life, a providential course wholly at variance with that close identification between the National Church and the Nation. That the Movement's identity was a foreign body in the National Church Newman brought home in Lecture 2 by quoting prominent Anglo-Catholics, reflecting on the Movement as well as on the "present crisis." Even more forceful were the episodes portrayed by Newman to illustrate the instinctive hostility with which a society in tune with the National Church reacted against the mere appearance of Catholic views and practices. What the Anglo-Catholics had to understand was that even Archimedes demanded a platform different from the earth in order to move it. It was a mere dream to try to establish Catholic truth within the Established Church by remaining within it. To be retained by that dream was to jeopardize supreme realities: "Oh, my brethren! life is short, waste it not in vanities; . . . wake from a dream, in which you are not profiting your neighbour, but imperiling your own souls."

Clearly Newman assigned to his Lectures a purpose which infinitely surpassed the typical aims of mere theological discourses. These, at least in our times, do not end with the clarion call, "Learn to fear for your souls," which brought Lecture 3 to a close. There he showed, by quoting from his Anglican Sermons, that the spiritual inspiration they were filled with could not be reconciled with the polity of the Established Church. Yet, while that inspiration had some similarity with what some Puritan and Wesleyan "saints" (sorely absent in the Established Church) displayed in their most inspired hours, "the Catholic, and he alone, has within him that union of external with internal notes of God's favor, which sheds the light of conviction over his soul, and makes him both fearless in his faith, and calm and thankful in his hope."

By speaking of the "light" of conviction, Newman sufficiently hinted that the Movement was to be appraised not on the basis of subjective satisfaction but on the basis of truth. For, and this was the topic of Lecture 4, if the Movement had anything providential in it, it was its coming into conflict with the heresy of Erastus, the sixteenth-century Swiss physician. In English terms, the heresy that civil authority had authority over the Church was the doctrine of Royal Supremacy. Or, in even more English terms, the heresy was the surrender to the popular principle that "the English people is sufficient for itself; it wills to be Protestant and progressive; and Fathers, Councils, Schoolmen, Scripture, Saints, Angels, and what is above them, must give way." Anglo-Catholics had therefore to recognize that they were under a providential destiny, "the destiny of truth," and be ready to sacrifice, if necessary, even their livelihood.

Anglo-Catholics, Newman argued in Lecture 5, were deadly wrong in believing that there was a safe and cozy corner for Patristic thinking within the Established Church. Newman warned Anglo-Catholics that acting on that belief would turn them into "Patristico-Protestants." He reminded them that "Anglican divines *would* misquote the Fathers, and shrink from the very doctors to whom they appealed." As to Anglican bishops, they "fearlessly handselled their Apostolic weapons upon the Apostolic party [the Oxford Movement]. . . . It was a solemn war dance which they executed round victims, who by their very principles were bound hand and foot." In Lecture 6 Newman portrayed the radically Erastian nature of all Branch Churches, including Eastern Orthodoxies, to show that the Movement, so anti-Erastian in its inspiration, was never aimed at the formation of a Branch Church. Again, the precisely Catholic aspiration of the Movement militated against its taking the formation of a sect for its aim. Were they to become a sect, Newman warned Anglo-Catholics in Lecture 7, this would leave them far worse off, because sects thrive on that private judgment that makes everybody his own pope. This was not the first or last of Newman's animated strictures against private judgement in the Lectures. In fact, they contain his most detailed and incisive observations on private judgment as the distinctive feature of Protestantism.

The last five Lectures dealt with the claim of Anglo-Catholics that because of its moral faults, diversities, provinciality, and innovations the Roman Church did not possess the classic Notes—holiness, unity, catholicity, and apostolicity—whereby *the* Church was to be known. Newman carefully spelled out the special perspective within which he was to answer that claim. He reminded Anglo-Catholics that they themselves were admitting his principles to the point of almost admitting his conclusions as well, that they were "all but ready to submit to the Church." He begged them to judge the fruits of the Church "by her principles and her object, which you yourselves also admit; not by those of her enemies, which you renounce."

A warning of capital importance indeed, valid for all Catholic presentations of those Notes. They could but appear ineffective whenever Anglicans, in their debate with Catholics, were granted assumptions which they themselves had to disavow as long as they were taking seriously their Christian standing. Therefore, what Newman offered in Lectures 8-12 on the Notes should recommend itself not only because it is his longest discussion of them, but also because he handled the topic in his penetrating manner. In Lectures 8 and 9 about the holiness of the

Church, he showed that sanctity is not to be confused with civilization, however noble, and that moral defects were to be part and parcel of a Church exemplifying the very parables about the Kingdom of God. About the unity of the Church (Lecture 10), Newman evoked Church history as an uninterrupted series of divisive attempts, verifying Christ's and the Apostles' prophecies and warnings. Similar was the gist of his presentation of the Note on catholicity (Lecture 11). What he offered about the apostolicity of the Church (Lecture 12) will be taken up shortly.

In all this Newman kept insisting that Anglo-Catholics were more English than Catholic in their "tailoring" those Notes so that they might find excuses to resist the force of dogmatic truth. He bluntly drove this point home toward the end of the final Lecture: "It is no work of a day to convince the intellect of an Englishman that Catholicism is true." Fourteen years later, in the *Apologia*, he put the same and hardly complimentary observation almost brutally: "It is not at all easy (humanly speaking) to wind up an Englishman to a dogmatic level."[12]

In fact, he showed in the Lectures that the most basic dogmas of Christianity could be levelled to the lowlands of nature by the foremost defenders of the logic of the National Church. Among the most poignant points in the Lectures is Newman's quoting, in Lecture 6, Bishop Warburton's claim that the State should have supremacy over the Church because very little is known about the laws of eternal life, while almost everything is very clear about what ought to be the laws of civil society. Clearly, the Gorham Judgment was a foregone conclusion: "Behold the principle of the reasonings of the Committee of the Privy Council, and the philosophy of the Premier's satisfaction thereupon!"

On the positive side, those last five Lectures are Newman's most gripping form of ecclesiology. Here too, as elsewhere, Newman excels as a theological phenomenologist. Still unmatched are his portrayals of the Notes as phenomena that must of necessity include shafts of light as well as puzzling shadows, precisely because of that human nature which a divinely estab-

---

[12] *Apologia pro vita sua* (Doubleday Image Books, 1956), p. 291.

lished Church must have on earth. Those five Lectures on the Notes contain no trace of the vagueness that characterizes in this respect his dicta in his former Anglican Sermons, transfused as these Sermons are by a most genuine longing for the concretely supernatural.

In the Lectures, Newman shows himself to be one of those very rare theological phenomenologists who never lose sight of the ontological substratum of the phenomona under study. The portrait of the Church he presents in those Notes is never without a sharp reference to that substratum, and contains some of his finest ecclesiological one-liners. No wonder that "ecumenical" Newmanists prefer to keep under cover statements of his such as these: "The essential idea of Catholicism is the Church's infallibility;" "All depends on the fact of the supremacy of Rome;" and "The Church lives, the Apostolic See rules." Utter loyalty to Rome was ringing out from the Lectures from the very start where he spoke of the inability of the National Church to cope with the turmoils of history: "One vessel alone can ride those waves; it is the boat of Peter, the ark of God."[13]

So much for the theological gist of the "difficulties of Anglicans," that is, of Anglo-Catholics as Newman saw them. He insisted on dogmas as standing for the strictly supernatural, as against a nature ready to glorify the national temperament. This alone should make Newman's Lectures appear most timely at a time when in so many parts of the world, but especially in its highly developed parts, Catholics push for a Catholicism subservient to a nature which is American, Dutch, French, German, or what not, and look to Anglicanism for a pattern. They still have to ponder the reasons for the debacle unfolding under our very eyes within the Church of England, to say nothing of other Anglican Communions, a debacle against which Rome is the sole antidote.

A powerful antidote is served in the last Lecture against those efforts that, as will be seen later, are aimed at playing down the true spiritual dynamics of Newman's conversion. As Newman now disclosed for the first time in print, that conversion

---

[13] *Anglican Difficulties*, pp. 377, 349, 328 and 25.

was propelled by a vision of the Church of the Fathers as a Church singlemindedly bent on the pursuit of holiness. Newman's cry, "Be my soul with the Saints,"[14] so often quoted and hardly ever with a reference to its context, is from his last Lecture. Tellingly it is in that Lecture that he gave a glimpse of his own total dedication to that holiness which is a self-effacing care for souls, in this case for the souls of Anglo-Catholics. He could say without boasting: "Others have scoffed at you, but I never; others may have made light of your principles, or your sincerity, never I; others may have predicted evil of you, I have only felt vexed at the prediction." In this respect too, he practiced the virtues heroically.

It was not until the end of July that Newman could write: "I have only just got my Lectures off my hands."[15] The Lectures came out both individually, each with a separate title page, and also as a single volume with "Newman on Anglican Difficulties" on the spine. The last two words on the spine would have made a really effective title page as well. Once more Newman failed to find a compact title for a book of his. He should have perhaps called the book "Appeal to Anglo-Catholics," or "The Pitfalls of Anglo-Catholicism." In that respect he got no help from his publishers who perhaps did not even dare to come up with suggestions of their own.

The publishers Lambert and Burns in London brought out the first edition in 1850. A second edition (printing) followed the same year, and an American edition a year later. James Duffy, in Dublin, was the publisher of the "new and revised" edition in 1857, where the corrections related to minor clarifications. The fourth edition, still with further corrections, followed in 1872 and in a much enlarged format, containing as it did also Newman's reply (first published in 1866) to Pusey's *Eirenicon*. It was in 1876 that Newman gave the Lectures their definitive form as part of a two-volume set, the second volume containing the Letter to Pusey as well as the Letter to the Duke of Norfolk, or Newman's

---

[14] Ibid., p. 388
[15] To Mrs Bowden, July 29, 1850, *Letters and Diaries*, vol. 14, p. 22.

defense of the definition of papal infallibility against its misrepresentations by Gladstone.

The Lectures drew more than enough people to fill the accommodations at the Oratory, a far cry from the splendor of its successor at Brompton Street. Among the listeners were Thackeray, Doyle the *Punch* artist, and Robert Montgomery, a literary clergyman. Regularly present was also Richard H. Hutton, a young man of twenty-six, the future co-editor of the *Spectator*. Needless to say, in attendance were also Bishop Wiseman, who enjoyed the Lectures a great deal, and the Oratorians who enjoyed themselves even more.

Yet, though in a sense enjoyable throughout, the Lectures contained a most serious touch, with an ominous sting to some. Thackeray burst out at the end of one Lecture with the defiant remark: "It is either Rome or Babylon, and for me it is Babylon!"[16] One may bemoan the hold of Babylon or the secular world on Thackeray, but he sensed matters unerringly. Newman's vision of Rome as the true Church implied the alternative, Rome or atheism and even worse, an alternative he himself was to make explicit in the *Apologia*. Manning echoed this broader gist of the Lectures as he wrote on December 11, 1850, to James Hope: "It is Rome or licence of thought and will!"[17]

In reporting to the *British Critic*, an Anglican organ, Montgomery kept such deep vistas out of sight. His chief aim was to neutralize the denominational sting of the Lectures. He did so by focusing on the form at the exclusion of the substance. Even his praise of Newman's attractive delivery was coupled with the slur that it exuded a "spiritual melancholy such as emotional ladies delight to hear." Worse, Montgomery suggested that much of the charm of the Lectures was "artificially *put on* by Mr. Newman."[18] To support this insinuation of insincerity on Newman's part, Montgomery had to find a moral fault-line in the Lectures. It lurked, in Montgomery's eyes, in what has become the most often

[16] H. Tristram (ed.), *John Henry Newman: Centenary Essays* (London: Burns, 1945), p. 235.

[17] Purcell, *Life of Cardinal Manning*, vol. 1, p. 590.

[18] See M. Trevor, *Newman. The Pillar of the Cloud* (London: Macmillan, 1962), p. 519.

quoted (and misquoted) and, indeed, the most stinging utterance in the Lectures. In that passage, which duly entered the *Oxford Dictionary of Quotations*, Newman holds high a poor beggar woman, "not over-scrupulous of truth" but serious in her religious duties, as one with "a prospect of heaven, quite closed and refused to the State's pattern man, the just, the upright, the generous, the honourable, the conscientious, if he be all this, not from a supernatural power,—but from mere natural virtue."

The words, "not over-scrupulous of truth," were seized by Montgomery—and were to be seized again and again—as proof that Catholics were taught to be economical with truth. Kingsley was to make that charge most memorably and with an eye on the entire passage, which then Newman defended with no apologies in the *Apologia*. But the passage (and another to be quoted later) represented the quintessence of Newman's thinking steeped in the supernatural as something thoroughly superior to what is merely natural—however attractive, socially respectable, and, to use the modern phrase, "politically correct" it may otherwise be. That natural counterfeit of the supernatural corresponded, as Newman argued in unforgettable paragraphs, to that "moderation" which a National Church, controlled by the State (the latter always siding with the world as opposed to the Church), had to preach as a convenient substitute for the Gospel.

In the Lectures Newman refers to those hundred or so who followed him into the Catholic Church, after he himself took that step so painful and so demanding in many ways. Even fewer followed the animated and scrupulously argued appeal carried by the Lectures. Newman knew that by becoming a Catholic an Anglo-Catholic jeopardized his social standing (and forfeited his very home and living if he were a clergyman). Newman knew what it meant to leave Oriel, then the most prestigious home in an Oxford which was, like heaven on earth, a state of mind even more than the splendid place it has always been.

One of those who could not go that existential distance was Frederick Rogers (created Lord Blachford in 1871). Rogers, of whom Newman later spoke as his most intimate friend during the Tractarian years and who defended Newman with a pamphlet in 1845, was by now turning into a pillar of the Establishment. As such, he did his best to blunt the edge of Newman's argument in reviewing his Lectures in *The Guardian*. Rogers claimed that Newman had set too great a store by logic. Newman in turn saw that Rogers, like so many others, tried to "fence off." He found this kind of argumentation very unfair: "They dare not, won't say *what* they believe and *why.*" The charge of too much logic could easily be turned back: "Our Anglo-Catholic friends enjoyed my logic while it attacked the evangelicals . . . , but when it went *too far* then it was inexorable and I deteriorated."[19]

Catholics took the lectures for a signal cause to rejoice. Newman could take for a compliment Bishop Wiseman's complaint about the price of the book as preventing leading Catholics from giving it away in large numbers. The very title, "Rise, Progress, and Results of Puseyism," of Capes' review of the Lectures in the December 1850 issue of *The Rambler* suggested strong approval. By then Newman was busy preparing another set of lectures, this time in the Corn Exchange in Birmingham, on "Present Position of Catholics in England," a resounding public-relations success. Then came the Achilli trial, after that the time-consuming business of setting up the Catholic University in Dublin. Newman had no leisure to reflect systematically on the reception of the Lectures. Recent converts could find great and immediate help in the Lectures, but they represented a mere trickle with respect to the two major segments of English Catholics. Those who descended from the Recusants had known all too well that the National Church was, as Newman put it in the very first Lecture, but a "mimic Catholicism." Sustenance other than brilliant Lectures was needed by the vast crowds of immigrant Irish whom Providence confided to the zeal of Manning.

Newman poured cold water on the enthusiasm of Talbot, who, on his way to becoming a close advisor to Pius IX and eventually a nemesis to Newman, wrote to him from Pisa in mid-July 1850, about the merits of translating the Lectures into Italian. They, Talbot claimed, had made a "sensation all over Europe." Newman replied that the Lectures "were solely addressed to Puseyites about whom the good Monsignori and Padri of Rome

---

[19] Dec. 28, 1850, to Henry Wilberforce, *Letters and Diaries*, vol. 14, p. 179.

are about as ignorant as Protestants are about them."[20] At any rate, the Lectures were quickly crowned from Rome with a Doctorate of Divinity *honoris causa.*

Three months later Newman showed a similar reserve about the Lectures in his letter to Charles Russell. The Lectures, Newman wrote, were a "mere ephemeral publication, and I shall be far more than satisfied, if, as you think, they will do good for the moment."[21] He could not have suspected how much good they could do in the very distant future in the context of a very "present crisis" not only of Anglo-Catholics but of Catholics in England in particular, and elsewhere as well. Are not too many of them ready to go Erastian in the sense of taking the dictates of culture for the articles of true Cult?

Apart from the section of the *Apologia* already mentioned, Newman said little on the Lectures in his publications. Significant remarks are, however, contained in his correspondence, where he and others (Baron von Hügel among them) refer to the Lectures as "Anglican Difficulties." Newman ties to the Lectures his reminder about one's God-given duty to seek holiness as codified concretely in the Church established by Christ. His sense of this duty sets the tone of his answer to Charles Thynne, who, in April 1852, pointed out to him that there were many Protestants with great virtues. "What I said," Newman replied with reference to the Lectures, "does not at all interfere with an admission of the religious excellence of *individual* Protestants." The late Bishop Ryder's grandsons, he added, "are with us here" in the Oratory School.[22]

Such was on Newman's part a concrete instancing of the direction in which one had to answer the question he character-ized as a "most *serious question* to any one who wishes to have the blessings and benefits of redemption." Any such person had to ask himself: "How do I *prove*, against the common opinion of mankind, that I belong to that great spiritual corporation of which Saints and Martyrs in the early times were members?" He knew that the question was a most personal one for Lord Ryder:

[20] Aug. 11, 1850, ibid., p. 35.
[21] Oct. 2, 1850, ibid., p. 87.
[22] *Letters and Diaries*, vol. 15, p. 63.

"I remember you and Lady C. in Mass. God be with you. You will find in Clifton those who will help you. I know you will be led forward, *through whatever pain*. It is what you *pay* for the pearl of great price." Therefore he could press the question which during his entire career he kept in focus: "*Am I in the Church?* This is the question for *me*—others have not had this question brought home to them, I have. I am not as others."[23] Very un-Newman-like should therefore seem the effort of those Newman-ists who try to make it appear that he always meant to be something other than a fully committed Roman Catholic.

In 1862, Newman referred to the last of the Lectures as a place where he "strongly stressed" the same point relating to the logic of his conversion: "I certainly did not become a Catholic, as others have, on the ground 'Ubi Petrus, ibi Ecclesia,'—but because, whereas the Church is to last to the end of the world, unless that large Communion which happens to be Roman be the Church, the Church has failed."[24] Beneath this reasoning lay the logic so dear to Newman (and so firmly argued in the last section of the *Grammar*) that if there was a God, it was most unlikely that He left man without a specific guidance as to how to find his way back to the divine, that is, the supernatural. The Church was merely the specific embodiment of that specific guidance towards a target which was not of this world but was the realm of the supernatural and of sacramental holiness.

Newman's last significant epistolary reference to the Lectures related to his insistence there on the need of grace to make natural virtues meritorious. Once more he had to defend his contrast between the beggar woman and the State's pattern man against the charge, this time (October 1874) made by the Reverend Edward Paget, once a staunch Tractarian, that Newman made good evil and evil good, virtue vice and vice virtue. It was not difficult for Newman to turn the tables on Paget, though he did so indirectly, in a letter to Emily Bowles. The supreme defect of Paget's accusations, Newman wrote, lay in the fact that the Thirty-nine Articles, and the Thirteenth in particular, imposed

---

[23] Ibid.
[24] Oct. 15, 1862, to D. Radford, *Letters and Diaries*, vol. 20, p. 308.

on Paget a contrast even more extreme than the one he himself had drawn: Catholics do not have to go as far as to hold, with the Thirteenth Article, that "works done before the grace of Christ and the inspiration of His Spirit, *have the nature of sin*." Whereas, Newman added, "I have drawn out the differences between the *world* and Christianity, he [Paget] deliberately places himself, an Anglican clergyman, on the side of the world."[25]

Of course, Paget was not the first or the last Anglican clergyman to do so. But a broader aspect of the lasting instructiveness of the Lectures lies in the perennial temptation for Catholic priests and laity to do the same and to look for Catholic theologians (including some latter-day Newmanites) ready to approve. Not a few of them are responsible for an image of Newman now popular among educated Catholics: Newman ultimately stood for a "gentlemanlike" behavior and held high the pattern man, if not of the State at least of refined Society. In Newman's time that "broadmindedness" still had a theological name, "Latitudinarianism," for it. Today, it is hiding under the fashionable cultural labels of "openness," "renewal," and, of course, "progress." Catholic "salesmen" of these labels are busy dispensing them as they try to distract, by emphasizing the categories "reformist" versus "traditionalist," from a categorical confrontation of the difference between Truth and Error, both writ large.

That "broadmindedness" was not yet too noticeable among Catholics when Wilfrid Ward published Newman's first major biography in 1912. This may explain his nondescript handling of the Lectures. In the chapter "The King William Street Lectures," only four out of twenty-one pages deal with the Lectures, and of those four two are taken up by a long quotation from Richard Hutton's *Cardinal Newman*, published two decades earlier.[26] Most readers of Ward's book were still aware that Hutton had exerted an enormous influence in England and in the English-speaking world by being for many years the co-editor of the *Spectator*. But

[25] Oct. 15, 1874, *Letters and Diaries*, vol. 27, p. 138.

[26] W. Ward, *The Life of John Henry Cardinal Newman* (London: Longmans, Green, and Co., 1912), vol. 1, pp. 231-34. On Hutton's work see the next note.

only those who had read Hutton's book carefully could still recall that, contrary to Ward, his disagreement with Newman's argumentation had some important qualifications. Indeed, at times Hutton seemed to agree with Newman in the very essentials.

Had Hutton, the son and grandson of Unitarian ministers, not wished to agree with Newman he would not have written: "When Newman made up his mind to join the Church of Rome, his genius bloomed out with a force and freedom such as it never displayed in the Anglican communion." Nor would he have eulogized Newman as one whose life stood in strange contrast "to the eager and agitated turmoil of confused passions, hesitating ideals, tentative virtues and grasping philanthropies among which it has been lived." In fact, Newman stood higher, in Hutton's eyes, than any of his contemporaries: "No life known to me, in the last century of our national history, can for a moment compare with it, so far as we can judge of such deep matters, in unity of meaning and constancy of purpose."[27]

In all likelihood, Ward knew of the letter which Hutton wrote to Newman in late February 1863. Hutton, who by then had moved from Unitarianism toward Anglicanism, told Newman of his being grieved by the treatment Newman suffered from those "whose profession is liberalism." He meant some who tried to defend Kingsley's indefensible attacks on Newman. In concluding his letter, he let Newman know that he would consider it a privilege to learn from him if he were ever to preach in London again: "I have not heard you since your course to the Anglicans in 1850, I think, on which I was a regular attendant."[28]

Hutton must have remembered this wish of his when almost three decades later he was proofreading his book and word came of Newman's death. He must have felt a special poignancy in going over the passage in which he told about his first exposure to Newman the lecturer or preacher: "I shall never forget the impression which his voice and manner, which opened upon me for the first time in these lectures, made on me. Never did a voice

[27] R. H. Hutton, *Cardinal Newman* (Boston: Houghton, Mifflin and Co., 1890), pp. 11, 55, and 250.

[28] *Letters and Diaries*, vol. 21, p. 68.

seem better adapted to persuade without irritating. Singularly sweet, perfectly free from any dictatorial note, and yet rich in all the cadences proper to the expression of pathos, of wonder, and of ridicule, there was still nothing in it that any one could properly describe as insinuating, for its simplicity, and frankness, and freedom from the half-smothered notes which express indirect purpose, was as remarkable as its sweetness, its freshness, and its gentle distinctness."[29]

Ward's nondescript account of the Lectures, which he praised for their "brilliantly witty" character, but for nothing deeper, begins with his quoting Newman's remark that he was writing "intellectually against the grain more than I recollect doing anything."[30] For the first but not the last time, that remark was quoted out of context and used to suggest that Newman himself deprecated thereby the intellectual quality of the Lectures. What he truly meant by that remark was revealed in his reply to Hutton. About Hutton's praises of his poems Newman observed that he would indeed gladly have given himself up to writing poetry, since it never troubled him, while writing books always did: "Their composition has been to me, in point of pain, a mental child-bearing; and I have been accustomed to say to myself, 'In sorrow shalt thou bring forth children'."[31]

These words of Newman's, apart from other utterances of his, run counter to Louis Bouyer's contention in his *Newman: His Life and Spirituality*, that the Lectures were Newman's last work "to be conceived and written in a spirit so foreign to his own, to his real self, a spirit forced upon him by his quondam disciples."[32] Bouyer's glowing account of Newman's Anglican defense of the Via Media is certainly contradicted by the Lectures where Newman dismissed the Via Media as pure speculation that existed only on paper. Clearly, it would be presumptuous to ascribe to external pressure this most considered statement of Newman's which he was to repeat with just as much emphasis

[29] Hutton, *Cardinal Newman*, pp. 207-08.

[30] Ward, *The Life of John Henry Cardinal Newman*, vol. 1, p. 231.

[31] March 3, 1864, *Letters and Diaries*, vol. 21, p. 69.

[32] L. Bouyer, *Newman: His Life and Spirituality* (London: Burns and Oates, 1958). p. 290.

in the *Apologia*. While admitting that never before had the doctrinal inconsistencies of Anglicanism "been more pitilessly exposed," Bouyer failed to register the reason for the effectiveness of the Lectures. They had that quality because of a most benevolent spirit displayed in them toward Anglo-Catholics. For in each and every topic taken up by Newman the Anglo-Catholic view was presented in its best possible light in order to leave no room for what Bouyer aptly called "the slough of inconsistency." Far from being conceived and written "against the grain," the Lectures were animated by a most genuine zeal for the salvation of souls, the souls of Anglo-Catholics. The Lectures will, of course, sound negative and belligerent in the ears of anyone unable to see almost all of the Church of England as steeped in Protestant private judgment, as opposed to its slight Anglo-Catholic segment. To decry that Church, as Newman did in the Lectures, as a "counterfeit Church,"[33] was to counter its effort to appear as "Catholic" and keep confusing Anglo-Catholics in their longing for genuine Catholicism.

Newman's next major biographer, Meriol Trevor, did not quote the "intellectually against the grain" passage, let alone exploit it. This protects some sparkling gems in her account of the Lectures which she did not esteem highly. She found symbolic Newman's reference to his labors in preparing the Lectures, for the printer: "Let no one suppose that my books do not cost me labor—they are as severe a trial as hedging and ditching, though it is not one's back that aches, or one's muscles that are worked."[34] Trevor commented: "Hedging and ditching was an apt description for what he was doing in these lectures, in contrast to the ploughing and sowing of other works."[35]

That Trevor may not have seen deeply and far enough can be gathered from her view that Newman's paradoxically sharp denunciations of moral evil sounded shocking "because those of the Gospel had become too familiar to impress the imagination."[36] She could not mean that the blame lay with the Gospels. But she

---

[33] *Anglican Difficulties*, p. 315.

[34] Newman to Miss Holmes, July 15, 1850, *Letters and Diaries*, vol. 14, p. 11.

[35] Trevor, *Newman. The Pillar of the Cloud*, p. 522.

[36] Ibid., pp. 520-21.

failed to insist that those whom Newman blamed deserved it in full. Moreover, writing this as she did in the early 1960s, she might have noticed that there was a trend afoot among Catholics to paint a portrait of Newman as an enthusiastic friend of all humanness and of nothing essentially higher. Those portrayals contained few traces of that paradoxically sharp moral vision about the difference between the Kingdom of God and the World. Miss Trevor's next book, *Prophets and Guardians: Renewal and Tradition in the Church*,[37] was a case in point. Its concluding remarks on the papacy and episcopal collegiality run counter to what Newman emphasized in the Lectures and elsewhere about the overriding need for a real central authority, which is not merely a final arbiter in dispute but a perennially firm guiding hand.

The discussion of the Lectures in the recent major biography of Newman by Ian Ker is introduced with Newman's complaint that he could not remember ever before writing "so intellectually against the grain." Unlike Trevor, who was more interested in anecdotal, though telling details than in intellectual analysis, Ker labored to condense the rich contents of the Lectures in ten or so pages.[38] He made much of Newman's emphasis on the difference between two kinds of vision: One where reality is grasped, and another where it dissipates like a mirage or fairy tale. This difference between reality and unreality is indeed an ever-recurring theme in the Lectures and so is the use of vivid analogies as an indispensable, though at times imperfect means of showing that difference. An allied theme is the reliance on common sense and consistency. Indeed, the last letter printed as an Appendix on the very last page of the first volume of Ward's biography contains this reminder of Newman's in 1846 to an Anglo-Catholic: "I have ever made consistency the mark of a saint."[39] His cry, "Be my soul with the Saints!" already quoted from the last Lecture, certainly is in line with *that* consistency.

---

[37] *Prophets and Guardians: Renewal and Tradition in the Church* (Garden City, N.Y.: Doubleday, 1969).

[38] I. Ker, *John Henry Newman. A Biography* (Oxford University Press, 1990), pp. 350-59.

[39] To Henry Wilberforce, July 4, 1846, *Letters and Diaries*, vol. 11, p. 191.

It is through that consistent attention to the pursuit of holiness against the ever-present lure of naturalism that the Lectures reveal their ultimate thrust, as well as the principal and most timely reason why they should be rescued from oblivion and neglect. The timeliness has to do both with the Catholic Church of the last thirty or so years and with the Church of England of these very recent days. In the Catholic Church, too many theologians have made it a fashion not to appreciate what Newman added to the contrast he drew between the beggar woman and the State's pattern man. Unlike in his day, Newman would not find today a broad Catholic echo to his claim that the Catholic Church, and the Catholic Church alone, is right in holding that "it were better for sun and moon to drop from heaven, for the earth to fail, and for all the many millions who are upon it to die of starvation in extremest agony, as far as temporal affliction goes, than that one soul, I will not say, should be lost but should commit one single venial sin, should tell one wilful untruth, . . . or steal one poor farthing without excuse."[40]

These words clash with the "socially correct" thinking of many Catholics, including some members of their hierarchy, who speak as if that "socially correct" thinking sets the supreme standard in faith and morals. Only those Catholics who still cling to truly supreme standards can find solace in the fact that even today official Catholic teaching (the *New Catechism* is a case and, of course, the Encyclical *Veritatis splendor*) can be invoked in support of Newman's claim about sun and moon. That claim was bound to send shock waves through England's nice society (and any nice society) and through all those who try to be part of it even at the risk of the salvation of their souls.

Newmanists have so far failed to see something significant in the fact that Newman devoted one lecture each to three Notes, but two lectures to the Note on holiness. By doing so, Newman served further notice as to what was really reprehensible in the Anglican Church and what made most illogical the resolve of Anglo-Catholics to find in it their spiritual home. They had to decide whether they were taking with utmost seriousness the

---

[40] *Anglican Difficulties*, p. 240.

Apostle's warning that a Christian had to look beyond his earthly abode for another home, where God's own holiness sets the rule, and which it was the sole business of the Church to make available.

To decide this, Newman argued, they had to adopt a perspective that was simply outrageous to those who identified Christian virtues with gentlemanly behavior in a nice society. That nice society, Newman warned in the Lectures, professed to be scandalized by gaudily popular festivals in Catholic countries. But, Newman added, what would happen if one were "to set up a large Crucifix at Charing Cross"? In that case, Newman prophesied, "it would but excite the scorn, the rage, the blasphemy of the out-pouring flocking multitude, a multitude who in their hearts are unbelievers. Alas! There is no idea in the national mind, supernaturally implanted which the Crucifix embodies."[41]

Today, when the entire National Church counts only two million practicing members out of a population of fifty million, there would be no demonstration, only indifference. The Nation, as Newman put it in these Lectures, has become "unchurched" by its National Church, and those within it are uncertain as to what to practice unless ever-shifting practice is taken for the norm. That indifference speaks more loudly than would a frenzied shouting down of the gist of what Newman said: a National Church can be no better, can rise no higher than a modern Nation which is all too often committed to pursuing the line of least resistance and is ready to sink lower and lower through its political dynamics.

One would therefore miss the very thrust of these Lectures, which reverberate with the palpably deepest concerns of a saintly soul, if one were to take a technique used there for their chief and most instructive characteristic. The technique, as already noted, is the appeal to the imagination as the only means whereby truth can be conveyed in a vivid form. Newman uses that technique from the start, even when he points out the dangers of the imagination whereby the fanciful is taken for the real. But to break the spell of a misleading imagination, one

---

[41] Ibid., p. 284.

needs the eyes of faith: "For this is the truth: the Establishment, whatever its temporal greatness and its secular prospects, in the eyes of faith is a mere wreck."[42]

A wreck it is, wrecked by its own logic at work from the moment its foundations were laid. That logic finds today [1992] the opposition Parties holding a farcical advantage over the governing Tories. The Tories, following a series of shocking disclosures about some of their leaders' philanderings, desperately try to make it appear that by putting "family values" on their banner they did not have "private morality" in mind. Those in the Opposition draw huge political dividends from the fact that they sedulously keep mum on the morals that keep families together. But even in morally more consistent British times Newman had grounds to say that he could not see how the Established Church, insofar as it is an integral part of the wider national Establishment, "could rise above the level of its source (Henry VIII, I say)."[43]

Newman would rightly see something prophetic in the latest convulsions of that wreck. They take place in the immediate wake of the 500th anniversary of the birth of a lecherous and perfidious monarch. He went through five wives (sending two of them to the scaffold) and cold-bloodedly deceived tens of thousands of trusting Englishmen, still good Catholics, forming a "Pilgrimage of Grace." Five hundred years after his birth, new patterns of "family living" have become so popular within the larger Royal Family as to bode ill for that august ruling House. Against this backdrop the decision of the Duchess of Kent to become a Roman Catholic stands out all the more significantly.

The moral of all this will be slighted, albeit reluctantly, by most Anglo-Catholics. They find too powerful the pull of the Establishment, with all its pomp and circumstance, however fading. They tolerate the farce whereby the sacred matter of ordination turns into a free game between the sexes. They listen in hushed silence, but do not follow up with appropriate actions, when the diocesan synod of Inverness is told by its bishop that

[42] Ibid., p. 4.
[43] To A. Philipps de Lisle, March 9, 1866, in *Letters and Diaries*, vol. 22, p. 176.

"the Scottish Episcopal Church was about to press the self-destruct button."[44] They try to overlook what the run-of-the-mill Anglican does not notice at all, namely that the light of the candle which, so Latimer told Ridley at the stake, "by God's grace, in England, so I trust, shall never be put out,"[45] is now flickering. Yet, in spite of their theological logic, would Latimer and Ridley still be "of good cheer" when hardly anything is left for their latter-day disciples to cheer about in churches abounding in empty pews?

Latimer and Ridley would hardly be pleased if they heard the archbishops of Canterbury and York declare that the conversion of the Duchess is one of those journeys or "personal pilgrimages" that "quite commonly lead individuals across denominational boundaries." Nor would Latimer and Ridley be comforted by the words of the Cardinal Archbishop of Westminster that "we must respect a person's conscience in these matters [the conversion of the Duchess], partly because "the Duchess recognizes how much she owes to the Church of England." Can these words comfort some Anglo-Catholics reluctant to see the handwriting on their ecclesiastical walls? And what about Roman Catholics? According to the archbishops of Canterbury and York the relation between Anglicans and Catholics is "warmer and more cooperative than ever before."[46] Should Roman Catholics therefore think that, contrary to Vatican II, their Church is but one of the many denominations and take this for good news?

In giving his answers to such questions Newman would be enormously pained, though not groping for words even for a moment. He would once more go right to the heart of the matter. Already in the very first of these Lectures he warned: "Logic is a stern master."[47] The phrase stands at the end of his tracing the logical trend within Protestantism toward that most alluring form of naturalism which is pantheism. Today it is, of course, dis-

---

[44] *The Scotsman*, August 24, 1993, p. 3.

[45] J. G. Ridley, *Nicholas Ridley. A Biography* (London: Longmans, Green and Co., 1957). p. 418.

[46] These statements, made in the wake of the Duchess' conversion in January 1994, were widely reported in the press on both sides of the Atlantic.

[47] *Anglican Difficulties*, p. 31.

guised as aesthetic reverence for a Nature writ no less large than the Creator Almighty, whom it aims to replace! In the Lectures he also drew the pathetic portrait of those driven by that trend: "Surely, they will find no resting-place anywhere for their feet, and the feet of their disciples, but will be tumbled down from one depth of blasphemy to another, till they arrive at sheer and naked atheism, the *reductio ad absurdum* of their initial principles."[48]

Only what he added to the words "logic is a stern master" may need some revision. He felt that those driven by that naturalistic trend still protested against that stern master: "They feel it, they protest against it; they profess to hate it, and would fain dispense with it; but it is the law of their intellectual nature."[49] Today, he would sadly register that they merrily go along. Witness their enthusiastic caving in to naturalism along the entire spectrum of sexual ethics and challenges of a bioethical nature. Instead of condemning them, Newman might say that we witness, and all Catholics should see this for what it truly is, the unfolding of another chapter written by a most painful logic at work in ecumenism. It is not a logic of easily hopeful vistas, while it does full justice to some momentous warnings.

Such warnings—most generous as well as most serious—did not fail to come from the highest forum. Generosity reached unusual heights when Paul VI seated Dr. Ramsey, the first archbishop of Canterbury to visit Rome in more than four hundred years, on a chair of equal rank with his. In his visit to the Canterbury Cathedral, John Paul II prayed on the same *prie-dieu* side-by-side with Dr. Runcie. As late as September 1992, Dr. Carey, the present archbishop of Canterbury, was allowed to offer a chalice to the Pope as a token of hope for an eventual concelebration of Catholic and Anglican clergy. A most generous gesture of goodwill it was. The Pope knew all too well that only a day or two earlier Dr. Carey had voiced, and in Rome at that, his full support of women who claimed for themselves the right

---

[48] *Anglican Difficulties*, p. 31.
[49] Ibid., pp. 31-32.

to consecrate the Eucharistic bread and wine, this central function of sacramental priesthood.

Already Dr. Ramsey had not taken as truly serious Paul VI's warning that an Anglican ordination of women would forever bar the road to reunion. By saying that he would not be surprised if Rome would follow suit, Dr. Ramsey proved that he knew Rome very little, a point which Newman could now illustrate by evoking situations from the past as anticipations of the present. Even more importantly, Newman might say today that in his unfathomable wisdom God allows Protestant logic to come suddenly to its final *dénouement* even in that (Protestant) Church which appeared to many to still have the reality of priesthood as understood in Roman Catholicism and Eastern Orthodoxy.

These Lectures provide the ground for second-guessing Newman in this matter. For just as he began the Lectures by pointing out that what appeared to be a rich reality was in fact a mirage ready to vanish, he handled in the same way the views of the Anglo-Catholic clergy about their presumed priestly status. He had once shared those presumptions of theirs with all the emotions thrown in for good measure: "Can I wipe out from my memory, or wish to wipe out, those happy Sunday mornings, light or dark, year after year, when I celebrated your communion-rite in my own church of St. Mary's?"[50] But all that noble experience had no substance to it. And he asked Anglo-Catholics to admit his explanation of the fact, since he was the last to deny the fact itself. However, once that explanation had been accepted, it was impossible not to conclude, as Newman was to do in the *Apologia*, that the Anglican Church, once "a great objective fact" in his eyes, turned before his very eyes into "the veriest of nonentities."[51]

The decision of the Church of England to "ordain" women to the "priesthood" illustrates both Newman's analysis of Anglican logic and the logic of his conversion. His remark, "In 1854 I had not that utter distrust of the Anglican Orders which I

---

[50] Ibid., pp. 81-82.
[51] *Apologia pro vita sua*, p. 368.

feel in 1870," was preceded by his pointing out that he had become a Roman Catholic because "I knew it was necessary, if I would participate in the grace of Christ, to seek it there where He had lodged it."[52] Newman, who hoped that a pope would eventually settle the question of the validity of Anglican Orders, would have greatly rejoiced in the chief argument in Leo XIII's decision. For Newman's distrust rested precisely with the difficulty of assuming a proper intention on the part of Anglicans in the performing of ordinations and in the celebration of the Eucharist. The pope's decision chiefly rested with considerations about Anglican intentions concerning holy orders and not with questions relating to the continuity of Anglican orders with the Catholic ordinations preceding them.

As is well known, Leo XIII's decision prompted some Anglican bishops to have themselves re-consecrated by Orthodox and Old-Catholic bishops. While this may be taken on their part for a proof of right intention, the same can hardly be said of each and every Church of England bishop, although almost all of them can now trace their own episcopal consecration to one or another of those re-consecrations. As can be judged from the continued obeisance to the Thirty-nine Articles as well as from the prevailing Anglican theology of ordination and eucharist, the general status of intention remains just as unconvincing. This was fully brought out by the drastic inadequacies (from the Catholic viewpoint) of the final report of the Anglican-Roman Catholic Interfaith Commission (ARCIC) on ministry and sacraments.

Whatever there remained of convincing character, it has now become drastically compromised by the decision to consider women as valid recipients of the sacrament of priesthood. Six years ago "the question of the ordination of women to the priesthood and the episcopate" could still appear but a theoretical problem, though "from a Roman Catholic point of view" one of the "matters pertaining to faith."[53] The problem is now turning into another chasm and bodes ill for the hopeful perspectives which the Roman Catholic Bishop Cormac Murphy-O'Connor

---

[52] To E. Husband, July 17, 1870, *Letters and Diaries*, vol. 25, p. 160.

[53] Certainly so after John Paul II issued his Apostolic Letter, "Ordinatio sacerdotalis," on May 22, 1994.

offered in a letter to the readers of *The Times*: "I do assure your correspondent that the Holy See and Lambeth have reopened the question of Anglican orders and regard it as a most important and urgent one."[54] The decision to ordain women (and its forthcoming implementation at the first appropriate ordination season this coming Eastertide) shuts a door hardly ajar and does it with a bang, however unintended.

Newman's words, referring to the 1870s, that Christians never desired a reunion more, but "never were the obstacles greater or stronger that divide them,"[55] has now an eerie timeliness. For incomparably greater strength is needed to reverse an error than to yield to its lure in the first place. The decision shows that the Church of England does not have the intention of doing what the Church has always been doing in ordaining. For almost two millennia now the Church has taken only men as priests. John Paul II has reconfirmed that policy on many occasions. One of them was his address to the American bishops during his second visit to the United States. He brushed aside an American archbishop's all too transparent suggestion that women be granted "full discipleship," with a mere seven words: "Women are not called to the priesthood." Newman would today point out that prominent laymen and laywomen who cry out "This is not a Church!" as they leave the Church of England merely accept his arguments about that Church not being Catholic.

What they leave has now revealed itself to be a *very partial* realization of the Church. Whether that expression would please Newman is doubtful. He would stress that with its decision to ordain women the Church of England has served another proof of the enormous extent to which it is part of an Establishment, taken for political structure and popular consensus. He would find an amusing confirmation of his view in a letter to *The Times* whose writer praised the spiritual insight of the bishops into God's will and found it a pity that the same will "must now be approved by Parliament, a predominantly lay body."[56] Newman

---

[54] *The Times*, August 19, 1988, p. 13.

[55] To the Rev. David Brown, October 24, 1872, in *Letters and Diaries*, vol. 26, p. 187.

[56] P. Birdsall, *The Times*, Nov. 17, 1992, p. 17.

would add that many in that political body have no faith in God, let alone in bishops.

A Church so much the prisoner of a largely agnostic Parliament will not see that a two-edged sword is at work in the logic of what has happened. A plain lay communicant of that Church can rejoice, again in the form of a letter in the same issue, that the bishops' judgment means that God "erected yet another barrier as a sign of His objection to any further attempt to unite the Anglican Church with the Church of Rome."[57] But a Roman Catholic steeped in Newman's perspectives can register another page written in what may be called God's ecumenism. By allowing the Church of England to break with a universal (catholic) tradition about the valid recipients of holy orders, God himself has called attention to the pitfalls of ecumenism.

Such pitfalls reveal more and more of their treacherous depths through the mechanism whereby the supreme seal is put on the bishops' judgment. The seal is not at all theological but political. Needless to say, theological rhetoric is used to the full to give the opposite impression. As he pleaded, in late October 1993, to the House of Lords to pass the bill authorizing the ordination of women, Dr. Carey referred to the well over a thousand women deacons "who are offering their skill and gifts to the service of Christ and many of them see this legislation as offering the fulfillment of their ministry."[58] With the Royal Assent given, on November 5, 1993, to the measure for the Ordination of women, it became the law of the land, though hardly the law of Christ's Church. In his un-rabbinically high esteem of womanhood, Christ certainly could have given, had He wanted to, more than one hint about the eventual inclusion of women in the Apostolic College, especially if He meant that College to be in bondage to the State or society. Rather, Christ emphatically denied to Caesar appurtenances which, inasmuch as they are strictly supernatural, such as the sacrament of priesthood, ought to pertain to God's ordinances alone. Otherwise Christ would

---

[57] T. G. Oliver, letter to *The Times*, Nov. 17, 1992, p. 17.
[58] *The Times*, Oct. 28, 1993, p. 2.

have put the Church in bondage to that unredeemed society over which the State rules supreme.

That the Church of England is in bondage, and willingly so, to a political Establishment, Newman would find grippingly illustrated in the contradictoriness of the comments by Richard Harries, the Anglican bishop of Oxford, who voted for the ordination of women. In an essay written for the *Observer* the bishop confessed: "Though we may have the legal authority to decide, we do not have the spiritual authority to do so."[59] The bishop should have spelled out that the legal authority rested with the Parliament. Worse, the spiritual authority, so the bishop added, could only come from a wider consensus, implying the consensus of a catholic or universal Church. Therefore he had to admit that those "who find their Christian identity as part of the wider Church" have no choice but to reconsider their membership in the Church of England. However, if such was the case, it made little sense on the part of the bishop to call one of his priests, Father Martin Flatman, ready "to seek entry into the Roman Catholic Church," his "fellow Catholic." The bishop should have seen that he and his priest meant two very different things by the same word "Catholic," unless equivocation was to be part of theology.

Newman would have no patience with the bishop's efforts to gloss over such a difference, nor would he be amused by the failure of prominent Anglo-Catholics, such as Dr. Graham Leonard, retired bishop of London, to see some crucial difference. For all his readiness to accept the Roman magisterium, Dr. Leonard still referred to some "responsible people in the Roman Catholic Church" who argue the revisability of Leo XIII's decision about Anglican orders.[60] Their "responsible" thinking does not include attention to the policy (unconditional re-ordination) which Rome has invariably followed regarding Anglican clergymen who become Catholics. Last but not least, Newman would pity, with tears in his eyes, Anglo-Catholics who with Olga Maitland, a member of the Parliament, begged Dr. Carey "to

[59] *The Observer*, Nov. 15, 1992, p. 24.

[60] *The Times*, Nov. 20, 1992, p. 5. [Dr Leonard has since become a Catholic and was ordained a Catholic priest.]

guide the Church to so conduct its affairs as to take into account our deep anguish." About her self-pity, "To be punished for seeking to stick to the truth and thus to ensure our salvation is hard to bear,"[61] Newman would remark that too many Anglo-Catholics have been for too long too willing to bear the unbearable. Thus Eric Mascall, a theological stalwart of Anglo-Catholicism in our times, did not take heed on realizing that the Church of England had no real use for him and his kind.

A chief and, in the context of the women's ordination, a most specific reason for Mascall's and other Anglo-Catholics' discomfiture is an equivocation, similar to the one with the word "catholic," which guides those led by Dr. Carey about the validity of orders conferred on women. In fact, even less than equivocation was offered by Dr. Carey to the 7 bishops and about 700 clergy who, on February 24, 1994, published their declaration of loyalty to Rome.[62] To these, who were fully convinced about the intrinsic invalidity of women's ordinations, Dr. Carey offered the next day a mere sop instead of theological reality, when he assured them that they would "continue to have a full and honoured place in the Church."[63] Some honor . . . , one would be prompted to think, some place . . . . As for the thirty-two woman-deacons who were ordained in Bristol cathedral on March 12, they could find no theology, even if interested, but only a mixture of psychology and sociology in Dr. Carey's encomium of their patience in awaiting and joy over receiving "their just reward." Theological ecclesiology was honored in the breach when Dr. Carey continued: "Now we look forward as a Church to a future in which all, *whatever their views on this issue*, can unite in proclaiming the gospel to a world in need" (italics added).[64] Social gospel has indeed no room for Christ's words: "Truth will set you free."

In view of this, Newman would be fully entitled to warn us against reading too much into his joy over some changes for the

---

[61] Letter to *The Times*, Nov. 17, 1992, p. 17.

[62] *The Times*, February 24, 1994, p. 1, under the headline, "Bishops Lead Exodus to Rome."

[63] *Church Times*, February 25, 1994, p. 1.

[64] *The Times*, March, 12, 1994, p. 5.

better that took place in the Church of England during his last years. When in 1876 the possibility of an Anglican Uniate Church was put forward by some, Newman welcomed it as a "means of drawing to us so many good people, who are now shivering at our gates."[65] He did not write this out of ecumenical sentimentalism so that a painful fact might get out of focus. It was his view, not weakened by the sight of a spiritual revival brought about by Charles Gore and others within the late-19th-century Anglican Church, that it was "only a matter of time, how long the Anglican Church retains any part of the Faith."[66] He saw that, regardless of such developments, the Anglican Church was on its way to being "so radically liberalized . . . as to become a simple enemy of the Truth."[67] He had already said the same again and again, though in different words, in the Lectures.

To see that Church as an "enemy of the Truth" may be a particularly harsh view, even when taken along the lines of mere theologizing. But in the Lectures Newman had already pointed out that it had been a trend among Anglican divines "to speak kindly of the heretical communities of ancient history, and at least obliquely to censure the Councils, which, nevertheless, they profess to receive."[68] These words of his, whose context included a pointed reference to Arius and Arianism, took on a prophetic character a few years ago when a Regius Professor of Divinity, who had done his utmost to show Arius in the best possible light and had dismissed Newman's classic book on Arius in a line or two, was raised to the Anglican episcopate.

The real harshness of the phrase, "enemy of the Truth," comes into focus when one thinks of the Bible's description of Satan as that enemy. Newman would not be taken aback if pressed on this point. He would recall the contrast he had drawn up in the Lectures between the World and the Church. There he

---

[65] To A. Philipps De Lisle, Jan. 27, 1876, *Letters and Diaries*, vol. 28, p. 20.

[66] April 5, 1872, *Letters and Diaries*, vol. 26, p. 55.

[67] To Canon Walker, Nov. 17, 1864, *Letters and Diaries*, vol. 21, p. 299. Immediately preceding this, Newman made a no less penetrating remark, again in full conformity with the thrust of the Lectures: "As to the Church of England, I cannot conceive the possibility of its being *removed*, while Monarch and Aristocracy remain."

[68] *Anglican Difficulties*, p. 389.

made much of the fact that the world disbelieves in hell so much that "it spits upon, it abominates, it curses its very name and notion. Next, as to the devil, it does not believe in him either." The Church, however, has "a foe in view; nay it has a battle-field to which the world is blind; its proper battle-field is the heart of the individual, and its true foe is Satan."[69] And if Newman were asked today to illustrate further the logic of that sad liberalization leading to the imprisonment of truth, he would find it dramatically illustrated in the suspicions of an Anglican bishop from Malaita, Melanesia. Not tainted yet by the comforts of civilized affluence, the Right Reverend Willie Pwaisho told the 1988 Lambeth Conference that the trend toward the ordination of women was possibly a satanic device within an Anglican Church unable to resist the feminist tide of naturalism.[70]

Satan is, of course, too clever not to rely on nature, or rather, to omit presenting nature as the only thing one should rely upon. For the devil has only one principal aim: to discredit that supernatural which takes the natural not only for a basis on which to build the edifice of grace but also for a factor that should be constantly resisted. As a nature that has fallen, it has its own law of a fearfully downward direction.

So much in support of the perennial value and sudden timeliness of these Lectures. In their time they could not have had as sustained an appeal to Catholics as did the *Development*, the *Apologia*, and the *Grammar of Assent*. These they took as written above all for them and found them invaluable. They could not see so much direct profit in Newman's analysis of the predicament of Anglo-Catholics, as set forth in these Lectures. But the Lectures remain an indispensable document to anyone interested in the development of Newman's philosophical and theological thinking. They witness, in gemlike phrases, his thoroughly objectivist epistemology and his insights into the strange dynamics of the human intellect. They contain some of his best pages on what formal faith, or submission to apostolic authority

---

[69] Ibid., p. 236.
[70] *The Times*, Aug. 2, 1988, p. 4.

is truly about, as distinguished from a merely material faith, or unreflecting acceptance of the creed as a social consensus.

In addition to Newman's insistence on imagination as the means that gives flesh to the body of formal reasoning, the Lectures also contain forceful anticipations of passages that make the *Apologia* and the *Grammar* so highly esteemed. The reader of the Lectures finds in them a skillful reliance on analogies as means whereby the force of a real fact, be it historical or natural, is suggested and perceived. In the *Grammar* Newman would set forth the same point, only in an analytical and systematic way. Last but not least, Newman exploited in the Lectures with great effectiveness, and well ahead of the *Apologia,* the analogy between the factions on hand in the early Church and the Churches of his own time: "What the See of Rome was then such is it now; . . . what Arius, Nestorius or Eutyches were then, such are Luther and Calvin now; what the Eusebians or Monophysites then, such the Anglican hierarchy now; what the Byzantine Court then, such is now the Government of England, and such would have been many a Catholic Court, had it had its way."[71]

Catholics of Newman's time, and for some time afterwards, did not have to be reminded of this. They were all too aware, and certainly in England, of the centrality of the Center. Today Newman might feel the pressing need to drive that point home, even to Newmanists. Too many of these have, during these last decades, put forward an image of Newman as if that point had been to him a secondary point which Roman Catholics, Anglicans, Lutherans, and "Catholic" Neomodernists could discuss with equal ease. This image of Newman was the gist of much written about him as the guiding spirit of Vatican II, and even more so of much published in connection with the centenary of his death. A curious performance indeed, especially in view of the fact that the centenary witnessed the declaration of his having practiced in a heroic degree the virtues befitting a Christian. But where was the flood of publications about his having answered in a heroic way the call of duty—a duty which he felt to be *his*

---

[71] *Anglican Difficulties*, p. 379.

God-given duty to bring home to any and all—to belong to the Church which alone was established by Christ?

Apart from being an unintended warning against such un-Newmanian developments, the Lectures recommend themselves by their immediate subject matter and the manner of their presentation. To quote Hutton again: "In matter and style alike these lectures were marked by all the signs of Newman's singular genius . . . I think the *Lectures on Anglican Difficulties* was the first book of Newman's generally read among Protestants, in which the measure of his literary power could be adequately taken. . . Here was a great subject with which Newman was perfectly intimate, giving the fullest scope to his powers of orderly and beautiful exposition, and opening a far greater range to his singular genius for gentle and delicate irony than anything which he had previously written."[72]

While it would be wrong to say with Hutton that the book "adds but little to our insight into his [Newman's] mind," his further remark, that "it adds much to our estimate of his powers,"[73] remains very true. The Lectures are an indispensable source for studying that power which Newman displayed in energizing the Oxford Movement for almost ten years, and English Catholics and Catholics all over the world ever since. Of course, Newman owed that power to the power of God's grace about which he could write that he never sinned against its light, its guidance, however slightly. In a form very different, though as valuable as the form displayed in the *Apologia* (and fourteen full years before he wrote it), he offered in these Lectures a consummate apology and in a perspective most dear to him: His conversion was sparked, nurtured, and decided by the consideration that if there was a divinely established Church, there had to be a divinely imposed obligation to belong to that same One Church.

He never shirked the often ungrateful task of reminding others of that obligation whenever opportunity arose. But it was not a "little war"[74] that he wanted to wage with the Lectures. Ten

---

[72] Hutton, *Cardinal Newman,* p. 207.

[73] Ibid.

[74] Letter to W. Faber, Oct. 28, 1849, in *Letters and Diaries,* vol. 13, p. 276.

years after their delivery he summed up their aim as a matter of logic: "I have, in my Lectures on Anglicanism, professed no more than to carry on the 'children of the movement' to their legitimate conclusions."[75] Shortly afterwards, he repeated this point and did so immediately after emphasizing that he had "never acted in direct hostility to the Church of England."[76] Only those in the grip of a misguided ecumenism will find in the reprinting of the Lectures an inopportune, nay a hostile act. They are the ones who do their best to keep under cover Newman's most impressive declaration of faith in Peter's Chair, his "Cathedra sempiterna," written in 1853, three years after the delivery of these Lectures. Owing to its almost complete unavailability, it is reprinted here as an Appendix, in a testimonial to the unity of his life's course.

That unity had to have hidden blemishes in the eyes of those who should have followed him but did not, as they watched him pay unreserved obeisance to that Chair. One of them was the Rev. John Allen, an Anglo-Catholic to the end. In late 1850, he tried to turn the tables by suggesting that Newman was beset with doubts and in search of peace of mind. Newman replied: "You are under a mistake in conjecturing that I am not at rest. I have not had a moment either of doubt or anxiety, ever since I became a Catholic."[77] More than a quarter of a century later, Allen, by then Archdeacon Allen, still speculated and theorized on Newman's being beset with doubts. The Lectures must have been in Newman's mind as he replied: "My dear Sir, I have stood where you stand, and I understand you—you have never stood where I stand and cannot understand me—but God help you for your good intentions."[78]

[75] To Canon E. Estcourt, June 2, 1860, *Letters and Diaries*, vol. 19, p. 353.

[76] To Estcourt, June 14, 1860, ibid., p. 360.

[77] Nov. 10, 1850, *Letters and Diaries*, vol. 14, p. 124. There he referred to the Lectures as a "Refutation of Anglo-Catholics." Allen was making objections ("protests") to various passages in Newman's *Development*, which Newman took for an evidence that Allen himself was in a state of doubt: "By your making them, I conjecture you are not at ease yourself—nor will you be my dear Sir, take my word for it, till you are a Catholic as I am."

[78] Oct. 10, 1876, *Letters and Diaries*, vol. 28, p. 121. As to Allen's assurance of his prayers that Newman might return to the Church of England, Newman

This is precisely what Owen Chadwick, the chief contemporary Anglican interpreter of Newman, fails to take to heart. Worse, he is one of those many Anglicans about whom Newman wrote in 1875 to a private correspondent: "It is astonishing that Anglicans will not believe my words, and it seems useless to attempt to inflict them upon unwilling ears."[79] They do not believe his most emphatic assertions, made in private and in print, that he never had a moment of doubt about the correctness of his having become a Catholic. His most prominent printed assertion is in the Postscript to his great defense of Papal Infallibility against its misconstructions by Gladstone.

As a "Newman expert" Chadwick cuts a sorry figure in speaking of Bremond's *Mystery of Newman* as the first book by a Catholic where the Anglican Newman is treated with full sympathy. Bremond wanted his own modernist proclivities mirrored in an artificial image he painted of Newman as forever an Anglican, that is, a Catholic who can act the Modernist or, preferably, the Neomodernist. Chadwick is utterly indefensible in his very recent book, *The Spirit of the Oxford Movement*.[80] There he refers to many books by Newman—six antedating his conversion, nine postdating it. Of Newman's Lectures Chadwick makes no mention at all! Does this mean that he takes those Lectures, undoubtedly the most thematic and authoritative interpretation of the Oxford Movement, as irrelevant to its very spirit? Such a performance on the part of an author proud of his scholarship can but force one to sigh—some author, some spirit . . . .

More than a sigh is in order over Chadwick's remark that *Oxford Apostles* (a book depicting the Tractarians as being driven, without perhaps knowing it, by homosexual urges) is the best book on the Movement. This not only would pain Newman beyond words but might also prompt him to write a second Apologia that would do to Chadwick what the *Apologia* did to Kingsley.

replied: "It is very kind of you to think of me, and I pray to God that He may return your prayers into your own bosom" as being prayers that cannot be "pleasing to God."

[79] To J. B. Robertson, July 23, 1875, in *Letters and Diaries*, vol. 27, p. 333.
[80] Cambridge: University Press, 1990. See Index, p. 323.

Undoubtedly, the *Lectures on Anglican Difficulties* bring home most painful difficulties to Anglican Newmanists such as Chadwick. They still try to take cover in the Fathers against the Catholic Newman as if Newman had not decried, in these very Lectures, the "Patristico-Protestants" who injected into the Fathers the principle of "private judgment."[81] Chadwick's chief contribution to the centenary of Newman's death consisted in giving a "scholarly" aura to typically Protestant thinking: Compelling as Newman's reasons were, patristic and other, for becoming a Catholic, they were primarily personal, that is, largely subjective. In other words, business as usual along the rosepath of ecclesiological relativism. Chadwick could take comfort from the fact that "business as usual" was the immediate semi-official English Catholic understanding of the news about Anglican ordination of women. Some business . . . , some understanding . . . .

The Lectures here reprinted were, still are, and will for a long time be a powerful channel for a far different understanding. The latter is the fruit of the seven gifts which God, through his Holy Spirit, bestowed on the One He sent to us. He in turn founded but One Church so that those within it may always have the gift of grace as He thought of it and meant to channel it. That gift is not the gracefulness of comfortable and civilized living on earth but the grace of an understanding that enlightens in order to secure eternal salvation.

That such indeed is the perspective in which Newman saw the Lectures and wanted others to see them has its most authoritative confirmation in his *Apologia*. Its concluding page, which a George Eliot, hardly sympathetic to Newman and to Rome, could never read without tears, lists those to whom Newman dedicated that magnificent spiritual confession of his. They were all Tractarians, that is, Anglo-Catholic allies of his. Newman first listed by name those who had not only followed him into the Catholic Church, but also into the Oratory. He specially dwelt on Ambrose St. John as the symbol of everybody dear to him in Oxford. In the last sentence of the *Apologia* Newman turned to those whom he summed up as a "whole company," in indication

[81] *Difficulties of Anglicans*, p. 154.

of the deep union he had always felt for them. They were the
Anglo-Catholics for whom he wrote (very much "against the
grain," that is, no matter what an effort it took on his part) and
delivered the Lectures. With no apologies, and not even with a
touch of fear that he might thereby hurt their "sensibilities," he
voiced a hope dearest to him: "And I earnestly pray for this
whole company, with a hope against hope, that all of us, who
once were so united, and so happy in our union, may even now
be brought at length, by the power of the Divine Will, into one
Fold and under One Shepherd."[82]

---

[82] *Apologia pro vita sua*, p. 353.

7

Newman's Logic and the Logic of the Papacy

The Oxford where young Newman wanted to live and work for the rest of his life was not yet as positively identified with logic as was the case a century later when logical positivism became its trademark. But prowess in logic could deliver much, even in the Oxford of young Newman. The assurance of lifelong livelihood there came to him when, at the exam for fellowship in Oriel, he far excelled his competitors in a field, mathematics, whose closeness to logic was by then drawing growing attention. He was far from being adversely disposed to Oriel by the advanced warning that the Common Room there "stank of logic."[1] The Oxford of those days was certainly proud of having a logician of the stature of Richard Whately, who in turn quickly discovered a potential intellectual heir in the new Fellow at Oriel.[2]

Newman's logical powers became in fact one of his two famed characteristics. The other was the sincerity with which he pursued an often heroic course of reflection and action. One of

[1] *Apologia pro vita sua*, ed. David J. DeLaura (New York: W. W. Norton, 1968), p. 136. All subsequent references to the *Apologia* are to this critical edition.

[2] Whately, whose *Elements of Logic* became a bestseller after its publication in 1826 and eventually made an impact on such pioneers of mathematical logic as Boole and De Morgan, bestowed his highest praise on Newman when he spoke of him as the clearest mind he knew. Newman closely assisted Whately in giving the final form to the latter's articles on logic for the *Encyclopedia Metropolitana* which later appeared as the *Elements*. See Meril Trevor, *Newman* (London: Macmillan, 1962), vol. 1, p. 48.

Newman's foes who berated both his logical powers and sincerity in one and the same stroke was Queen Victoria's chaplain Charles Kingsley, whose denunciation of Newman triggered the writing of the *Apologia*. Although urged by *Macmillan's Magazine* to rebut that masterpiece, Kingsley declined on the ground that it was useless to waste time on one who had amply demonstrated his illogicality by accepting the dogma of the Immaculate Conception and who believed in papal infallibility. Nor did Kingsley wish to become the victim of Newman's unconscionable use of his powers in logic: "I cannot be weak enough to put myself a second time, by a fresh act of courtesy, into the power of one who like a treacherous ape, lifts to you meek and suppliant eyes, till he thinks he has you within his reach, and then springs gibbering and biting at your face."[3]

Cardinal Manning, the chief among Newman's foes within the Church, had similar and no less vehement reservations about Newman. Nine years after Newman had been raised to the cardinalate, Manning still felt it to be a horrible mistake for which he laid the lion's share of responsibility on Bishop Ullathorne. Much of their last conversation was taken up by Manning's reiterating the charge: "You do not know Newman as I do. He simply twists you round his little finger; he bamboozles you with his carefully selected words and plays so subtly with his logic that your simplicity is taken in. You are no match for him."[4]

Friends of Newman and the no less vast circle of his admirers have not, of course, failed to be impressed by the combination of his logic and sincerity. Gladstone, who warned his fellow Anglicans about their failure to grasp the true measure of the loss Newman's conversion inflicted on them,[5] described Newman's mind as "hard enough to cut the diamond and bright as the diamond which it cuts."[6] Newman's logic enabled him to

---

[3] Quoted ibid., vol. 2, p. 344.

[4] Quoted ibid., vol. 2, p. 555.

[5] W. E. Gladstone, *Vaticanism: An Answer to Reproofs and Replies* (New York: Harper and Brothers, 1875), p. 12.

[6] G. B. Smith, *The Life of the Right Honorable William Ewart Gladstone* (New York: G. P. Putnam, 1880), p. 499.

make a new approach to the development of dogma and to explore a field previously untouched, the complex structure of the act whereby one assents to a proposition. In both cases Newman displayed two main aspects of the inner power of logic. One is the attention to the many nuances and ramifications of a leading idea, the other, the relentless drive whereby its ultimate implication is unfolded.

This second aspect of one's bent on logic can easily go hand in hand with an impulse to be a leader in the pursuit of a most specific goal. Newman certainly had that impulse. That in his younger years he loved to dwell on Wellington's exploits revealed his penchant for the role of commander or at least of chief of staff. He naturally became the unofficial leader of the Oxford Movement and engaged it in a campaign aimed at nothing less than the restoration of the Church of England to its status as the ideal Church. By that restoration he meant to implement what he used to call, in his *Parochial and Plain Sermons*, the "imperial" notion of the Church as a visible continuation of Old Testament theocracy.[7] He opposed anything that would compromise that restoration—not only the liberalism and secularism of many Anglican churchmen but also the emancipation of Catholics.[8] He saw that theocracy as an empire acting with power in all but one respect: it was not to wield weapons.[9]

After his conversion, Newman lived for years in the belief that a spiritual campaign issuing in the conversion *en masse* of Anglican clergymen and lay leaders could be brought about. The final stage of that phase of Newman's thinking was the course of lectures he gave in 1850 on the *Difficulties of Anglicans*. From a distance of forty years the memory of those lectures evoked to one present the combination of unmistakable sincerity and irresistible logic. The sincerity, R. Hutton remembered, came

---

[7] Carefully analyzed in ch. vii, "The Imperial Image of the Church," in *Papacy and Development: Newman and the Primacy of the Pope*, by P. Misner (Leiden: E. J. Brill, 1976).

[8] See *Discussions and Arguments on Various Subjects* (Longmans, Green and Co.: London, 1897), pp. 59-60.

[9] Even as far as from Sicily Newman wanted to know about the implemen tation of "the atrocious Irish sacrilege Bill." See Trevor, *Newman*, vol. 1, p. 120.

through the delivery "singularly sweet, perfectly free from any dictatorial note." But the relentless return to the incoherence of the Anglican position as a mere instrument of the Establishment was clearly characteristic of a victorious strategist for whom it was sufficient to unfold the self-destructive predicament of his opponents. Newman succinctly put that predicament in a metaphor: "The Anglicans had reared a goodly house, but their foundations were falling in. The soil and masonry were bad."[10] This phrase, which Hutton found the most representative of the whole book, had much more to it than was perceived either by him or by any other of Newman's interpreters, or even by Newman himself for that matter.

Meanwhile, Newman most energetically turned to the task of injecting intellectual and theological vigor into the Catholic Church in England and Ireland. *The Idea of a University* was aptly called an intellectual strategy worthy of an "imperial intellect."[11] Newman was not allowed to remain the chief of staff of that strategy. But the failure of his rectorship in Dublin only helped him to redirect his energies, first to defend the honesty of the Catholic clergy. He did so in a lawsuit that drew national attention and, precisely because of his losing it, earned him a major victory. No less important a mouthpiece of the establishment than *The Times* was forced to admit that Roman Catholics could not yet count on the impartiality of the British Courts.[12] Then came the undivided concentration of Newman's energies on the Oratory in Birmingham. There he could act, if necessary, in the manner of a ruler who would be declared a despot today, in this age when, in the name of "due process," festering abuses among the clergy and religious are protected for years from quick "surgical" interventions. Even in his eighties, Newman could entertain thoughts of vast new strategies, strategies that only popes could conceive of. Were he to be elected pope, he

[10] R. H. Hutton, *Cardinal Newman* (1891; new ed.; London: Methuen, 1905), pp. 208-09 and 211. The quotation is from the fifth lecture on *Anglican Difficulties*.

[11] D. Culler, *The Imperial Intellect: A Study of Cardinal Newman's Educational Ideal*, (New Haven, Conn.: Yale University Press, 1955).

[12] See Trevor, *Newman*, vol. 1, p. 600.

said in 1884, he would set up a number of high level commissions concerning the most urgent questions relating to the present state and immediate future of the Church.[13]

If his fiercely independent character is an indication, he would, as pope, hardly have acted as a mere moderator of commissions of cardinals, bishops, and theologians. On that ground alone it is quite possible to envision Newman as a pope who would reply to an inquiry about a controverted document lying in front of him as did Pius IX: "I have not yet read it, so it cannot be condemned. For I am the captain of the ship."[14] But there are other grounds, too, far more telling and very factual for believing that the idea of a pope with the undisputed powers of a ship's captain on the high seas was very germane to Newman's thinking. Just about the time when the campaign of Ultramontanes was getting in high gear on behalf of a declaration of papal infallibility, Newman told Pusey in a long letter that the ecumenical program "Eirenicon" advocated by him was an invitation for Catholics to "commit suicide." The reason for this was, Newman argued, that the Church Pusey envisaged was a "dead thing, a paper code" unworthy of being "the object of faith." The latter was *not* simply "certain articles A. B. C. D. contained in dumb documents, but the whole word of God, explicit, and implicit, as dispensed by his living Church. On this point, I am sure, there can be no Eirenicon; for it marks a fundamental, elementary difference between the Anglican view and ours, and every attempt to bridge it over will but be met in the keen and stern temper of Cardinal Patrizzi's letter."[15]

Newman's approving reference to a "keen and stern temper" was only introductory to something far more astringent. While Pusey raised an apparently practical question about the Pope's limited jurisdiction in a future ecumenical church, Newman rushed with his logic from practicality to principles. By principles he meant even more than "true doctrine," although that was

---

[13] See W. Ward, *The Life of John Henry Cardinal Newman* (London: Longmans, Green and Co., 1912), vol. 2, pp. 476-77.

[14] Ibid., vol. 2, p. 211.

[15] Quoted in Ward, *The Life of John Henry Cardinal Newman*, vol. 2, pp. 222-23.

always very precious in his eyes. "Doctrine is the *voice* of a religious body, its principles are of its *substance*. The principles may be turned into doctrines by being defined; but they live as necessities before definition, and are the less likely to be defined *because* they are so essential to life."[16]

The reality of life was not, however, likely to be defined by Newman in the form of principles, if he viewed life with the romantics as an ultimately elusive feeling. For him life meant unrestricted specific implementations in line with his idea of an "imperial" church, that is, the kingdom of God on earth, as was, *mutatis mutandis* the Davidic kingdom of God's covenant. The pope's "universal jurisdiction" followed from his function, which was not to be a mere figurehead. The pope was not to act "as a man of straw" but "as a bond of unity."[17] Clearly Newman meant a bond that was not mere sentiment but a strict constraint if necessary.

Ready to run along with the force of logic, Newman was prepared to spell out in specifics what was meant by universal jurisdiction. It not only extended over all Christians but over all matters connected with their stand in a real world as the arena of spiritual struggle for eternal salvation: "Now the Church is a Church militant, and, as the commander of an army is *despotic*, so must the visible head of the Church be; and therefore in its idea the Pope's jurisdiction can hardly be limited" (italics added). Since this was sheer logic, the logician could unabashedly make himself seen: "I am not dealing with antecedent arguments. I am accounting for a fact. It is Whately's 'a' is not 'A'. I have proposed to draw out the facts as a matter of principle, not of doctrine."[18]

The Newman of this long letter can hardly be pictured as one who would countenance an ecumenical platform restricted to the tenets of the Nicene Creed, or to the definitions of the first eight ecumenical councils. Were he alive today Newman would have no less harsh words for suggestions that would make "elective" all doctrines that owe their specific solemnity to papal acts, from the dogma of the Immaculate Conception to the dogma

16 Ibid., p. 221.
17 Ibid., p. 223.
18 Ibid.

of the Assumption. But was not Newman's holding high the idea
of a despotic papacy only a momentary stance, provoked by
Pusey's importuning him with an issue that he had already
answered in a book-length letter?[19]
   Such a possibility is difficult to reconcile with two factors:
The first, Newman's extraordinary respect for Pusey, and the
second, his awareness that with Pusey all his words would count
heavily. If there was anyone on earth it was Pusey whom
Newman would not have wished to alienate with rash words.
Nor should one overlook the various shades of meaning
applicable to the word "despotic." Newman, whose phraseology
owed much to biblical and patristic Greek, was hardly unaware
of the title "*despotes*" given in the Greek Testament to God and to
Jesus Christ,[20] though hardly in a sense evocative of a Darius or
Ramses II. Yet without envisioning a pope à la Genghis Khan,
Barbarossa, or Henry VIII, Newman certainly meant by "despotic"
a sovereign whose decision could overrule any majority, real or
apparent.
   This idea of papal sovereignty, which did not depend on
soliciting advance approval for its decision, was not the momentary product of a particular provocation in Newman's case. It
had rather been a constant theme with the Catholic Newman, who
could easily recognize it as the logical fulfillment of that King-
dom-ecclesiology he had preached in season and out of season
both as a curate and a Tractarian. For if the "despotic" papacy
means an "absolutist" one, it is plainly in sight in Newman's
argument in the *Development* on behalf of an "absolute need of a
monarchical power in the Church."[21] The argument in fact is so
"absolutist" as to suggest (reverentially, of course) an impossibility on God's part to decree "the rise of a universal Empire" and

---

[19] A positive answer to this question is implied by Misner who presents
Newman's characterization of papal jurisdiction with the words "unlimited
and despotic" as something that "cannot be pressed . . . because Newman
was exasperated at Pusey and his unrealistic hopes for corporate reunion at
the time." *Papacy and Development*, p. 137.

[20] See *despotes* in Kittel's *Theological Dictionary of the New Testament*.

[21] *An Essay on the Development of Christian Doctrine* (new ed.; London: Basil
Montagu Pickering, 1878), p. 154.

not to decree "the development of a sovereign ruler" within it.[22] This impossibility rested on the logical connection between the revelation of truth and its truthful guaranteeing across space and time.[23] The organ of guarantee had therefore to speak with "one voice"[24] and to be always faithful to itself, that is, "incorrigible,"[25] to recall an emphatic word of Newman which evokes precisely the comportment of a despot. Moreover, Newman of the *Development* was courageously logical in spelling out a necessary corollary of the "divine provenance" of the "incorrigible" papacy. While not all its actions were infallible, "it was ever to be obeyed."[26]

The Newman of the twelve lectures forming the *Difficulties of Anglicans* was no less "despotically" outspoken. In fact it was there that he spoke out most firmly against his own great attempt to salvage the Anglican position as a "via media" between Catholicism and Protestantism. He had to recognize that a council of private judgment, dressed as it could be in liturgical paraphernalia and quartered in fine monuments of tradition, was still a private judgment compounded, most unworthy of divine Revelation, which has to be Truth incarnate. If only the Catholic Church bore witness to the truth it was because "its essential idea was the Church's infallibility."[27] This note of "despotism" ringing throughout the last of those lectures received its specific interpretation in the immediately preceding one where Newman opposed to private judgment the God-given duty "to submit to the supreme authority of the Holy See." And in a perhaps even more "despotic" spirit he calmly spelled out the consequences, namely,

---

[22] Ibid., p. 155.

[23] Ibid., p. 79, where Newman admits that the revelation of truth and its guaranteeing may often be distinct *in fact*, but that this distinction of fact does not apply in the case of Christianity, which comes to us "as a revelation, as a whole, objectively, and with a profession of infallibility."

[24] Ibid., p. 322.

[25] Ibid., p. 442.

[26] Ibid., p. 86. The See of Peter, Newman continues, "is not in all cases infallible, it may err beyond its special province, but it has in all cases a claim on our obedience."

[27] *Certain Difficulties felt by Anglicans in Catholic Teaching* (London: Long mans, Green and Co., vol. 1, p. 377.

the "inevitable constant rising of the human mind against such authority." He showed no readiness to soften the fearful alternative as he presented the tableau of

> not merely individuals casting off the Roman Supremacy (for individuals, as being of less account, have less temptation, or even more opportunity, to rebel, than collections of men), but, much more, the powerful and the great, the wealthy and the flourishing, kings and states, cities and races, all falling back upon their own resources and their own connections, making their house their castle, and refusing any longer to be dependent on a distant center, or to regulate their internal affairs by a foreign tribunal.[28]

As always, here too the present was for Newman prefigured in the past. In the next breath he described the breaking away of the Oriental Churches, with its moral anticipated by Saint Paul's "There must be heresies. . .," and added: "A command is both the occasion of transgression, and the test of obedience. All depends on the fact of the Supremacy of Rome."[29]

It was that unbending Newman, so triumphalistically "unecumenical" as one would say today, who celebrated the unity of Catholics as having reached in 1850 a degree unparalleled beforehand: "The Church lives, the Apostolic See rules. That See has greater acknowledgment than ever before, and that Church has a wider liberty than she has had since the days of the Apostles. The faith is extending in the great Anglo-Saxon race, its recent enemy, the lord of the world, with a steadiness and energy, which that proud people fears, yet cannot resist."[30] The provenance of these quotes from the last three lectures of the twelve forming the *Difficulties*, indicates their ascending thrust and gives a clue to an earlier statement of Newman's about "the thousand subordinate authorities round that venerable Chair where sits the plenitude of Apostolic power," authorities either "planted by that Chair" or having issued from it. "Hence, when she would act, the blow is broken, and concussion avoided, by

[28] Ibid., pp. 348-49.
[29] Ibid., p. 349.
[30] Ibid., p. 328.

the innumerable springs, if I may use the word, on which the celestial machinery is hung."[31]

The point of this passage, the context of which is not about dogma or morals, but about the confrontation between two jurisdictions, ecclesiastic and political, was a favorite with Newman. He loved to recall that only a real power utterly sure of itself can afford the luxury of softening its "blows," as if with built-in shock absorbers, to wax a bit modern. He made that point in the *Apologia*: "Zosimus treated Pelagius and Coelestius with extreme forbearance; St. Gregory was equally indulgent with Berengarius; by reason of the very power of the Popes they have commonly been slow and moderate in their use of it."[32] But a power it was and of gigantic proportions. It was "as tremendous as the giant evil which has called for it."[33] Consequently, Newman once more felt entitled to cast infallibility into its harsh "despotic" light:

> The initial doctrine of the infallible teacher must be an emphatic protest against the existing state of mankind. Man had rebelled against his Maker. It was this that caused the divine interposition: and the first act of the divinely accredited messenger must be to proclaim it. The Church must denounce rebellion as of all possible evils the greatest. She must have no terms with it; if she would be true to her Master, she must ban and anathematize it."[34]

Of course, Newman meant by rebellion the one constituted by sin, especially by the sin of pride. And he quoted three of those texts from his *Difficulties of Anglicans* for which he had been particularly pilloried by mainstream Christians, to use another modern phrase. One was about the Catholic Church's holding that the willful committing of a mere venial sin is a far greater catastrophe than the starvation of millions.[35] The other was about the value of a "filthy beggar-woman, though chaste, sober, cheerful, and religious," a value incomparably greater than that

---

[31] Ibid., p. 180.
[32] *Apologia*, p. 205.
[33] Ibid., p. 192.
[34] Ibid., p. 190.
[35] Ibid.

of "an accomplished statesman, or lawyer . . . however upright, generous, honourable and conscientious," without the grace of God in his heart.[36] The third was, and in the same breath, a similarly unbending estimate of the relatively small matter of a lie in comparison with a lustful thought, as the latter, in Christ's judgment, was tantamount to plain adultery.

Were he alive today, Newman would undoubtedly give unbending support to *Humanae vitae* and warn about the potential pitfalls in the latter-day Catholic rush to the Bible. For, according to him, only an infallibility embodied in a concrete person can do what the Bible cannot: The Bible "cannot make a stand against the wild living intellect of man, and in this day it begins to testify, as regards its own structure and contents, to the power of that universal solvent, which is so successfully acting upon religious establishments."[37] His would be a prophecy fulfilled in this age of born-again Christians who ignore that only a living infallible organ can make specific truths for the intellect out of the divine command, "You must be born again." Such was the gist of Newman's rephrasing that command: "Your *whole* nature must be reborn, your passions, and your affections, and your aims, and your conscience, and your will, must all be bathed in a new element and reconsecrated to your Maker, and, the last not the least, your intellect."[38]

Such a despotically unbending contrast between the spirit of the world and the infallible organ that alone can effectively counter it was not only conceptually identical with the one Newman set forth in his letter to Pusey, but also almost coincided with it. Both the *Apologia* and that letter mark the moment when Newman and many others suddenly became preoccupied with rumors about a coming Council and with the rapid rise of voices demanding a solemn declaration of papal infallibility by that Council.

As is well known Newman repeatedly declined invitations (from the English hierarchy, from the famed bishop Dupanloup of Orléans, and even from Pius IX) to be a theologian at the

[36] Ibid., p. 191.
[37] Ibid. p. 188.
[38] Ibid., p. 191.

Council. No less resolutely did he resist promptings to join with publications in the increasingly heated debates between infallibilists and those favoring the status quo. Only his private correspondence reveals the extent to which he loathed and dreaded the prospect of a definition of papal infallibility. His letters written between January 1, 1868 and December 1873[39] contain many times his emphatic assertion that he had always held that doctrine, though he did not rate it higher than a theological opinion with which one could honestly disagree. He also insisted that there was no need for definition, a point of utmost importance, as in his view the development of dogma always had for its motive force urgently felt needs. Only in one letter did he acknowledge one such need which, typically enough, evoked a Church that needed to act despotically: "In the present state of the world," he wrote on August 29, 1869, "the Catholic body may require to be like an army in the field, under strict and immediate discipline."[40] But he added that he saw "more reasons for wishing it [the definition] may *not* be laid down by the Council, than for wishing it should be." The opposing reasons, of which more later, must have been extremely grave in his eyes because he never made a secret of the gravity of the threat posed to Christianity and the Church by the agnosticism, liberalism, and rationalism responsible for "the state of the world."

On almost all occasions when he took up the subject with his correspondents in those years he spoke scathingly about the unscrupulous faction that pushed for the definition and hinted at the divine judgment in store for them.[41] In fact he saw God's punishment for the definition both in the violent thunderstorm that engulfed St. Peter's on the day of the definition[42] and in the loss of the Pope's temporal power.[43] Most revealingly, he felt

[39] They are included in volumes 24, 25, and 26 of *The Letters and Diaries of John Henry Newman* (Oxford: Clarendon Press, 1973-74). All these three volumes had Charles S. Dessain and Thomas Gornall for editors. Each of these volumes will be referred to as *Letters and Diaries*.

[40] *Letters and Diaries*, vol. 24, p. 325.

[41] *Letters and Diaries*, vol. 25, p. 205, "A heavy retribution still may await the perpetrators of the act." (Sept. 14, 1870).

[42] *Letters and Diaries*, vol. 25, p. 262.

[43] *Letters and Diaries*, vol. 25, p. 245. "The definition of July involved the

confident even as late as June 28, 1870, that there would be no definition.[44] After it had passed he tried to withhold consent as long as he could. First he thought that the departure of a hundred or so bishops from the Council just before the definition cast doubt on the moral consensus needed for its validity.[45] Then, on seeing that the minority did not organize, he anchored his hope on the planned reopening of the Council in October.[46] When this failed to come about, he seized on the advanced age of Pius IX.[47] A new pope might balance things, for according to Newman the exact meaning of *ex cathedra* was still to be defined.[48] Even with a great master of logic, the danger of hair-splitting was not necessarily too far removed.

Yet in all this perplexity, intellectual and emotional, Newman had several considerations to fall back on. One was an

dethronement of September" (Dec. 12, 1870).

[44] Ibid., p. 153. "I will not believe that this definition about Papal Infallibility is passed, till it actually is passed."

[45] *Letters and Diaries*, vol. 25, p. 167. He contrasted "the mere majority" to "moral unanimity" in the same letter (July 27, 1870, to Ambrose St John). His hesitation was, however, balanced with a reference to the great historical argument derived from the authoritative actions of the popes.

[46] Ibid., p. 171 (August 3). Furthermore he told his correspondent (F. Rymer) that the plans for October should be kept secret: "We must take care not to *tell* our opponents what we want and what we don't."

[47] In writing on November 7, 1870, to the parents of a boy at the Oratory school in Edgebaston, that the boy's problem would be better treated at home during the next year's summer vacation beginning June 17, he suddenly switched his train of thought, in indication of what was his dominant concern: "Although that day was still a great way off, if the common belief is true, the Pope will not live till that day." By then Newman had met his moment of truth when an Anglican reminded him that "at least you Catholics are as much divided in opinion as we Anglicans—you are divided in questions of faith. We thought certainty your special boast." In reporting this on November 1 to Bishop Moriarty of Kerry, Newman confessed: "On this I assure you I feel quite ashamed, and know not what to say" (*Letters and Diaries*, vol. 25, p. 223). Apparently Newman had no second thoughts on the theological wisdom of trying to restore the theological status quo at almost any price.

[48] *Letters and Diaries*, vol. 25, p. 224. One wonders whether this helped the perplexity of Lady Simeon, the recipient of the letter. Clearly, Newman meant what he wrote on June 18, 1870: "It seems to me a duty, out of devotion to the Pope and charity to the souls of men, to resist it, while resistance is possible" (ibid., p. 153).

unconditional trust in the divine guidance accorded to the Church. This he never failed to impress on his correspondents troubled with the infallibility question, both before and after the Council. Another was the overriding role of loyalty. Or as he concluded his letter of Year-end to Archbishop Darboy of Paris: "If by some fiction those who love me will have it that I am a teacher of the faithful, I am above all a disciple of the Church, doctor fidelium discipulus ecclesiae.[49] Still another was his recall, after the definition, that his acceptance of papal infallibility was in part anchored in history, namely in the magisterial, authoritative acting of not a few popes, even early popes: "The fact," he wrote on July 27, 1870, "that all along for so many centuries, the head of the Church and the teacher of the faithful and the Vicar of Christ has been allowed by God to assert virtually his infallibility, is a great argument in favour of the validity of his claim."[50] On August 15 he referred to the "self assertion, the *ipse dixit* of the Popes for 1800 years," as "a great and inspiring argument for the validity of their claims."[51] The next March, in writing to Mrs. Froude, widow of a closest friend from Tractarian days, he offered the same argument in even more graphic words, making infallibility almost synonymous with "despotic." There a reference to Pope Stephen's rebuke of St. Cyprian, who rejected the validity of baptisms administered by the *lapsi*, helped Newman to present two points: One is the stage at which a doctrine, still "obscurely held," manifests itself through action; the other is the attributes of the action through which alone papal infallibility can transpire:

> The Popes acted as if they were infallible in doctrine—with very high hand, peremptorily, magisterially, fiercely. But when we come to the question of the analysis of such conduct, I think they had as vague ideas on the subject as many of the early Fathers had upon portions of the doctrine of the Holy Trinity. *They acted in a way which needed infallibility as its explanation.*[52]

---

[49] *Letters and Diaries*, vol. 25, p. 259.
[50] Ibid., p. 168.
[51] Ibid., p. 186.
[52] Ibid., p. 299.

Toward the end of that year he again stated that the infallibility of the Popes had always been transparent in their conduct.[53] By then he had acknowledged a new aspect of the expediency of the definition. It was to prevent the reappearance of Gallicanism and Jansenism, and to forestall the resurgence of the Branch theory.[54]

All this reveals both a most generous measure of sincerity with his correspondents, a sincerity coupled with an indifference to possible indiscretion on their part. It also reveals some illogicality in a mind acclaimed as well as feared for its prowess in logic. The latter problem is made more acute by Newman's own comments on two theological roads to infallibility. One he explicitly labelled "logical," the other may not improperly be called "phenomenological." The former he described succinctly in the last paragraph of his letter of May 8, 1869, as consisting in focusing on the role which Rome exclusively had in turning the Christian communities into a real communion: "Union with Rome is the logical *differentia* in the Church." The role was equivalent to the proposition that "Rome is the center of unity," a proposition which Newman "believed as a doctrine, taught by the Church, and indispensable." Yet though he recognized the intimate connection between the "See of Rome as the center of unity" and the infallibility of that See, he held that only the former had to be believed as a *doctrine* taught by the Church. The latter he would believe as a doctrine only "if the Church so determined—and I believe a General Council is to be her *Voice* in determining—and I don't believe that a General Council can decree anything which the Divine Head of the Church does not will to be decreed."[55] The "phenonemonological" way was in the forefront when on December 15, he informed another correspondent that he held the Pope's infallibility on the basis of general consensus "as having the suffrages of most people in this day,"

[53] Ibid., p. 447.

[54] Ibid., p. 259. This too was part of his letter to Archbishop Darboy. There Newman characterized the Branch theory as the means "by which the Catholic-minded members of a Protestant church claim the blessings of Catholicism."

[55] *Letters and Diaries*, vol. 24, p. 253. The recipient of this important letter was Sir John Simeon, one of the only two Roman Catholic MPs at that time.

but that he "cannot defend it in a set argument" and that he "never would use it as the instrument of bringing inquirers into the Church."[56]

Clearly, the "logical" road was not logical enough for a great logician, although even the "phenomenological" way, as gathered from the general consensus, imposed it precisely because of its logicality. In a letter written the next day he conveyed something of the illogicality of his own understanding of that "logical" way by equating it with building a church—St. Peter's in Rome, to wit—from the top down. First he registered his satisfaction that many congregationalists and Wesleyans were fond of reading his books, whatever their repudiation of his dogmatic doctrines. He took their interest for an evidence that he was

> contributing to lay the foundation of principles which may tend as a first step to bring towards Catholic Truth the various separated communions of this country. To begin with the doctrine of the Pope is to begin to build St. Peter's from the cross and ball. We must begin from the bottom—not even only from the foundations of the building, but from the soil in which the foundations must be placed—If I succeed merely in this, to contribute to the creation of a sound material on which the stone work of the edifice of faith is to be placed, I shall think myself highly blest, and to have done as much as I can wish to do.[57]

Of course, Newman was right about the soil or the broader mental disposition conditioning one's assent to a given proposition. (He was just completing his *Grammar of Assent* on which he had been working for the previous ten years. It was partly for fear that it would never be completed that he had declined the invitation to participate in Vatican I. Another reason was the pressing task of putting his vast correspondence in order, a concern for which he deserves the gratitude of all posterity, Christian and other). But as a logician he should have perceived that it was one thing to be concerned about the subjective soil that was to receive the stone edifice of faith, yet another to see the difference between foundation and edifice, and still another

---

[56] Ibid., p. 390.
[57] Ibid., p. 391.

to set forth the logic whereby the entire character and solidity of a structure is determined by the very nature of its foundation stone, especially if it is a single individual rock! Newman's speaking in his *Difficulties of Anglicans* about "foundations falling in" may now reveal its broader significance. Was it not a subconscious failure of his to distinguish between foundation and edifice that made him speak of what is hardly possible for a foundation, namely, its "falling in," which only walls and roofs can do, and certainly not a rock foundation? Did he suspect that a rock can at best disintegrate or pulverize but not fall in? Was he so enthralled by the spread of exquisite archways, facades, and spires in Oxford as never to think of their foundations, enveloped in dark, cold mildew, and seen, if ever, by servants alone?

A better clue to this multiple oversight on Newman's part is provided by his sincerity. By insisting that it was not the "logical" but the "phenomenological" way that brought him into the Church, he amply revealed the predominance of the visual or imaginative component in his thinking over the logical. Only a very high esteem of Newman's logical powers will help one to appraise the overriding power of the imaginative factor at work in him. To be sure, that factor was not an addiction to fancy. But his logic was at its best whenever it could work within an image or a vision grasped intuitively. Once possessed by that image, such as that of an "empire" church established by God to spread concrete holiness all over the world, his logical powers could unfold with ease and penetration countless connections and nuances. But the imaginative intuition always had the most satisfactory last word for him. A stunning case of this is provided in that letter in which, as already noted, he admitted one expedient reason on behalf of the declaration of infallibility. Its last paragraph deserves to be quoted in full:

> Now the very reason I became a Catholic was because the present Roman Catholic Church *is the only church* which is like, and it is very like, the primitive Church, the Church of St. Athanasius . . . . It is almost like a photograph of the primitive Church; or at least it does not differ from the primitive Church nearly so much as the photograph of a man

of 40 differs from his photograph when 20. *You know it is the same man.*[58]

An uncanny self-portrait, too, it was about Newman the MAN writ large who was, however, but a man with limited talents and perceptions, however extraordinary. To begin with, he was an Oxford man who saw the world through Oxford. One wonders whether he would have loathed the prospect of the definition of infallibility had it not made even more hopeless the setting up of a Catholic house of studies in Oxford. It was that work which he wanted more than anything else, a work, as he put it, best suited to his abilities, and exactly the work that was denied to him by Rome acting under the advice of some in the English hierarchy.[59] He must have foreseen for years what he spelled out in a letter to J. Spencer Northcote on April 7, 1872. On the one hand, he saw Oxford and the Anglican Church increasingly becoming a "whirpool of disbelief." On the other hand, he took the view that since "the infallibility of the Pope has simply thrown down the gauntlet to the science and the historical research of the day," any official Catholic presence in Oxford was bound to be involved "in a mortal fight." Worse, any Catholic scholar there, forced to defend historically the Pope's infallibility, was bound to make inevitable mistakes "on the stage of a great theater." But would the intellectual chances of Catholics in Oxford have really been so much better had they had to account only for what happened at Trent three hundred years earlier? Were they really as unprepared as "newborn children," so many offspring of a new Council? Was not Newman taking Oxford for the world? A study in depth not so much of Newman at Oxford as of Newman *the Oxonian* might unfold more than meets the eye.

At any rate, there can be little doubt about the immense usefulness of his reference to the similarity between two photographs of a man taken twenty years apart, for understanding Newman's attitude toward papal infallibility. No expertise in

---

[58] Ibid., p. 325. See note 40 above.

[59] "The only one [place or office] I am fit for, the only one I would accept, a place at Oxford, he [Manning] is doing all he can to keep me from," wrote Newman on Jan. 3, 1866; see Ward, *The Life of John Henry Cardinal Newman,* vol. 2, p. 124.

conceptual graphology is needed to discover the identity of the author of the great *Letter* explaining infallibility to the Duke of Norfolk, written at 75, of which more later, with that of the *Development* written at 45, or even with that of some of the Parochial sermons on the church delivered ten years earlier. They all bespeak the same man seized by the vision of a visible edifice, vast in space and keeping its essential features across time, the vision that brought him to the Church and kept him in it. The spectacle was magnificent in the ultimate analysis because it represented God's plan and will, which one could either reject or obey. This was the consideration that overruled in him all doubts and objections looming oppressively large two days before the solemn definition of infallibility on July 18, 1879. The oppressiveness was given an added touch through a letter he received on July 17, in which Edward Husband, a well-known convert to Catholicism, informed Newman about his having left the Church on account of infallibility and said he expected Newman to follow suit. To his correspondent's taunting question, "Have you found what you hoped and longed for?", Newman had the following answer:

> That depends on what I 'hoped and longed for'. I did not hope or long for any thing except to do God's will, which I feared not to do. I did not leave the Anglican church, as you think, for any scandals in it. You have mistaken your man. My reason was as follows: I knew it was necessary, if I would participate in the grace of Christ, to seek it there where He had lodged it. I believed that that grace was to be found in the Roman communion only, not in the Anglican. Therefore I became a Catholic. This was my belief in 1845, and still more strongly my belief now, because in 1845 I had not that utter distrust of the Anglican Orders which I feel in 1870.[60]

The metaphor of a lodging for grace should seem of utter importance, especially since it stood for a structure as universal or Catholic as befitted the God of the universe. Its persuasiveness is attested by countless converts who found Newman's "phenomenological" road into the Catholic Church eminently

---

[60] *Letters and Diaries*, vol. 26, p. 59.

convincing.[61] The shortcomings of that road received less attention, though they were no less positively instructive. They illustrate the fact that only a firm, sincere adhesion to a universal or Catholic Church that teaches no less universally can keep a great Christian thinker from falling into the ever gaping pitfalls provided by his background and intellectual predilections, however noble. In its elemental simplicity that Church was the organism from which one could not separate oneself under any circumstance without courting spiritual disaster. Newman said so to none other than the Carmelite Hyacinthe Loyson, a most influential preacher, who left the Church on account of the definition of infallibility, without wanting to become a Protestant. In writing to him that "nothing which has taken place justifies our separation from the One Church,"[62] Newman simply voiced, half-consciously or not, an immortal phrase of Augustine of Hippo.[63] Newman may have heard before he died that the "Eglise Catholique Gallicane," which Mr. Loyson set up in Paris, had degenerated into a cult of his wife, hardly a minor disaster.[64]

But to return to particular pitfalls, and especially to the kind connected with one's intellectual predilections. The latter, insofar as they were bearing on the infallibility problem, continually posed a mental block to Newman in those crucial years. In his letters he kept returning to the "securus judicat orbis terrarum" as the great test of theological truth.[65] The pattern certainly shows the extraordinary and lasting impact which that text began to make on him a few months after he was confronted with it in Wiseman's memorable article published in 1839.[66] He resonated

---

[61] *Letters and Diaries*, vol. 25, p. 160.

[62] Ibid., p. 235.

[63] "Non esse quidquam gravius sacrilegio schismatis, quia praecidendae unitatis nulla est justa necessitas" (There is nothing more serious than the sacrilege of schism because there is no just cause for severing the unity of the Church), *Contra. epist. Parmeniani*, lib. II, ch. 11, in Migne *Patrologia Latina*, vol. 43, col. 69.

[64] See "Loyson" in Index of names to *Letters and Diaries*, vol. 24, p. 419.

[65] For instance in *Letters and Diaries*, vol. 35, pp. 164, 172, 186, and 235.

[66] That on his first reading of Wiseman's article Newman, according to his own reminiscences (see *Apologia*, p. 99), failed to see the crucial importance of that Augustinian phrase shows the extent to which even the keenest mind can be locked in the perspectives of its preferences.

to it all the more because it appealed to his visual grasp of a picturesque reality, natural or supernatural. But a grasp it was also in the sense that it blocked his vision in other no less crucial directions. He was never seized, for instance, by the image of that Rock into which Christ turned Peter as the foundation of His church.[67] Nor was Newman ever impressed by the visual imagery of the Keys of the Kingdom entrusted to Peter.[68]

For this a great deal of blame may lie with the Anglican and Protestant sublimation of those two hard and concrete things into a "faith" of which invariably the subjective side was played up against the objective tenets in which one was to believe. It took Newman many years to purge his thinking of the Protestant notion of an Antichrist associated with the Romish Church in general and with the Papacy in particular. He was less successful with respect to the re-concretization of Rocks and Keys. His view in the *Development* of the great Petrine texts as "more or less obscure" anticipations of the papal claims[69] remained unchanged for the rest of his life. He was not struck by the authentic interpretation of those passages in *Pastor aeternus* (the Vatican I document on papal infallibility) as something that should have called for an explanatory note in the new edition (1878) of the *Development* which contained, in his own words, "important alterations" in its text too,[70] to say nothing of its notes.

[67] In view of Newman's appreciation of visual imagery, he might very well have seized on the relevance for the interpretation of Mt 16:16 of the magnificent drawings of a huge wall of rock just outside Caesarea Philippi in *Picturesque Palestine* (4 vols.; London: Virtue & Co., 1880-84), had that work been available twenty or thirty years earlier. For further details and reproductions, see my *And on This Rock: The Witness of One Land and Two Covenants* (Notre Dame, IN.: Ave Maria Press, 1978), pp. 32-34; 2nd enlarged edition: Manassas, VA: Trinity Communications, 1987 pp. 30-33; 3d enlarged edition, Front Royal, VA: Christendom Press, 1996, pp. 24-30.

[68] Did Newman ever suspect that Christ's words to Peter, "I *give* you the keys of the Kingdom of Heaven," were conditioned by the fact that by then the huge unwieldy keys that had to be put on one's shoulders (see Isaiah 22:19-25) had been replaced by small metal keys embodying all the "modernity" of keys in common usage in his time? For further details and illustrations see my *The Keys of the Kingdom: A Tool's Witness to Truth* (Chicago, Ill: Franciscan Herald Press, 1986).

[69] *Development*, p. 156.

[70] Ibid., p. viii.

That he was not struck by that definition either should seem most baffling, indeed. He rather added to his often quoted dictum from his *Letter to the Duke of Norfolk* that "the Vatican Council left him [the Pope] just as it found him,"[71] variants such as "very little was passed," "very little was added," "nothing of consequence was passed," "as little as possible was passed."[72] He took some time before he indirectly tried to reconcile these brave statements of his with the crucial words *ex sese* and *non ex consensu ecclesiae* in the definition that frightened him when he learned about their presence in the draft eight months before they became the essence of the definition. In his letter of November 21, 1869, he described those words as "an alteration in the fundamental dogma," and a "throwing away one of the human means (the pope acting with the bishops) by which God directs him." The infallibility of the pope's own words "made the system more miraculous," something "like seeking a bodily cure by miracle when human means are at hand."[73] His first discussion of *ex sese* postdates the definition by a year and a half, and it is almost a soft-pedaling of the issue, if not a dust cloud raised from a logician's specious distinctions. After pointing out that even the Gallicans had admitted the infallibility of the pope's solemn utterance "if the Bishops did no more than keep silence," he added that "all that is passed last year, is that *in some sense* he may speak per se, and his speech may be infallible—I say some sense, because a bishop who voted for the dogma tells me that at the time an explanation was given that in one sense the pope spoke per se, and in another sense not per se."[74]

History was to show that Newman underestimated the change in its importance as well as the need for it. The proof of this is the sudden resurgence of Gallicanism in the guise of the bishops' collegiality as soon as John XXIII made his intention known to call a Council. This is not to say that the majority of

[71] *A Letter addressed to His Grace the Duke of Norfolk on Occasion of Mr. Gladstone's Recent Expostulation* (London: D. M. Pickering, 1875), p. 62.

[72] *Letters and Diaries*, vol. 25, pp. 216, 220, 224, 262 (letters written between October 20, 1870 and January 2, 1871).

[73] *Letters and Diaries*, vol. 24, p. 377.

[74] *Letters and Diaries*, vol. 25, p. 447.

bishops wanted a collegiality on whose approval or consensus would have depended the truth of the infallibility of the pope's solemn utterance. But a very influential group of theologians, aided and abetted by several bishops, used all ruse and equivocation to secure on collegiality in the Dogmatic Constitution on the Church (*Lumen Gentium*), a wording that would lend itself to studied ambiguity. It was through that strategy that they wanted to claim after the Council that collegiality meant, first, episcopal democracy, ruled by a majority vote, an easily manipulable commodity; then, a presbyteral-lay democracy, a commodity even more prone to manipulation through artfully contrived opinion polls. The strategy is now widely known,[75] together with its sudden failure, as if God had miraculously foiled the devil by letting him slip unmiraculously on the trivial instrumentality of a letter, a thing potentially more slippery than a banana peel. A private note containing that strategy became, by being entrusted to a confidential friend, a sure means of quickly disclosing a secret supposed to be most carefully kept.

The disclosure was nothing short of a shock treatment for Paul VI, whose awe for theological commissions exceeded even that of a typical professional theologian, which he was not. He suddenly realized that he had been deceived in his defense of a pivotal theological commission, in spite of highest-level warnings. He broke down in tears, but had not much time for weeping and lamenting. The final voting on collegiality was only three days away. The Council could easily be thrown into turmoil by withdrawing a text repeatedly discussed, amended, and approved. Paul VI chose as a way out of the dilemma a direct message to the Council Fathers. In that message he notified all of them about the *only* meaning which they were allowed to attribute to the subtly ambiguous text on collegiality.[76] The

[75] Largely through *The Rhine Flows into the Tiber: A History of Vatican II* (Rockford, Ill.: Tan Books and Publishers, 1985), by Ralph W. Wiltgen; see especially pp. 230-33.

[76] According to the allowable meaning, the college of bishops was not the inheritor of the apostles' power in that full sense in which the pope is, and whereas that college can exercise its power only when convoked by the pope into an ecumenical council, the pope "as supreme pastor of the Church . . . can always exercise his authority as he chooses, as is demanded by his office

meaning was that of the infallibility of the pope *ex sese* and *non ex consensu ecclesiae*, that is, not through the consent of bishops, and certainly not through the consent of periti, of priests, and of the public.

The papal letter containing that message was to be placed at the head of *modi* (official interpretations) of the text on collegiality in *Lumen Gentium*.[77] This directive was honored in the breach by most translators and editors of *Lumen Gentium* in particular and of the documents of Vatican II in general, to the point of not being printed at all.[78] Behind such a strategy, in direct contravention of an explicit papal order, there must have been a very strong resolve. Collegialist-ecumenists were resolved to keep out of focus the papal letter's vision of "despotic" papacy without openly condemning that letter to the theological wastebasket. In the "ecumenism" of that move Newman would certainly recognize the one offered to him by Pusey, which he thought equiva-

itself." See pp. 90-101 of the English translation quoted in note 78 below.

[77] No mention is made of the fact that the interpretation to be prefixed to the *modi* of chapter 3 of *Lumen Gentium* was a message from "higher authority," that is from the Pope himself, in *Vatican Council II, The Conciliar and Post-Conciliar Documents*, ed. A. Flannery (Collegeville, Minn.: The Liturgical Press, 1975), pp. 432-34. Its printing in *The Documents of Vatican II*, ed. Walter M. Abbott S. J. (New York: Guild Press, 1966) is suggestive of a less than unreserved obedience. The admission (p. 99) that that Secretary of the Council made clear to the Council Fathers the provenance of the message from "higher authority" is "balanced" with an emphasis on the "great advances" made by Vatican II in the understanding of the importance of the episcopal office!

[78] Most sinister is the absence of that papal letter in the Study Club edition of *The Constitution of the Church* (Glen Rock, N.J.: Deus Books, Paulist Press, 1965), edited by E. H. Peters, which contains a foreword by the then Abbot (subsequently Bishop) Basil C. Butler, and a commentary by the then still Augustinian priest Gregory Baum. In a manner that goes directly counter to Newman's keen awareness of chronic human weakness as the very reason for a firm, authoritative, supreme guidance in the Church, Abbot Butler was dreaming in his foreword about a "presidency in charity of the See of Rome," (p. 14) as if that See would henceforth be spared rank abuses of its charity, to say nothing of rebellions against its God-given authority. In his commentary Baum spoke of that letter as the fruit of the resistance of a "small minority of bishops and cardinals to the doctrine of collegiality almost till the end" (p. 32). The silence of Baum, who was one of the ultraliberal *periti* at the Council, about the true story (of which he could hardly be unaware) behind that letter should seem nothing short of being deliberately tendentious.

lent to an invitation for Catholics "to commit suicide." He could perceive the essential identity between two ecclesial phenomena that were separated by centuries and not merely by a mere hundred years.

After that it would be the turn of his keenness on sincerity. The sharp adjectives—unscrupulous, wilful, intolerant—that he had applied to the "infallibilists" would now have for their target the "collegialists" and especially those among them who used him for a foil. It was behind that foil that they sowed everywhere in the supernaturally monarchical Church the most un-Newmanian seeds of theological "democratism" and "liberalism." With his mind so attentive to probabilities, especially to their antecedent kind, he would have found antecedently impossible not to see a pattern in the four Letters to the Editor of *The New York Times*, in its September 14, 1986, issue. All four letters were on the Vatican's declaration that Charles A. Curran was no longer a "Roman Catholic" theologian and therefore had no right to teach theology at the Catholic University of America, a Pontifical University. Each of the authors of the two letters that criticized the papal decision invoked Newman. One of them wrote: "Cardinal Newman once noted how silly the Church would look without the laity. Soon we may see how silly some Catholic universities look without faculty, students, or academic freedom."[79]

Such a reference to Newman perfectly suited those ignorant of his ringing declaration that "the essence of religion is to protect from error"[80] and of his most considered dicta on laity and university in their relation to the See of Peter. In the first of his lectures delivered before the faculty and students of the incipient Catholic University of Dublin, he sounded his call for a wholehearted support of a project in which "the possible and the expedient" seemed to be wide apart, with the uncompromising statement:

[79] *The New York Times*, Sept. 14, 1986, p. E24, cols. 5-6.

[80] *Letters and Diaries*, vol. 25, p. 259; from his letter to Archbishop Darboy, already quoted.

It is the decision of the Holy See; St. Peter has spoken, it is he who enjoined that which seems to us so unpromising. He has spoken, and has a claim on us to trust him . . . If ever there was a power on earth who had an eye for the times . . . such is he in the history of ages, who sits from generation to generation in the Chair of the Apostles, as the Vicar of Christ, and the doctor of His Church. These are not the words of rhetoric, Gentlemen, but of history. All who take part with the Apostle, are on the winning side . . . The past never returns; the course of events, old in texture, is ever new in its colouring and fashion. England and Ireland and the United States, one should add are not what they once were, but Rome is where it was, and St. Peter is the same.[81]

As for the newfangled "infallible" role of laity in the Church, spread with a reference to his famous article on the laymen's role in the Church,[82] his correspondence from those stormy years around "infallibility" contains his briefest and most authentic specification of what exactly he meant: Only two weeks after the definition of infallibility he referred in a letter to the consensus of the Universal Church (the *securus judicat orbit terrarum*) "as the ultimate guarantee of revealed truth," but hastened to add that

---

[81] *The Idea of a University Defined and Illustrated* (London: Longmans, Green and Co., 1888), pp. 23 and 17-18.

[82] That article, "On Consulting the Faithful" (1859), has indeed become the Trojan horse in the hands of those who tried to cast Vatican II in a light that for Newman would have been the evidence of the presence of the Prince of Darkness. The only comfort he would not find, say, in the book, *The Infallibility of the Laity: The Legacy of Newman* (New York: Herder and Herder, 1967), by S. D. Femiano, is the admission in the Foreword by Gregory Baum that "the reinterpretation of the self-identical Gospel in a new cultural context" is "not the idea of a homogeneous development of the doctrines once defined" which "was Newman's position" (p. xii). That this admission could be made unabashedly in 1967 shows the rapidity with which logic unfolds itself. It took only six years to reach that position of open defiance of Newman while making capital of his article, following its reprinting (on the very eve of Vatican II) in a book form (New York: Sheed and Ward, 1961) by J. Coulson, with almost as long an introduction (49 pp) as the article itself. Coulson apparently failed to see that his balancing of Newman's idea of the pope "as a ruler, not a philosopher" (p. 34) with a "deeper and more theological analysis" of the role of the laity, could but invite a lopsided glorification of those who are to be taught over the one who is to teach, and in the very name of Christ.

"according to my recollection, my paper in the *Rambler* is not in point. I think the paper was on the *sensus*, not the *consensus* fidelium—their voice was considered as a witness, not as an authority or a judgment. I compared consulting it to consulting a barometer for a fact. Thus it was a *fact* that the *fideles* in Arian times were for our Lord's divinity against their bishops, but in the Article, I think, I expressly reserved the 'magisterium' for the authorities of the Church." It was only that magisterium which could claim the phrase, *securus judicat*, with the latter word underlined by Newman himself.[83]

Of course, he would easily notice that behind the newfangled boosting of laity there lurks the glorification of private judgment, the source of all evil in his eyes. He would have no patience with that judgment, even when presented as the sacredness of conscience. Nothing was more sacred to him than that inner voice about the morally good and morally evil which, in his most considered judgment, was the most direct evidence of God. But he had no use for the culturally sanctioned meaning of conscience, which he branded publicly as a "miserable counterfeit" in his *Letter to the Duke of Norfolk* explaining to all Englishmen the meaning of papal infallibility. There he described that counterfeit conscience as:

> the right of thinking, speaking, writing, and acting, according to their judgment or their humour, without any thought of God at all. They do not even pretend to go by any moral rule, but they demand, what they think is an Englishman's prerogative, to be his own master in all things, and to profess what he pleases, asking no one's leave, and accounting priest or preacher, speaker or writer, unutterably impertinent, who dares to say a word against his going to perdition, if he like it, in his own way. Conscience has rights because it has duties; but in this age, with a large portion of the public, it is the very right and freedom of conscience to dispense with conscience, to ignore a Lawgiver and Judge, to be independent of unseen obligations. It becomes a license to take up any or no religion, to take up this or that and let it go again, to

---

[83] *Letters and Diaries*, vol. 25, p. 172. Aug. 3, 1870 to F. Rymer already quoted.

go to Church, to go to chapel, to boast of being above all religions and to be impartial critic of each of them. Conscience is a stern monitor, but in this century it has been superseded by a counterfeit, which the eighteen centuries prior to it never heard of, and could not have mistaken for it, if they had. It is the right of self-will.[84]

He had respect only for a conscience which was the very opposite to a "longsided selfishness" and "to a desire to be consistent with oneself." True conscience was rather

> a messenger from Him, who, both in nature and grace, speaks to us behind a veil, and teaches and rules us by His representatives. Conscience is the aboriginal Vicar of Christ, a prophet in its informations, a monarch in its peremptoriness, a priest in its blessings and anathemas, and, even though the eternal priesthood throughout the Church could cease to be, in it the sacerdotal principle would remain and would have a sway.[85]

Could there be a real conflict between such a conscience and the infallible Pope? Newman's answer to that question is pivoted on Aquinas' dictum that conscience "is the practical judgment or dictate of reason, by which we judge what *hic et nunc* is to be done as being good, or to be avoided as evil." Introductory to that quote was Newman's declaration that conscience is "not a judgment upon a speculative truth, any abstract doctrine, but bears immediately upon conduct, on something to be done or not done." To Aquinas' dictum he added: "Hence conscience cannot come into direct collision with the Church's or the Pope's infallibility; which is engaged only on general propositions, or the condemnation of propositions simply particular."[86]

What was to be done, according to Newman, when in a particular instance the sacred or second kind of conscience approved by him urged one to go against a papal ordinance? First, one was to apply oneself to prayer and study in a most serious and conscientious way. Second, one was to realize that the *onus probandi*, a very difficult burden, weighs in all such cases on the individual conscience. Third, one was to be conscious of

---

[84] *Letter to the Duke of Norfolk*, p. 58.

[85] Ibid., p. 57.

[86] Ibid., p. 62.

one's duty to give all the benefit of doubt to the Pope and to act as much as possible in the spirit of loyalty owed to him. Last but not least, one was to purge oneself of the spirit of disobedience in all its disguises:

> He must vanquish that mean, ungenerous, selfish, vulgar spirit of his nature which, at the very first rumor of a command, places itself in opposition to the Superior who gives it, asks itself whether he is not exceeding his right, and rejoices, in a moral and practical matter, to commence with scepticism. He must have no wilful determination to exercise a right of thinking, saying, doing just what he pleases, the question of truth and falsehood, right and wrong, the duty if possible of obedience, the love of speaking as his Head speaks, and of standing in all cases on his Head's side, being simply discarded.

Such was Newman's "necessary rule" for the problem, and he felt that if it were observed "collision between the Pope's authority and the authority of conscience would indeed be very rare."[87]

The applicability of that "necessary rule" to one's attitude toward, say, the moral precept laid down in *Humanae vitae*, should be all too clear: Since that precept is of general validity, Newman would necessarily call for unconditional acceptance of it. To try to distill another directive from Newman's utterances on papacy, Church, and conscience, taken either from his *Letter to the Duke of Norfolk* or from his letters and publications postdating it,[88] is to attack Newman's logic and the logic of the papacy by one and the same stroke. The chief proof of this was provided by Newman himself two years after he published that *Letter*. In the long preface he wrote to the third or Catholic edition of the *Via Media*, he emphatically stated that what he had written there as an Anglican about the Church as a Mystical Body should in no way diminish the validity of the imperial notion of the Church as pivoted on a ruling papacy:

> I will but say in passing, that I must not in this argument be supposed to forget that the Pope, as the Vicar of Christ,

---

[87] Ibid., p. 64.

[88] As done most emphatically by Misner in the last two chapters of his *Papacy and Development*.

inherits these offices and acts for the Church in them . . .
Christianity, then, is at once a philosophy, a political power,
and a religious rite: as a religion, it is Holy; as a philosophy, it
is Apostolic; as a political power, it is *imperial*, that is, One
and Catholic. As a religion, its special centre of actions is
pastor and flock; as a philosophy, the Schools; as a *rule,* the
Papacy and its Curia (italics added).[89]

That to the very end of his days the logic of the papacy included
for Newman even the pope's Curia may be a bitter pill for many
latter-day Newmanists to swallow, but it is the only logic which is
truly Newmanian.

[89] *The Via Media or the Anglican Church* (new ed.; London: Longmans, Green
and Co., 1896), vol. 1, p. xl. The first sentence in this quotation is left out in
the middle of a passage quoted by Misner on the same page. Needless to say,
he did not quote (*Papacy and Development*, p. 181) the remainder of the
quotation although with its words *imperial* and *Curia* it must have stared him
in the eye!

8

Faith and Church History

For a convert like Newman, Christian culture could only mean the cultivation of true cult as embodied in the Catholic Church. This logical connection rules Newman's dicta on Church history. It is the logic of faith searching into its past. For sacred as true cult or worship can be, embody as it may the highest eternal realities, it still shares in the universal predicament of all created entities: They all have a history. Indeed, they exist only inasmuch as they exist in history, that is, exist through time and in time. They are all time-conditioned. Time in turn means change. Not to be subject to change is to be above time, a condition strictly reserved for one being, the Creator.

There can be no greater difference than the one between a condition of change and that of absolute changelessness. In a divinely inspired form, Psalm 101 sets forth this difference as it contrasts the Creator with the heavens and the earth, or the sum of all things: "They will all wear out like a garment. . . . But you neither change, nor have an end."

Those things include everything which is not God, and therefore we must count among them even our ideas and concepts. Yet in stating this, the human mind asserts something changeless in the welter of change. Change presupposes permanence. The question then arises whether permanence can be spotted better if we look at the beginning of change or at its unfolding. Or, in other words, is it the early phase of the history of a process that reveals better what remains permanent under change, or rather is it the ever later phases of history?

A classic answer to this question is given by Newman as he ponders the history of doctrine. That history, he states, cannot be likened to a stream, crystal clear at its origin and increasingly muddied as it pursues and broadens its course. On the contrary, an idea or a belief reveals its strength as it meets ever new challenges. Any idea changes with the challenges it meets, "in order to remain the same. In a higher world it is otherwise, but here below to live is to change, and to be perfect is to have changed often."[1]

These words, needless to say, are from Section I of Chapter 1 of Newman's *The Development of Christian Doctrine*. There Newman searches into faith's past in order to show that true Christian faith has always remained true to itself. In that book he often takes up events from Church history as so many manifestations of doctrine. But with Church history as such he does not deal in that book. Four years later, we are in 1849, Newman toyed briefly with the idea of choosing Church history for the subject of a series of lectures, which Bishop Wiseman, not yet a cardinal, asked him to deliver in London, during Lent of 1850. Newman dropped the subject of Church history on the ground that he was not a historian.

Yet his series of lectures, known eventually as *Anglican Difficulties*, was a masterful probing of faith into its history.[2] The faith in question was the faith of his comrades-in-arms in the Oxford Movement. Less than ten percent of them, if that many, had recognized with Newman that only by uniting with Rome would they do justice to the deepest motivations, aims, and gradual unfolding of the Oxford Movement.

Newman gave in those lectures the best kind of historical account of an event or process from the past. He gave that account as the story's chief participant. Ranke, the most remembered historian of the 19th century, would have had to agree on the merit of such an account. After all, it was Ranke who claimed

---

[1] J. H. Newman, *An Essay on the Development of Christian Doctrine* (London: Basil Montague Pickering, 1878), p. 40. In the subsequent notes this work will be referred to as *Development*.

[2] See my introduction to the Real View Books reissue, 1994, Reprinted here as Chapter 6.

in a now famous phrase, that the historian's real task is to reconstruct the past "exactly as it happened."[3]

There are no doubt dangers in such a definition of the historian's task, and the same can be said of Ranke's other precept, namely, that the historian should use only documents that were produced during the phase of the past under investigation. Yet although Newman's *Anglican Difficulties* were written five years after the Oxford Movement had come to a close with Newman's conversion, any effort to write the history of that Movement with no proper attention to that work would be greatly mistaken indeed.[4] Whatever a historian of the Oxford Movement may think of this, it is not possible to doubt that in those lectures Newman searched the Oxford Movement with the purpose of unfolding true faith by probing into its recent past.

To see this it should be enough to recall a few gems from those Lectures. It was there that Newman first stated publicly that the study of the Fathers had made him a Catholic. It was there that he first went public with his innermost motivation: "Be my soul with the saints," meaning above all Saint Athanasius and Saint Ambrose. It was there that he gave his finest presentation of the four great Notes of the Church—its unity, catholicity, apostolicity and sanctity—all heavily illustrated from Church history.

In fact, nothing can illustrate, document, and demonstrate those Notes better than Church history. On the basis of his statement, quoted above, about the need to change in order to live well, Newman could have no other approach, even if another was possible at all. This is what made him a special historian and not the kind of antiquarian who is hesitant to say anything

---

[3] "Wie es eigentlich gewesen." See L. von Ranke, *Geschichte der romanischen und germanischen Völker von 1494 bis 1514: Zur Kritik der neueren Geschichtschreiber*, in *Sämmtliche Werke* (3rd ed.; Leipzig: Duncker und Humblot, 1885), vol. 33-34, p. vii.

[4] Authors of all important monographs on the Oxford Movement have failed to do justice to Newman's *Anglican Difficulties*, to say nothing of all major monographs on Newman's life and work. In his *The Spirit of the Oxford Movement* (London: Sheed & Ward, 1945), Christopher Dawson shied away from that book of Newman's for the most likely reason that most former High-Church Anglicans find it very painful to face up to the illusory character of High Anglicanism when taken for genuine Catholicism.

definite about the Greeks until all Greek inscriptions have been catalogued. He was certainly not like the historian who claimed that nothing certain could be known about the Civil War until all the voting records of all members of Congress from 1830 until 1860 had been fed into a computer and analyzed by it.[5] One can hardly imagine a better illustration of the dictum, garbage in, garbage out, however finely ground.

Emphasis on the broad vistas of the manifestations of faith characterizes Newman the historian. This is certainly true of his many essays on Church history, collected in the three volumes of his *Historical Sketches* and of his *Essays Critical and Historical*. While always keen on the significance of this or that detail, he never got lost in details. He had an inner assurance that he would not go wrong thereby as a Church historian. This is why he felt free to re-live the past of faith, and to commune with the great faithful of the past.

The reason for this assurance of Newman's lies in the fact that for him Church history was a history of faith, for if it was not, it was not Church history but a chapter in the historical branch of religious studies. Such studies exclude the question of the intrinsic truth of this or that religious proposition, let alone the dogmatic certainty of faith by which Newman set so great a store, as anyone should know who has read the *Grammar of Assent*. In that book one finds the reasons why Newman as a Church historian had to be a student of faith, that is, a theologian, and a most orthodox one at that. Orthodox means one who professes the right or true doctrine, and such a doctrine demands an assent which is firm and irrevocable, or else the act or habit of faith which offers the assent is not genuine. Yet although he speaks at length in the *Grammar* of the various degrees of certainties that can be acquired about events of the past, it is not in the *Grammar* that he set forth his method of faith's search into its past.

The phrase, faith searching into its past or history, should recall Saint Anselm's famous words, "fides quaerens intellectum," a phrase never seriously misunderstood until this century. It was

---

[5] Professor L. Benson of the University of Pennsylvania made that claim in a seminar at Princeton University, on May 11, 1967.

in this century that Karl Barth tried to give a new twist to that phrase of Anselm's, the twist of fideism. Fideism creates the object of faith and turns it thereby into a vehicle of subjectivism, ultimately severing faith from all history, indeed even from that recorded history of faith called the Scriptures.

Anselm was never a Barthian. He knew his Saint Augustine far better than did Barth and all the Barthians, including Catholic Barthians, these hapless examples of our "new" theology. As for Augustine, he certainly was not a Barthian. To see this, one does not need to peruse all the folio volumes of Augustine's works. It is enough to read a long letter of Augustine's, Letter 120, which is specifically on the relation of faith and reason. In that letter Augustine gave the rule which forever should guide all orthodox reflections on the subject. There he wrote that "intellectus aliquantulum semper precedit," because it is not possible to have faith in something unless one first has some idea about what to believe in a given proposition. Only when that embryonic knowledge is there can faith spur further probings into the proposition's conceptual contents.

Quite similar is the logic, I would say, the epistemological logic, of Newman's approach to Church history. That logic is riveted on facts, which for Newman were monumental facts. In claiming this, Newman also struck a blow at a fideist form of writing Church history. He delivered that blow in the Introduction to his *Development*: "History is not a creed or catechism, it gives lessons rather than rules; still no one can mistake its general teaching in this matter, whether he accept it or stumble at it. Bold outlines and bold masses of colour rise out of the records of the past. They may be dim, they may be incomplete; but they are definite." And he was so certain intellectually on this point as to risk its convincingness by adding an illustration: "And this one thing at least is certain; whatever history teaches, whatever it omits, whatever it exaggerates or extenuates, whatever it says or unsays, at least the Christianity of history is not Protestantism. If ever there were a safe truth, it is this."[6]

[6] *Development*, p. 7.

Whatever this statement is, it is the kind of statement about history that fully corresponds to what originally was meant by the act of discoursing about the past. In fact, when the word *historia* or rather its verb form, *historein*, was used by the Greeks of old, they did not restrict its use to the past. For them, whenever one offered a reasoned discourse, one engaged in the act of *historein*.[7]

Indeed for those who established among the Greeks the art of writing history—it should be enough to think of Thucydides and of his *Peloponnesian Wars*—the act of re-creating history was not a mere narrative, the art of adding one entertaining story to another, but a reasoned discourse about the past. It was in that tradition of historiography that there came to be formulated what I believe is still the best definition of historiography: history is philosophy drawn from examples.[8]

Reasoned discourse presupposes, however, some premises, some presuppositions, tacit or explicit, and a marshalling of facts or objects on behalf of a set of propositions. Reasoned discourse is therefore different from both its empiricist and its idealist versions. In the former one is guided by a method of induction that leads nowhere. In the second, one simply makes up facts to fit the theory, or one ignores facts that the theory cannot tolerate. Both Bacon, the empiricist, and Kant and Hegel the idealists, gave egregious illustrations of this running roughshod over the facts of history.

But back to Newman, or rather to the only and wholly ignored context in which he sets forth his own version of faith searching into its past as Church history. The context in question consists of five letters, four of them very long, written by Newman in 1875 and first printed in 1899, nine years after his death. Although they appeared in *The Contemporary Review*,

---

[7] To see this it is enough to look up in a better-grade dictionary of the English language, the etymology of the word *epistemology*, which means the study of understanding or reasoning. On separating it into its three components, *ep, istemo,* and *logy* one can immediately see that *istemo* comes from *istemi* (I understand or I reason) which in turn is the root of the word *istorein,* or to discourse in a reasoned manner.

[8] A rephrasing by Dionysius of Halicarnassus (fl. 25 B. C.) in his *De arte rhetorica* (xi. 2) of a dictum of Thucydides.

Britain's leading biweekly around the turn of the century, they were totally ignored, and certainly so by Catholic Church historians.

A century or so later, and in the wake of the centenary of Newman's death, to ignore those letters may be a high crime, intellectually that is. For it is an intellectual crime to dismiss a powerful compass and set of directives in the contestation for truth, especially historical truth. About truth of a more theoretical kind, little can be said in this age of deconstructionism and, what is even more dangerous, phenomenologism. Cultivators of phenomenology have always shied away from history, and this is also true of Catholic philosophers who feel they have found in the phenomenological method the philosopher's stone.

Newman was saved in advance from phenomenology. What saved him for the cause of objective truth was not just his preference for the illative method and for the concrete as opposed to the general. Actually, that preference of his, when coupled with his philosophico-theological motto, *unusquisque in sensu suo abundet* (everybody should cultivate his own preference), brought him—the *Grammar of Assent* is a witness—to the edge of an epistemological precipice.[9] What saved him from going over the edge and from being lost in the subjectivist or personalist abyss beyond it was his trust in the following reasoning: If there is God, and there has to be, it is not conceivable that He would have abandoned mankind to "an aboriginal calamity." If, however, God revealed to us a salvation history, He had to protect its truth by an infallible factor: the infallibility of the Church, with the infallibility of the Pope as its seal and assurance.[10]

What follows from this for faith's probing into Church history, or faith's search into its past? To have Newman's most considered and mature answer, and indeed his only systematic answer to this question, we must turn to those five letters of his,

[9] See my essay, "Newman's Assent to Reality, Natural and Supernatural," in *Newman Today* (San Franscisco: Ignatius Press, 1989), pp. 189-220, reprinted here as Chapter 9.

[10] While Newman felt very strongly that the definition was inopportune and did so even after the definition became a fact, he had repeatedly stated, and well before Vatican I, his belief in papal infallibility.

or first rather to John Rickards Mozley, to whom Newman wrote those letters between March and December 1875. Mozley did not initiate the correspondence in order to have an argument, although he was an intellectual of the first rank. A brilliant student at Eton and Cambridge, Mozley became in 1869, at the age of twenty-nine, professor of Pure Mathematics at Owens College, Manchester. More important than that, Mozley was the son of Newman's sister Jemima. In writing to Newman, Mozley therefore wrote to his own uncle, fully confident of receiving replies worthy of such an uncle who had returned to public eminence with his *Apologia* in 1864, and again ten years later with his defense of papal infallibility, his *Letter to the Duke of Norfolk*. Nobody dreamt yet at that time that within five years Newman would become the kind of eminence that a cardinal is.

While the nephew-uncle relation on his mother's side seemed to be very promising for Mozley, the same was not true on his father's side. Two of Mozley's paternal uncles were among those allies of Newman's in the Oxford Movement who had refused to follow him to Rome, and both eventually gave memorable explanations for their refusal. In 1875 one of those uncles, James B. Mozley, Regius Professor of Divinity at Oxford, published a lengthy criticism of Newman's *Essay on Development*, or of Newman's argument that far from introducing new dogmas, Rome merely unfolded the contents of doctrines it had held from the start.[11] The other uncle, Thomas Mozley, also a theologian, was working on reminiscences of his Oriel days in Oxford. When published in 1882,[12] his work was taken by Anglicans as the essential corrective to a number of points in Newman's *Apologia*.

Clearly, John Rickards Mozley grew up in a family circle where it was persistently argued that Newman's conversion lacked intellectual cogency, even if it did not lack personal honesty. Mozley's letters had therefore to appear of some

---

[11] J. B. Mozley, *The Theory of Development: a Criticism of Dr. Newman's Essay* (London: Rivington, 1847), reprinted from the January 1874 issue of *Christian Remembrancer*. Further editions in 1878 and 1889.

[12] T. Mozley, *Reminiscences, Chiefly of Oriel and the Oxford Movement* (London: Longmans, Green and Co., 1882), 2 vols.

moment, and all the more so because he asked his uncle to answer these two questions that ran between the lines of his letters: Since you are of such a keen mind and undoubtedly of a most sincere soul, how can you see in the Church of Rome the Church of Peter and Paul? Are you really alive to the many evils perpetrated by the Church of Rome, often with the popes' direct connivance? Such questions could seem all the more acute because only a year earlier Newman had published his famed defense of papal infallibility, *Letter to the Duke of Norfolk*, which within four months had been reprinted as many times. There Newman argued, and most emphatically so, that not one of the popes' wrongdoings—political, intellectual, or moral—could be construed as a counterargument to Rome's claim of being the Church of Peter and Paul.

In fact, as John Rickards Mozley later disclosed, it was Newman's stark, unapologetic listing of indefensible papal acts in the *Letter to the Duke of Norfolk* that brought home to him the magnitude of what appeared to him a sadly one-way vision plaguing Newman. John Mozley was not the first to feel that way. A generation earlier, F. D. Maurice, a convert from Unitarianism to Anglicanism and Professor of Divinity at King's College, London, went on record with the following comment on the freshly published *Development of Christian Doctrine*, Newman's major historical work: "The system Mr Newman believes in is presented to us in its darkest form; all that can be said against it is anticipated."[13] Maurice, too, wondered how Newman could then apparently disregard all the darkness he had painted so starkly.

The cogency of Newman's argumentation in defense of papal infallibility has stood the test of times. Half a century after its publication, Harold J. Laski, hardly one to be suspected of sympathy for Rome, described Newman's *Letter to the Duke of Norfolk* as "perhaps the profoundest discussion of the nature of obedience and of sovereignty to be found in the English language."[14] This is not to suggest that Laski was convinced by

[13] F. D. Maurice, *Epistle to the Hebrews* (London: J. W. Parker, 1846), Preface, p. liii.

[14] H. J. Laski, *Studies in the Problem of Sovereignty* (New Haven: Yale

Newman's argumentation, but to say that he certainly recognized in it an ever fresh challenge to any decent intellect. But even if one accepted that Newman argued cogently, the question still remained whether the error-free intellectual consistency on the part of the popes could offset their moral failures, or simply the at-times widespread moral failures of Catholics. Those failures could hardly be reconciled, as Mozley put it in 1899, "with that spirit of morality and goodness which should mark a divine example and a divine teacher."

Mozley continued with his reminiscences: "I pointed to facts in the history of the Church which appeared to me to be symptoms of a faulty nature. I referred to the condition of the countries most obedient to Rome—Spain under Philip II, France up to the first Revolution, Italy up to the middle of the nineteenth century—as exhibiting a tremendous total misdoing, partly traceable directly to the influence of the highest authorities of Rome, partly permitted by them without protest or repudiation .... How came it that the members of an organisation to which the divine promises were believed to have been entrusted, should not only have committed such grave offences in the past, but should be so unwilling to confess them in the present, except as bare facts, and without any sense of the disrepute thereby attaching to themselves, and to the society they looked upon as divine?"[15]

In his first letter to Newman, Mozley described himself as being "perplexed and even curious." He found it difficult to "understand how a man like you, who have had time and opportunities for observation and thought should be able to put up with a one-sided view of Rome."[16] As befitted a highly polished Englishman, Mozley knew how to extol Newman's intellectual stature by commending it and yet, at the same time, to cast doubt on it.

University Press, 1917), p. 202.

[15] J. R. Mozley in his Introduction to those five letters of Newman's in *The Contemporary Review* 76 (Sept. 1899), p. 357. The letters cover pp. 358-370. They are, of course, available in *Letters and Diaries of John Henry Newman*, vol. 27. Here the references are to the text in *The Contemporary Review.*

[16] Ibid.

Newman gladly obliged his nephew, although the subject had many ramifications. Actually it took eight months for the correspondence to run its course, because the month-long sickness and death (on May 25) of Ambrose St John, his fellow Oratorian and best confidant, put severe demands on Newman's time and energy.[17] There was, of course, nothing original in Mozley's centering on the behavior of the Church in Inquisition times to prove that the Church's actual behavior compromised and discredited her claims, sublime as they could appear when taken in the abstract. The evils, real and imaginary, of the Inquisition have never failed to provide a particularly telling argument against the Church's exalted spiritual status.

But the reality of evil could be construed not only against the Catholic Church, but also against any form of Christian or Jewish belief, indeed against any form of belief in a personal God as a moral governor. The real issue, according to Newman, was not the evil, but the good. If there was a God and He gave a revelation in the form of establishing a visible society, it followed that this society achieved some good that no other society could achieve. "There must be visible tokens of sanctity in the Church, if the Church is to be considered divine," although, Newman wisely added, "as the Spirit bloweth as it listeth, so its manifestation in works [is] according to no laws and cannot be reckoned on."[18]

Then Newman quoted secular as well as Protestant historians who acknowledged that the Catholic Church could indeed claim special moral credit during all her history.[19] Clearly, Newman was not one of those latter-day Catholic Church historians who seem to lay on the Church the blame for all real and imaginary evils in history, past and present. Although ready to acknowledge the dark side, he insisted that "its good has been more potent and permanent and evidently intrinsic to it than its

---

[17] Thus Newman's fifth and especially long reply to John Mozley could not come until early December.

[18] Ibid., p. 360.

[19] They were Lord Russell, Gibbon, Voigt, Hurter, Guizot, Ranke, Waddington, Bowden, Milman, and Neander.

evil."[20] These are words of capital significance. They show that, according to Newman, faith could confidently search into its past and find there incontrovertible evidence of its divine origin and of a divine force that does not cease working in it.

Even more startling should appear to some liberal Catholic Church historians Newman's second letter to Mozley. There Newman reiterated his point that attention should be focused on the good if any meaningful conclusion was to be arrived at. Still, he was willing to refocus on the bad in the Church. He held it to be a consequence of the fact that the Church consisted of human beings and therefore was a visible, indeed a large, visible society. As such the Church had to exercise power, including the punishment of heretics. He warned that the Church's use of the power of the sword would appear an unmitigated evil only to those who found fault with the endorsement of capital punishment throughout the Old Testament. They, Newman added, should first find fault with Saint Paul's endorsement of the use of the sword on the part of the secular magistrate.

Thus Newman found an excuse even for the Pope, Gregory XIII, who had hastened to approve the St Bartholomew massacre. No, Newman would not go so far as to say, although it could have been said for good reason, that if the Huguenots had not been massacred, they would have massacred the Catholics. Newman merely said that the Church, being a large, visible society, has to wield power, political power, a most risky venture at all times: "A large society, such as the Church, is necessarily a political power, and to touch politics is to touch pitch."[21]

Now, one may add, if this was true of the Catholic Church as a political entity, what about Churches that were and are mere appendices of the political State? What about States themselves, such as the United States, that practice in the extreme the principle of separation between Church and State? Don't they become thereby a mere political entity, which, if touched, blackens one's hands with pitch that also smells foul in the extreme? Would it not therefore be proper, one may ask, to have

---

[20] Ibid., p. 360.
[21] Ibid., p. 363.

for a big newspaper not the motto "all the news that's fit to print," but Newman's words: "to touch politics is to touch pitch"? Might not one include in that pitch—an ugly and gluey black substance—the editorial politics as well?

If all these implications of what Newman stated appeared startling, even more so had to appear the inference which Newman drew from Mozley's demand, namely, that "the Popes ought publicly to confess, when it is proved they have gone wrong."[22] Newman first asked whether Mozley would expect Queen Victoria to apologize for the sins of George IV? Should loyal children denounce their parents? Should not private memoirs be withheld from public eyes at least for some decades? Can any party be kept together if there is no reticence? Anyone with a clear mind and with a reasonably clean conscience could find that these questions of Newman's would today hit secular entities long before they would hit, say, the Vatican's Secret Archives. These questions of Newman's may also suggest that he would wonder at today's trend when apologizing for long-past mistakes has become a virtue.

By not asking the Church to apologize, Newman did not wish to defend the bungling of Churchmen in matters political, economic and financial. Nor did he want to defend the deplorable backwardness of Latin countries as compared with England. But he minced no words about the fact that infidelity started from prosperous England and had its stronghold there in his day. And since it was not the temporal success, talent, and renown of the Papacy, or in sum its cultural achievements that made him a Catholic, he wrote to Mozley, "its errors and misfortunes have no power to unsettle me."[23]

But, as one may expect, Mozley's mind was riveted on the wrongs perpetrated by leading Catholics, above all, the Popes. Had Newman called Mozley's attention to the distinction to be made between individuals and the Church itself, he would not have said much that was new. But he went on to insist on the good: "I maintain that it [Church] has done an incalculable

[22] Ibid., p. 363.
[23] Ibid., p. 364.

amount of good, that it has done good of a special kind, such as no other historical polity or teaching or worship had done, and that good has come from its professed principles."[24]

Such is an unusual challenge to those outside the Church, making hay for themselves of its history. It is also a challenge to liberal Catholic Church historians who would consider Newman's words, "incalculable amount of good," to be a crime of brazen triumphalism with respect to Church history. What he added is a challenge to some conservatives who look at the past as a token of inevitable triumph for the future: "Things are so constituted in this world that the power of doing good has a maximum [limit]." Although in what follows Newman had in mind secular moral "authority," there is much food for thought there for such Catholics who expect any major papal encyclical to bring about a total change of heart and mind: "I am disposed to deny that as time goes on the authoritative view of moral and religious truth becomes clearer, wider, and more exact."[25]

Still he insisted on that incalculable amount of good and on its special character, such as that only the Catholic Church could produce. Today, when so many Catholic ecumenists expect from Protestant churches the cure for the ills and woes of the Catholic Church, Newman's following words should sound as the voice crying in the wilderness of our newfangled ecclesiology: "If it is a great work to preserve Christianity in the world, this I think the Church has done and is doing: and at this moment Christianity would be dying out in all its varieties were the Catholic Church to be suppressed."[26]

In a short reply (May 16) to Mozley's fourth letter, Newman excused himself with a reference to the heavy blow he had just suffered through the death of Ambrose St John. His final communication, which came on December 6, 1875, was a gem of ecumenical courage. He found that his able nephew still would not go "to the bottom of the matter." Moreover, Newman felt that "it would not consist with that truth and frankness due to all

[24] Ibid., p. 365.
[25] Ibid., p. 366.
[26] Ibid.

men, and especially to one with whom I am so united in affection as yourself, not to say so."[27]

Newman then performed faith's deepest conceivable search into its past. He did so by stating what should pass for a rank discrimination today when everybody is viewed as being equally virtuous, when Brigitte Bardot is fined in France for having declared Muslims not to be animal-friendly, when Christians of all varieties are held to be equally holy, when voodoo rites are taken for means of sanctification. But without flinching, Newman wrote to Mozley that difference between Catholics and Protestants, or rather pure Protestants and pure Catholics, is basically an ethical difference, and that "this difference is radical and immutable, as the natures of an eagle and a horse are."[28] Anything else, including dogmatic differences, let alone cultural differences, is strictly secondary by comparison.

Then, in support of this sweeping generalization, Newman listed four facts that were, as he put it, "historically undeniable." The first of these facts was that, unlike Protestantism, Catholicism preserved that ethical character which was the hallmark of Christianity from its very start. One could hardly find for certain papal encyclicals a better justification than Newman's words: Christianity "arose with a certain definite ethical system, which it proclaimed to be all-important, all necessary for the present and future welfare of the human race, and of every individual member of it, and which is simply ascertainable now and unmistakable." Liberal Catholic moral theologians, echoing the tunes of their main-line Protestant counterparts, were disavowed by Newman well in advance and roundly as he wrote: "This ethical system . . . is the living principle also of present Catholicism, and not of any form of Protestantism, whatever." He held that ethical principle or vitality to be "the essential life" and "vigorous motive power" of Catholicism. Without that principle or system "Catholicism would soon go out," and in virtue of it alone "Catholicism makes itself manifest, and is recognized."[29]

---

[27] Ibid., p. 367.

[28] Ibid.

[29] Ibid., p. 367. Of that difference between Catholics and Protestants Newman said, "I have [of it] a clear perception, clearer and clearer as my

The second fact consisted, according to Newman, in Catholic ethics' utter variance with the ethical character of secular society, or, as we would say today, with the momentary majority opinion, or with the soon-to-be-engineered majority opinion about what is ethical and unethical. Certain proof of this can be found in any issue of our big dailies as they report about the morality of the cloning of humans or about the morality of doctor-assisted suicide. Such moralities are made to order by the media and are always at cross purposes with the moral stance of the Catholic Church. Far less certain is whether Newman could say today without a moment of hesitation that Catholics by and large form a Church militant on earth. He would sadly say that too many Catholics make a virtue of laying down their arms and engaging in theological draft-dodging.

In looking at Mother Teresa and her nuns (or at many other unpublicized heroic groups of religious), Newman would be able to repeat his third point, or rather fact, that Catholics oppose the world out of love and not out of hatred. It is the love issuing from our Lord's injunction, that we must love our enemies even though the world will keep hating us. He quoted to that effect passages from the Synoptics, from St Paul, and from St John's Gospel and epistles. What he said in conclusion should send a chill down the spines of our champions of a new moral theology, who are busy launching peace missiles to the world: "After avowals such as these in our primary authorities, it will be a hard job to discover any Irenicon between Catholicity and the moral teaching of this day."[30]

---

own experience of existing religion increases." Today the starkest reminder of this is to be found not in the plain caving in of all mainline Protestant Churches to the immorality of the day, but in the hapless tactic of those Protestant groups that fight pornography tooth and nail but say not a word about contraception. They remind me of those antidrug crusaders who denounce the use of heroin but advocate the availability of marijuana, although the use of the latter invariably leads to drug addiction.

[30] Ibid., p. 369. Newman's use of the word "Irenicon" harked back, of course, to Pusey's famed public letter under that title and to Newman's reply to it, both reprinted in the volume attached to the *Anglican Difficulties* in the Longmans edition of his works. "Ecumenicon" would be its present-day equivalent.

The fourth fact Newman listed was related to the resolve of the world "to make the most of this life." This resolve was at total variance with the duty of Catholics to focus on eternal life. Protestants, Newman added, had largely lined up with this worldly resolve. Hence Newman could but repeat: "You can no more make the Catholic and Protestant *ethos* one, than you can mix oil and vinegar."[31] His final words should seem particularly memorable in this age of science: "Although our opposition to science, etc., ceased ever so much, we should not thereby be more acceptable in our teaching to the public opinion of the day."[32]

In saying all this about faith's searching into its past, which is always its present and the token of its future, Newman, who was not a Church historian, did not say anything different from the great Church historians of his century. I mean Hergenröther, Janssen, and their followers, Pastor, Denifle, Grisar, to mention only the chief ones, and Lebreton, Jedin, Fliche and Martin in our century. They all searched Church history in the firm conviction that they would find there what Newman repeatedly called in those letters, "the incalculable amount of good."

That amount is a fact. It is a fact recognized even by those who do not have faith but do not close their very eyes. One of these was Voltaire who doubted whether it was possible to find Sisters of Charity outside the Catholic Church. Facts will prevail, and one can do nothing better than to find oneself on the side of facts. Among facts none is more striking than that incalculable moral, intellectual and cultural good which the Church delivered to mankind for the past two millennia. But let us not forget that the incalculable good is a very special good, which only the true Church can deliver. Any other approach to Church history is mere muckraking. It can earn the Catholic Church historian kudos from the secular academia but will not turn his work into what it should be, faith's search into its past.

There in that past, both remote and recent, bold outlines and bold masses arise. They are the mountain ranges of the incalcula-

---

[31] Ibid. p. 370.
[32] Ibid.

ble good delivered by the Church. The vista of those mountains should make us resonate with the Psalmist who saw God's help come to him from the mountains, once he raised and fixed his eyes on them. Such is the first and foremost task for anyone who with Newman would search into faith's past. He or she must be convinced that such a past, though rippled with shortcomings and failures, is still full of an incalculable good which only the historical Church could and did deliver to human history.

9

Assent to Reality:
Natural and Supernatural

On Tuesday, March 15, 1870, Newman's *Essay in Aid to a Grammar of Assent* came off the press and sold out on that same day.[1] A week later, to Newman's great surprise, there followed a second printing.[2] Still another ten days later *The Spectator* brought the *Grammar* to the notice of the intellectual and literary world with a long review of it. The reviewer, Richard Holt Hutton, began with characterizing the title as being "superfluously modest and a deprecation by Dr Newman of extravagant expectations on behalf of his readers."[3] Pressed by a correspondent about the title, Newman pointed in its defense to the difference between an essay and a grammar. The word "essay" meant mainly an "analytical" probing, which his book was, instead of being a "systematic" work which any grammar was supposed to be.[4] Another justification he offered was that, as it stood, the title "would prepare people for a balk"[5] and diminish thereby the measure of their disappointment.

Whatever the defense of the title, Newman's remark that the book was a "semi-logical fancy" was subtly to the point. In the

---

[1] As stated in the entry for that day in Newman's diary. See *Letters and Diaries*, vol. 25, p. 54.

[2] To Mrs. Mozley (Jemima Newman), March 21, 1870, ibid., p. 59

[3] "Dr. Newman's *Grammar of Assent,*" *The Spectator*, Apr. 2, 1870, p. 436.

[4] To Canon J. Walker, Apr. 8, 1870: "You see I called it an Essay, as it really is, because it is an analytical inquiry—a Grammar ought to be synthetical." *Letters and Diaries*, vol. 25, p. 84.

[5] To Jemima, Feb. 21, 1870, ibid., p. 35.

Grammar Newman aimed at unfolding the distinction between mere assertions and assertions that were so many assents, not so much from the logical as from the phenomenological or psychological viewpoint. Not that he put this clearly when six weeks before its publication Newman warned Bishop Ullathorne that the *Grammar* was about a "dry logical subject, or semi logical Assent."[6] However, insight into the logical peculiarity of assent was, in Newman's own admission, the factor that enabled him to write the book. In his letter of February 21, 1870, to his sister Jemima, he recalled his having been seized, while on vacation in Switzerland, with the meaning of assent: "We went up to Glion, and then suddenly the idea came into my head, which have [sic] been a clue to the treatment of my subject; and my first pages stand pretty much as I wrote them in August 1866."[7]

In those first pages of the *Grammar* Newman offers some distinctions, almost pedantic at first sight. He tells his reader that a verbal proposition is either a question, or a conclusion, or an assertion. But then he warns that when we conclude we still argue, but when "we assert we do not argue."[8] In other words he warns that we must be most logical with words, that we must take them in their pristine meaning, a point that should seem prophetic in this age when respect for meaning is being atrophied by advertising, the media, and analytical philosophy. Newman then lists the three mental acts—doubt, inference, and assent—corresponding to those three verbal propositions. The *Grammar*, he states, will deal almost entirely with assent, with inference hardly, and with doubt not at all. Finally he points out the difference between assenting to a notional or abstract proposition and assenting to a concrete fact, especially to one vividly visual. Throughout the *Grammar* Newman lays much emphasis on the primacy of the sense of vision over the other senses. Indeed, from the very start he stresses the superiority of

[6] To Bishop Ullathorne, Jan. 28, 1870, ibid., p. 19.

[7] To Jemima, Feb. 21, 1870, ibid., p. 35.

[8] See pp. 25-31 in the Image Book (Garden City, N.Y.: Doubleday, 1955) edition of *An Essay in Aid of a Grammar of Assent*, which, in addition to being its most widely available edition, also has the extra feature of a penetrating introduction by Etienne Gilson.

single facts as objects of sight over universal notions, a strategy that has not failed to perplex philosophically sensitive minds.

Another and rather different account given by Newman about the genesis of the *Grammar* is worth recalling for two details in it. One shows Newman's own recurring perplexity: "I felt I had something to say upon it [assent], yet, whenever I attempted, the sight I saw vanished, plunged into a thicket, curled itself up like a hedgehog, or changed colours like a chameleon." The other is the importance which Newman attributes to his having found the right start after so many tries. Once more he refers to the visit to Glion, where "a thought came into my head as the clue, the 'Open Sesame', of the whole subject, and I at once wrote it down, and I pursued it about the Lake of Lucerne. Then when I came home, I began in earnest, and have slowly got through it."[9]

Newman's references to the *Grammar* as "disappointing,"[10] as a "Lenten reading for one's mortification,"[11] as a "dry and humdrum" discourse[12] that would make people ask, "what is it all about?"[13] could be disappointing to not a few. Even more so his warning that the book would not be a refutation of rationalism on a grand scale. To be sure, instead of combating such representatives of the day as Huxley, Tyndall, and Lyell, "or anything necessarily of this day," the book was on a "far more abstract level." But then, almost as if to contradict himself, he added that the book "combats views of friends of my own rather than any popular orthodoxies.[14] As will be seen, those views were quite rationalistic and very much the product of the day.

That in writing the *Grammar* Newman had some friends of his in view was an almost open secret in the circle of his confidants. Few of them knew, however, the long story of the making of the *Grammar*. In that letter to Jemima, already quoted,

[9] To Aubrey de Vere, Aug. 31, 1870, *Letters and Diaries*, vol. 25, p. 199.

[10] Ibid., pp. 24, 35, 43, 46.

[11] Ibid., pp. 38 and 39.

[12] Ibid.

[13] To Jemima, Feb. 21, 1870, ibid., p. 36.

[14] To Canon Walker, Jan. 25, 1870, ibid., p. 14, and also to Bishop Ullathorne, Jan. 28, 1870, ibid., p. 19.

Newman speaks of a most laborious tunneling process,[15] and elsewhere he describes it as a *work* that, unlike many of his other writings, was a toil for him.[16] He expected its reading as well to be a toil.[17] To a correspondent who read it twice, he wrote: "To have read it once is a real kindness; I take it as a personal one— but it is more than kind to have read it twice." Then he indulged in another superfluously modest self-deprecation: "Of course I can't tell the worth of it myself."[18] Yet Newman never for a moment doubted the importance of the *Grammar*. He kept telling his correspondents that time will prove the full worth of so laborious a work.[19]

A labor it was and a labor of a love that excels by patient endurance. Newman spoke to Jemima about the half-dozen versions dating back to 1846, 1850, 1853, 1854, and 1865.[20] Even from 1866 on he rewrote parts of the *Grammar* several times. He spoke of those years as a particularly taxing period in his life. But his resolve to resume the ever heavier task of writing had more to it than the urge to accomplish: "All I know is that I was unhappy till I had done it. I felt it a sort of duty on my conscience."[21] Rarely was conscience invoked in a fuller sense. For, as will be seen, Newman rested the objective truth about assent more on the objectivity he ascribed to the voice of conscience than to the objective truth of the external world. Such an esteem of the voice of conscience called for a heroic measure, both in sensing the magnitude of responsibility and in the resolve to live up to it. Once more the burden assumed proved the truth of his often-quoted words: "I have never sinned against the light."[22]

---

[15] Ibid., p. 35.

[16] Ibid., pp. 10 and 12.

[17] Ibid., p. 65.

[18] To Sir Frederic Rogers, June 30, 1870, ibid., p. 155.

[19] Ibid., pp. 160 and 279.

[20] Ibid., p. 35. Newman gives elsewhere (p. 155) the years "1846, 1847, 1850, 1853, etc."

[21] Ibid., p. 155.

[22] In the context of his first reminiscences of his almost fatal sickness in Sicily. See *Letters and Correspondence of John Henry Newman during his Life and in the English Church*, ed. A. Mozley (London: Longmans, Green and Co., 1890), vol. 1, pp. 365-66.

Indeed he never refrained from taxing himself if he could save a soul. The one who kept saying in later years that he was neither a philosopher nor a theologian was wont to identify himself as a mere "controversialist."[23] Such was a touch of saintly modesty on the part of the shepherd of souls he was. In the entire "General Staff" of the Oxford Movement, he alone engaged in down-to-earth pastoral work. Newman senior, a banker, was shocked on learning that his son, an Oriel don, regularly visited the often illiterate working-class families of Littlemore. In doing so, Newman pursued the same goal which he did in writing, publishing, and disseminating the Tracts. They were to alert souls to their being called to holiness as the sole reason for the existence of the Church. It was most logical that the *Grammar* should come to a close with an encomium on holiness. Newman presented holiness as the chief characteristic of the assent given by the first Christian martyrs to the truth, natural as well as supernatural, of the existence of God the Creator and especially as the Moral Lawgiver.

Working with simple souls, Newman, great logician that he was, could not help noticing the difference between their vast ignorance of the proofs of the Christian faith and their firm, unshaken attachment or assent to it. They were never absent from his mind as he struggled in writing the *Grammar*, which in fact is aimed at defending the mass of the faithful against the accusation of fideism. In making this appraisal of the *Grammar*, Fr. Charles Stephen Dessain could have quoted not a few passages from it. Fortunately for those far away from the manuscript treasures of the Birmingham Oratory, he quoted from a draft of the *Grammar* dated January 5, 1860: "Mrs L comes and says, 'I want to be a Catholic.' Her catechist is frightened, for he can find no motivum. . . , a factory girl comes and can only say, 'So and so brought me,' etc. . . a boy comes and says he wishes to get his sins forgiven."[24] Yet, for all his concern for these simple folks, Newman did not expect them to read the *Grammar*. Its readers were to be above all some of his friends who, the more

---

[23] *Letters and Diaries*, vol. 25, p. 100.

[24] Quoted from a draft (Jan. 5, 1860) of the *Grammar* by C. S. Dessain, *John Henry Newman* (new ed.: Oxford University Press, 1980), pp. 152-53.

they had learned about the proofs of the Christian faith, the more they refused to give their assent to them.

One of those friends was William Froude, (1803-1879), a prominent civil engineer who saw his wife and later his four children, one after the other, become Catholic. For Froude this was a protracted trial which he bore with great tactfulness. Although everybody expected him to become a Catholic and countless prayers were said for his conversion, he stuck by his argument that the complete assent implied in the Catholic faith presupposed absolutely certain proofs that no theologian could provide.[25] But no philosopher, however rationalistic, could provide such a proof either. This point, which Newman made all too clear in the *Grammar,* was not to make a dent on Froude's thinking.

Newman was very much privy to the spiritual drama enveloping the Froudes. For over twenty years he hoped to work out an argument to his own satisfaction that would help the conversion of Froude and others trapped in the fallacy of that rationalist argument. The counter argument was to show that absolute assent is given on countless occasions in daily life as well as in general intellectual and moral domains though absolute proofs are not on hand. Dispensing with "absolute" proofs would but invite a shift toward tactful persuasion. Thus Newman did not send a copy to William Froude, but rather to his son Edward. "Thank Eddy," he wrote to Froude, "for his letter, for me—and tell him I mean to send him my book—I don't send it to you, lest I should seem controversial."[26]

Still another point, very important for understanding the *Grammar,* is that it may appear a systematic abdication of scholarship. Today the very first thing expected from a scholar is to serve evidence that he has indeed read everything available on the subject. Newman was resolved not to read anything that others had written on a number of subjects pertaining to the

---

[25] See P. Flanagan, *Newman, Faith and the Believer* (London: Sands, 1946), pp. 92-95. Froude's argument was called "equationism" by F. R. Ward in his review of the *Grammar,* in *The Dublin Review* (17 [April 1871], p. 255), of which he was the editor.

[26] To W. Froude, Jan. 31, 1870, *Letters and Diaries,* vol. 25, p. 22.

Grammar although, to quote his words, "there has been much written in this day." Newman gave two reasons for this rather unusual policy. One was that he would have been drawn too much into controversies with others to the detriment of clarity. The other was outspokenly personal and personalistic: "my own work would vanish."[27] In the words of the *Grammar*, it was his most personal book in which he wanted to offer arguments that moved him personally. A consequence of this, again pointed out by him, was that far from being systematic, the *Grammar* contained seemingly unnecessary digressions.[28] He could not therefore mean systematic philosophical strength when he listed the *Grammar* as one of his five "constructive" books that do not have controversy for their chief aim.[29]

A book with many digressions, necessary or not, is bound to appear obscure. This is one of the reasons why the *Grammar* has remained Newman's least read and hardly ever digested major work. Half a century after its publication, Father Henry Tristram of the Birmingham Oratory, an authority on Newman's thought, felt the need to write an article to facilitate the reading of the *Grammar*. He recalled that some had spoken of it as "one of the most obscure books ever written" and that some "distinguished philosophers" had openly avowed that "they could make nothing of it." Fr Tristram admitted that the book was obscure "by its outward appearance" and because "of the eagerness with which its critics fasten upon irrelevant side issues when discussing it."[30]

In trying to dissipate the apparent or real obscurity of the *Grammar*, Fr Tristram urges one to concentrate on the enormous

[27] Ibid., p. 36.

[28] *Grammar*, p. 172.

[29] *Letters and Diaries*, vol. 25, p. 11. He refers to them as 2 Protestant and 3 Catholic. In another letter (*ibid.*, p. 35) he begins describing them with the *Grammar* as "the hardest, though all have been hard—my Prophetical Office [*Via Media*], which has come to pieces—my essay on Justification, which stands up pretty well—and three Catholic—Development of doctrine— University Education, and the last which I have called an Essay in aid of a Grammar of Assent."

[30] F. J. Bacchus, "How to Read the *Grammar of Assent*," *The Month* I (1924), p. 106.

degree of its originality for which, as he rightly puts it, most of its readers were unprepared. This unpreparedness should seem even greater in these times of ours when more than ever science is viewed as the exclusive source of rational certainty. A much broader and deeper view of certainty was, according to Fr Tristram, the *Grammar*'s chief contention as well as originality. Warnings, such as the one by the editor of *The Month*, one of the earliest reviewers of the *Grammar*, that Chapter Seven on certitude holds the book together,[31] may, because of that unpreparedness, remain ineffective in allaying the perplexity caused by the *Grammar*.

Another and very different source of the perplexity about the *Grammar* is a series of barbs in it aimed at metaphysics, barbs that undoubtedly gave some pleasure to Newman himself. Otherwise Charles Meynell, professor of theology at Oscott College, near Birmingham, who helped in reading the proofs of the *Grammar*, would not have thought of congratulating Newman for having defied the scholastic system of argumentation:

> Since you look at man in the concrete, it is not so much for you to reconcile yourself with metaphysics as for the latter to reconcile itself with you. If metaphysics doesn't account for the concrete man, I say so much the worse for metaphysics! As for the writer who says that *the book* does not follow the scholastic system, I say What is the scholastic *system?* I never heard of it. The ultra-realism of the writer who considers the *ideas* as separate *entities* was not held by *all* the scholastics, nor is it held by the modern Catholic metaphysicians. And Liberatore and the Sacred congregation suspect it.[32]

All this can only whet one's curiosity about Newman's handling in the *Grammar* of basic philosophical or epistemological questions, especially that of the universals, the chief target of Meynell's remarks. Newman did not handle the universals with gloves in hand or with much consistency, except that whenever he felt himself being carried to the edge of the precipice of unorthodoxy, he consistently and resolutely pulled back. If he had the strength to do so, that strength had much less to do with

[31] *The Month*, 1 (1870), p. 360.
[32] May 24, 1870, *Letters and Diaries*, vol. 25, p. 39.

philosophy, or with logic for that matter, than with his quest for holiness, a quest anchored in his enormous sensitivity and faithfulness to the voice of conscience, a principal point in the *Grammar*. But this is to anticipate. Thus the very same Newman who repeatedly and emphatically stated that assent was an intellectual act, that the illative sense (a term which he did not invent but certainly made popular) was an intellectual operation, and that certitude was supremely intellectual,[33] also pleaded a personal dislike, in fact a plain incompetence, for his not giving philosophical answers to essentially philosophical and fundamentally epistemological questions. Thus at the very start of Chapter 9 on the illative sense, in a sense the philosophical finale of the *Grammar*, Newman invokes a sort of philosophical agnosticism as he tries to defend the very objective of the *Grammar*:

> My object in the foregoing pages has been, not to form a theory which may account for those phenomena of the intellect of which they treat, viz. those which characterize inference and assent, but to ascertain what is the matter of fact as regards them, that is, when it is that assent is given to propositions which are inferred, and under what circumstances.[34]

In the hands of most present-day phenomenologists this passage might serve as their endorsement by that very high authority which Newman has become. The phenomenologists in question are, of course, those who forget that the methodical avoidance of ontological and metaphysical questions does not prove the non-existence of those questions. But those forgetful of the inevitability of metaphysics may derive ample support from Newman's apparent agnosticism as he hints at the impossibility or unfeasability of epistemology (the genesis of reasoning that gives a hold on the real insofar as it is intelligible) on the ground that even the "acutest minds"[35] could not convince their opponents. Did Newman remember, as he wrote this, that he repeatedly argued in the *Grammar* against those who took widespread

[33] *Grammar*, p. 86.
[34] Ibid., p. 270.
[35] Ibid.

disagreement for proof that it was impossible to reach the truth, and with certainty?

In the same context Newman, who certainly opposed those philosophers who admitted only probabilities but no certainties, refused to accept the aid of philosophers who held high the trustworthiness of intellectual certainty about physical and spiritual realities. He was not impressed by their efforts whereby "in order to vindicate the certainty of our knowledge," they take recourse "to the hypothesis of intuitions, intellectual forms, and the like, which belong to us by nature, and may be considered to elevate our experience into something more than it is in itself." As he distanced himself firmly and almost contemptuously from even the good philosophers, Newman made an appeal, most unphilosophical on a first look, to public opinion: "In proof of certainty, it is enough to appeal to the common voice of man-kind."[36] An ironical appeal it was, and easily turned into a boomerang, a point which Newman could hardly be unaware of.

The *Grammar* is a storehouse of evidences not only of Newman's keeping some very good philosophers out of sight, but also of his strange choice of philosophical heroes. Not once does he quote Aquinas. His sympathy for Aristotle is restricted to the author of *Nicomachean Ethics*, who makes much of the personal characteristics of each intellect, according to its aim and profession.[37] On none of the three different occasions when he speaks of Francis Bacon, "our own English philosopher," does Newman note the chinks, very fateful ones, in the intellectual armor of Lord Verulam. He praises Bacon for having inculcated the maxim that "in our inquiries into the laws of the universe, we must sternly destroy all idols of the intellect,"[38] but fails to note that Bacon's empiricism could not lead to a single law and much less to the assurance that there is a universe ruled by laws.[39] As he

[36] Ibid.

[37] Of the eight references in the *Grammar* to Aristotle, four deal with the shortcomings of syllogisms and four with the *Nicomachean Ethics*. It is among the latter that one finds Newman endorsing Aristotle as "my master" (p. 335).

[38] Ibid., p. 275.

[39] On some fatal defects in Bacon's philosophy with respect to natural science, see chap. IV, "Empirical Scouting," in my Gifford Lectures, *The Road of Science and the Ways to God* (Chicago: University of Chicago Press, 1978).

recalls Bacon's separation of mechanical from teleological causes,[40] Newman does not so much as hint about the disastrous consequences of that separation for natural theology which for Newman very much includes a purposeful Providence, that, philosophically at least, is non-existent for Bacon.

One wonders whether Locke was ever put on a higher and more undeserved pedestal than the one provided by Newman. Clearly, if Newman had "so high respect both for the character and the ability of Locke, for his manly simplicity of mind and his outspoken candor," and if there was "so much in Locke's remarks upon reasoning and proof with which he [Newman] wholly concurred," then disagreement with Locke on any point could but be painful for Newman. Newman, the great logician, did not seem to perceive anything of the chain that made one particular point (very fateful in Newman's eyes) a logical consequence of Locke's basic presuppositions. Newman merely deplored Locke's "slovenly thinking" for not seeing a contradiction between two claims of his: One was that it was not only illogical but also "immoral to carry our *assent* above the *evidence* that a proposition is true" or to have a "surplusage of *assurance beyond* the degree of evidence." The other was that some first principles, though only most probable, were to be allowed "to govern our thoughts as absolutely as the most evident demonstration."[41]

Yet, Newman did not probe into either of two most pertinent aspects of the inconsistency which Locke espoused. One aspect related to the very root of that inconsistency, the other to its morale. There was more to that inconsistency than, as Newman put it, Locke's *animus*, or resolve to form men or human thinking "as he thinks they ought to be formed, instead of interrogating human nature as it is."[42] To give a glimpse, however brief, of the root of that inconsistency, would have been

---

[40] Actually, Newman speaks of Bacon's separation "of the physical system of the world from the theological" (*Grammar*, p. 282), which is a signal misunderstanding on Newman's part of Bacon's rejection of the "teleological."

[41] See *Grammar*, pp. 137-39. The quote is from Locke's *Essay on Development of Doctrine*, chap. VII. Later (p. 251) Newman remarks that Locke "does not tell us what these propositions are."

[42] *Grammar*, p. 139.

rather easy since Locke himself plainly stated, and prominent admirers like Voltaire loudly repeated, that he wanted to chart the human mind in the light of Newton's physics.[43]

Newman's failure to probe this point was all the more surprising because both in the *Grammar* and, many years beforehand, in a still not sufficiently appreciated writing of his, Newman spoke prophetically of the limitations of the quantitative method.[44] There he decried the fashionable infatuation with that method as a cultural curse and as the chief mental obstacle to the recognition of spiritual and ethical realities. But he would not on that score inculpate Locke in the *Grammar*, although Locke was most instrumental in spreading Newtonianism as the only sound form of philosophy.[45] There the quantitative method ruled supreme, with the consequence that complete certainty in any formal assent was legitimate only if a mathematical proof was on hand. The very opposite was Newman's chief contention in the *Grammar*, that on that basis human life would be both impracticable and unthinkable. Would it not have been most logical to exploit Locke's inconsistency as striking evidence of the traps opened up by mechanistic philosophy taken for reasoning? In fact it would have been most philosophical but this was the very posture Newman was not too eager to take in the *Grammar*.

Newman's disagreement on a particular point with Bishop Butler, his third favorite British philosopher, is equally revealing though in a positive sense. In speaking about the range of illative sense, a particular aspect of prudent judgment, Newman considers among various objections to its validity in matters

[43] For details on both Locke and Voltaire, see chap. 6, "The Role of Physics in Psychology," in my *The Absolute beneath the Relative and Other Essays* (Lanham, Md.: University Press of America and Intercollegiate Studies Institute, 1988).

[44] The importance that Newman attached to that writing, "The Tamworth Reading Room," a long critique addressed to the editor of *The Times* apropos a speech by Sir Robert Peel at the dedication of a public library in Tamworth in early 1841, can be seen from Newman's quoting from it at length in the *Grammar* (pp. 88-92).

[45] A fact all the more ironical as Locke had to gain assurance from Huygens that the *Principia* contained not only good mathematics but also reliable physics.

religious the rationalist Thomas Paine's claim that if there is a divine revelation, it should be as clear "as if it were written in the sun." The claim, Newman noted, appeals to common sense through an assumption which Butler would not admit because it is unphilosophical. The assumption is part of that probabilism with respect to the real which follows from Locke's seeking in philosophy full certainty in terms of quantitative or Newtonian exactness. While Newman here parts ways with Butler, he does not see that above all he is parting with Locke as he turns the tables on Paine and does so by endorsing "philosophical cogency." The Visible Church, Newman says, "was at least to her children the light of the world, as conspicuous as the sun in the heavens." Newman was willing to admit at most that "owing to the miserable deeds of the fifteenth and sixteenth centuries" some clouds may have come over the sun, yet he would not allow that "the Church fails in this manifestation of the truth any more than in former times." While the countenance of the Church, Newman continues, "may have lost something in her appeal to the imagination, she has gained in philosophical cogency."[46]

Rarely in the history of philosophy did a great mind speak so emphatically of "philosophical cogency" and speak with so little conceptual cogency about its very foundation. The foundation, here as in many other cases, is the question of universals. The answer to that question controls whatever generalization is offered about the real as universal truth. This point is forcefully brought home in our times by the reluctant awakening of Darwinists to the fact that all talk about species, genera, classes, phyla and kingdoms is talk about universals before it becomes scientific talk. Another modern aspect of the fateful presence of universals relates to the impossibility of talking rationally about such ethical problems as abortion and euthanasia without coming to terms with the reality of human nature as a universal. Much less can certitude be claimed about universal truth (Newman's chief task in the *Grammar*) without setting forth the truth about the universals.

[46] *Grammar*, p. 295.

To be sure, Newman holds high universal truth throughout the *Grammar*, and especially in that pivotal chapter on certitude: "Truth cannot change; what is once truth is always truth."[47] In the section on complex assent leading to the chapter on certitude, Newman defines certitude as "the perception of a truth with the perception that it is a truth."[48] Newman is defending the universality of truth when he distinguishes it from the "conclusiveness of a proposition."[49] Even when he extols probability as the practical guide in life and reasoning, he takes pains to point out that "probability does presuppose the existence of truths which are certain."[50] He has no patience with the claim that "truth need not be universal."[51]

Yet the "universals" without which there can be no consistent discourse about universal truths fare badly in the *Grammar*. Newman does not refer to the word itself as he states that comparing and classifying things are among the "most prominent of our intellectual faculties." There he also states that those functions act "instinctively" and "spontaneously" even before we set about apprehending "that man is like man, yet unlike; and unlike a horse, a tree, a mountain, or a monument, yet in some, though not the same respects, like each of them." Without having studied Thomas' doctrines on universals and the analogy of being, Newman almost articulates them. Yet, almost in the same breath he undercuts his insights. By being reduced to the class *man*, he states, the individual man, is "made the logarithm of his true self, and in that shape is worked with the ease and satisfaction of logarithms."[52]

[47] Ibid., p. 181.
[48] Ibid., p. 162.
[49] Ibid., p. 158.
[50] Ibid., p. 192.
[51] Ibid., p. 196.
[52] Ibid., pp. 44-45. Whereas some of the first Catholic reviewers, Fr. Harper, S.J., in particular, expressed deep concern about Newman's cavalier treatment of the universals, little trace of such concern is found in the studies of the *Grammar* written recently by Catholics who cannot be suspected of anti-Thomist preferences. That Newman was inconsistent on the problem is set forth in some detail by Dr. Zeno, the Dutch Capuchin Newmanist, in his *John Henry Newman: Our way to Certitude: An Introduction to Newman's Psychological Discovery: The Illative Sense and His Grammar of Assent* (Leiden: E. J. Brill,

The remark is a descriptive marvel and a philosophical near-disaster. Well in advance of their times, logical positivists received in that remark a devastating portrayal but at the same time Neothomists too were dealt a great injustice. In the latter respect the only saving grace was Newman's admission about his remark's being a "harsh metaphor." For when Newman explicitly speaks of universals, he comes very close to denying any real content in them. "There is no such a thing as a stereotyped humanity," he declares.[53] He has little use for general man, which he calls the *auto-anthropos*. For him universals are wholly subservient to individual things: "Let units come first and (so-called) universals second; let universals minister to units, not units be sacrificed to universals." A middle road could not seem important to the one who had just declared: "What we aim at is truth in the concrete."[54]

Newman was so much taken up with the concrete, tangible facts, as to create time and again the momentary impression of being a latter-day follower of Ockham, if not a replica of Mister Gradgrind teaching but facts and nothing but facts. "Experience," Newman declares, "tells us only of individual things."[55] He ties belief "to things concrete."[56] His stated preference is "to go by facts" not by abstract reasoning.[57] The weak point of logic is, according to him, that "it does not give us to know even one individual being."[58] Newman's world is a "world of facts, and we use them; for there is nothing else to use."[59] On a cursory look it

---

1957), pp. 63-75. The problem, which Dr. Zeno calls "Newman's inconsistency," is passed over by E. J. Sillem in his long study preceding his edition of *John H. Newman: The Philosophical Notebooks* (New York: Humanities Press, 1969) and is not discussed by I. T. Ker in his long introduction to his meticulous critical edition of the *Grammar* (Oxford: Clarendon Press, 1985).

[53] *Grammar*, p. 224.

[54] Ibid., p. 223.

[55] Ibid., p. 44.

[56] Ibid., p. 87.

[57] Ibid., p. 136.

[58] Ibid., p. 226.

[59] Ibid., p. 272. Such and similar emphases put by Newman on objective truth found no echo in N. Lash's introduction, which disgraces the edition of the *Grammar* by the University of Notre Dame Press (1979). Lash sees in Newman's thinking an anticipation of T. S. Kuhn's evaluation of all

is a world of empiricism that beckons, not surprisingly, also in the *Apologia* which Newman wrote by putting aside momentarily the writing of the *Grammar*. The latter comes to a close with an apotheosis of the Roman Catholic religion as not so much a religion of notions as a religion of facts, and for this reason the only true religion. In the *Grammar* Newman turned this insistence on facts as pregnant with universal truths into a coherent philosophical proposition much less convincingly than he did in the *Apologia,* a difference very revealing indeed.

Resolute insistence on facts may have immediate advantages. Thus in dealing with Gibbon's famous "five causes" of wholesale conversions to Christianity in late Imperial Rome, Newman certainly scores with his question: "Would it not have been worth while for him [Gibbon] to have let conjecture alone, and to have looked for facts instead?"[60] Yet, how would Newman have countered the objection that the imbalance between his praise of facts (individual things) and his overt suspicion about universals makes him a mere conceptualist? Did he realize that conceptualism failed to prevent Protestant thought from being fragmented and caught in subjectivism? Was it fragmentation and subjectivism that he tried to overcome by reading Catholicism into the Thirty-nine Articles? Did he not recognize that the *Via Media* was a mere system on paper precisely because it was ultimately an exercise in conceptualism? Would he not have protested from all his heart the claim that in espousing Roman Catholicism he had not embraced a universally valid reality?

As the author of the *Grammar*, Newman would have been entitled to offer two answers. Although philosophically neither could be satisfactory, both could be forceful to the point of dissipating any doubt about his orthodoxy, philosophical and

---

intellectual processes as a series of paradigm shifts without noting the latter's irrationalist character. The latter point was made in my Gifford Lectures, *The Road of Science and the Ways to God* (Chicago: University of Chicago Press, 1978; 3rd paperback edition, 1986), and subsequently by the professedly nonreligionist D. Stone, of the University of Sydney, in his *Popper and after: Four Modern Irrationalists* (Oxford: Pergamon Press, 1982), where Kuhn is described as a greater threat to rationality than Popper, Lakatos, and Feyerabend!

[60] *Grammar*, p. 358.

theological, and could cut short any future attempt (by modernists, neo-modernists, and phenomenologists) to misconstrue his
true position. In a way of answer he could have referred to some
forceful statements in the *Grammar* about objective truth, though,
if I may say so, they amount in each case to a sort of rescue
operations. Time and again, when he seems to commit himself to
mere empirical facts, he reasserts, and in a matter of fact way, the
validity of objective truths transcending those facts. The most
telling of such cases occur when he insists on the personal
conditions that decide whether a proposition is assented to or
not. But he immediately balances his act by asking, as if to
prevent any misreading of his train of thought: "Shall we say that
there is no such thing as truth and error?"[61]

All those personal features, color as they might one's assent
to a proposition, are subordinated to the truth of the proposition:
"Assent is the acceptance of truth and truth is the proper object
of the intellect."[62] Newman had no use for the principle of
universal doubt, perceiving as he did its contradictory character.
He held, and did so most reflectively, that the starting point in
reasoning was a plain surrender to the obvious, an assent "to the
truth of things, and to the mind's certitude of that truth."
Ultimately there was no other criterion for recognizing the truth
of the real than that sense which was primarily a good or
common sense rather than scientific. Behind that position of his
there lay a most considered stance: "I own I do not see any way
to go further than this."[63]

A particular aspect of that sense was that illative sense which
Newman defined as a judgment of prudence in which he saw a
pre-eminently personal characteristic. Whenever he noted that
the illative sense opened the door to subjectivism, he right away
shut that door: "Duties change, but truths never."[64] The
recognition that "the rule of conduct for one man is not always
the rule for another" did not prevent him from stating in the
same breath: "The rule is always one and the same in the abstract

---

[61] Ibid., p. 247.
[62] Ibid., p. 145.
[63] Ibid., p. 271.
[64] Ibid., p. 278.

and in its principle and scope."[65] Again, the fact that "men differ so widely from each other in religion and moral perceptions" does not prove, he warns, "that there is no objective truth."[66]

Newman's other answer could have consisted in referring to more than one place in the *Grammar* where the human mind is celebrated as made for truth, objective truth, that is. Of course, he knew that the human mind was not infallible. But if its errors were not to land one in wholesale doubt about reasoning, one had to have the highest esteem for the mind's structure as pivoted on truth: "It is absurd to break up the whole structure of our knowledge, which is the glory of the human intellect, because the intellect is not infallible in its conclusions."[67] This passage is from the section, "Indefectibility of certitude," where he anchors that indefectibility not in some intangible subjective disposition but in objective truth insofar as the human mind has an intrinsic affinity for it:

> Now truth cannot change; what is once truth is always truth; and the human mind is made for truth, and so rests in truth, as it cannot rest in falsehood... It is of great importance then to show...that the intellect, which is made for truth, can attain truth, and, having attained it, can keep it, can recognize it, and preserve the recognition.[68]

Newman must have been thinking of this passage when, after Leo XIII's *Aeterni Patris* redirected Catholic philosophers to the doctrine of Aquinas, he was asked about an eventual Thomistic scrutiny of his ideas: "I have no suspicion, and do not anticipate [any suspicion] that I shall be found in substance to disagree with St Thomas."[69]

---

[65] Ibid., p. 279.

[66] Ibid., p. 293.

[67] Ibid., p. 187.

[68] Ibid., p. 181.

[69] In a letter of Dec. 10, 1878, to Fr. R. Whitty, S. J., in *Letters and Diaries*, vol. 28, p. 421. Fr. Whitty's reply of Jan. 19, 1879 (ibid.), to a subsequent letter of Newman's is expressive of Newman's philosophical orthodoxy and also prophetic in view of the great popularity of transcendental Thomism among Fr. Whitty's latter-day confrères: "My own impression I confess was just what you mention—that the Pope having himself been brought up in the Society's teaching—knowing that some of our Professors in Italy and France

Newman certainly opposed doctrines irreconcilable with basic Thomistic positions. Newman's flat declaration, "by means of sense we gain knowledge directly,"[70] shows that his thinking is poles apart from Kantianism and even from that Aquikant- ianism which is transcendental Thomism. The Kantian principle whereby the mind's categories create reality is contradicted by Newman's statement: "We reason in order to enlarge our knowledge of matters, which do not depend on us for being what they are."[71] His most devastating anti-Kantian declaration is in a note which he took from one of his early Catholic sermons and attached to the *Grammar* ten years after its first publication. In that sermon Newman urges that assent to natural and to supernatural truths or realities (which may appear as sheer mysteries to rigid logicians) is based, we would say today, on the same epistemological considerations. Without ever having read Kant's *Critique* in its entirety, Newman hits its very core by his emphatic declaration: "When once the mind is broken in, as it must be, to the belief of Power above it, when once it under- stands that it is not itself the measure of all things in heaven and earth, it will have little difficulty in going forward."[72] Newman rejects the mind as the measure of things not only because he has moral sensitivity about fallen human nature, but also because of his readiness to assent to natural reality and truth as given independently of man.

Since Newman did not have Kant in mind why did he make statements so forcefully anti-Kantian? The answer is simple. In philosophy in general, and epistemology in particular, the basic options are few. Actually, there are only two fundamental

were leaving St. Thomas in certain points of *Philosophy*, and feeling that these were important points against the errors of the day—had expressed a wish that our teaching should return to the old lines."

[70] *Grammar*, p. 210.

[71] Ibid., p. 222.

[72] Ibid., p. 385. Newman considered this so characteristic of his thinking that he gave in italics part of the remainder of the quote, which is from his sermon "Mysteries of Nature and Grace," where he argued the epistemologically most pivotal point, that "belief in God and belief in His Church stand on the same kind of foundation." See *Discourses Addressed to Mixed Congregations* (London: Longmans, Green and Co., 1902), p. 260.

alternatives. In one the starting point is the objective thing, in the other the subjective ego. By casting his lot with the former, Newman inevitably had to censure the latter. This is why one finds in the *Grammar* gem-like phrases that cast a devastating light on such latter-day intellectual preoccupations as artificial intelligence, the subconscious, logicism, and the information explosion.

When Newman denounces the claim that "whatever can be thought can be adequately expressed in words,"[73] a basic assumption of artificial intelligence is denounced in advance. The same is true when Newman asserts that the acts of man's intellectual growth are "mental acts, not the formulas and contrivances of language,"[74] or when he notes that we arrive at our most important conclusions not by "a scientific necessity independent of ourselves, but by the action of our own minds, by our own individual perception of the truth in question, under a sense of duty to those conclusions and with an intellectual consciousness."[75] In fact, Newman sees intellectual activity in such a non-mechanical perspective (of which the "sense of duty to conclusions" operative in any assent is a graphic reminder) as to endorse what in our times has come to be spoken of as "tacit knowledge." He does so as he notes that in performing acts of the illative sense, the mind often perceives the connection of data with first principles "without the use of words, by a process which cannot be analyzed."[76] But this absence of explicit analysis did not mean a general falling back on the subconscious. On assent that comes subconsciously, Newman states, "I have not insisted, as it has not come in my way; nor is it more than an accident of acts of assent, though an ordinary accident."[77]

As great a logician as Newman was, he did not miss an opportunity to put logic in its place. If logical positivists had an advance antagonist, it was Newman. Close as was the connection between assent and logical conclusions, it was not closer than

[73] *Grammar*, p. 212.
[74] Ibid., p. 275.
[75] Ibid., p. 252.
[76] Ibid., p. 282.
[77] Ibid., p. 157.

the one "between the variation of the mercury and our sensation; but the mercury is not the cause of life and health, nor is verbal argumentation the principle of inward belief. If we feel hot or chilly, no one will convince us to the contrary by insisting that the glass is at 60. It is the mind that reasons and assents, not a diagram on paper." Then he points out the rank inconsistency of a "class of writers" who act upon as many a truth as do their unsophisticated neighbors, but pretend "to weigh out and measure" truths and warn them that "since the full etiquette of logical requirements has not been satisfied, we must believe those truths at our own peril."[78] It is not certain whether he meant by that "class" the followers of J. S. Mill or of Whately, but his strictures certainly apply to the claims and behavior of logical positivists.

Present-day academics, fond of dissecting and wary of assenting, are aptly described in Newman's reference to the claim of some in the Academies of ancient Greece who claimed that "happiness lay not in finding the truth, but in seeking it." Their abdication of finding the truth was as much an evasion of the duty to assent to truth, as is the claim, fashionable among modern academics that all intellectual pursuit is a mere game. Newman grants that in matters that do not "concern us very much, clever arguments and rival ones have the attraction of a game of chance or skill, whether or not they lead to any definite conclusion."[79] But in matters of grave human concerns, the claim, Newman argued, was as hollow as the alleged happiness of Sisyphus.

Taking all intellectual pursuit for a mere game, as an excuse for dispensing with assent, had in part to do, according to Newman, with what is called today the information explosion: "The whole world is brought to our doors every morning, and our judgment is required upon social concerns, books, persons, parties, creeds, national acts, political principles and measures. We have to form our opinion, make our profession, take sides on a hundred matters on which we have but little right to speak at

---

[78] Ibid., p. 151.
[79] Ibid., p. 171.

all."[80] Such is his prophetic anticipation of our educational and public situation, in which any and all are continually invited to offer their opinionated judgments as if they were so many assents. The result is the general feeling that assent can be readily reversed, the very point which Newman held to be impossible.

The very fact that Newman was writing the *Grammar* when he took out ten feverish weeks to write the *Apologia* may in itself suggest that the *Grammar*, too, was autobiographical in the sense of being very personal. The *Grammar* contains Newman's most personalist philosophical statements. He spoke of a sentiment that came over him habitually "about egotism as true modesty" when he turned to discussing inference and assent in the matter of religion, natural and supernatural: "In religious inquiry each of us can speak only for himself, and for himself he has a right to speak." Of course, here too, he immediately went to the rescue of objective truth. The individual "knows what has satisfied and satisfies himself; if it satisfies him, it is likely to satisfy others; if, as he believes and is sure, it is true, it will approve itself to others also, for there is but one truth."[81]

Precious and all-important as are Newman's almost instinctive moves to safeguard objectivity and the universal validity of truth, those moves are never systematic. The *Grammar* is as far beyond a mere treatise as concrete life is far beyond a book. Books come and go and their arguments will forever be controverted. Such a perennial pattern would least surprise the one who once spoke about the "wild living intellect of man."[82] The phrase is from the concluding part of the *Apologia*, which certainly has this in common with the theme of the *Grammar*, namely that religion is not about notions but about facts. No fact did ever command Newman's assent more than that of Original Sin, which he called "the giant evil."[83] A chief evidence of it was, in Newman's eyes, the cacophony of the human scene. To reconcile it with the evidence of God ("*if* there be a God, *since*

---

[80] Ibid., p. 191.

[81] Ibid., p. 300.

[82] *Apologia pro Vita Sua* (Image Book; Garden City, N.Y.: Doubleday, 1956), p. 322.

[83] Ibid., p. 326.

there is a God"), one had no choice but to assent that "the human race is implicated in some terrible aboriginal calamity. It is out of joint with the purposes of its Creator. This is a fact, a fact as true as the fact of its existence; and thus the doctrine of what is theologically called original sin becomes to me almost as certain as that the world exists, and as the existence of God."[84]

In the *Grammar* the last argument on behalf of the supernatural origin of the Christian religion is that "it has with it that gift of stanching and healing the one deep wound of human nature, which avails more for its success than a full encyclopedia of scientific knowledge and a whole library of controversy, and therefore it must last while human nature lasts. It is a living truth that never grows old."[85] Newman would find exceedingly illogical the present-day emphasis on the Church's healing power which under-emphasizes to a shocking degree the existence of that deep wound. This is certainly true about the intellectual part of that wound, the result of man's desire to become, through knowing, like God. In trying to rise above everything, man becomes bewildered by the variety of things, all of which clamor for his assent but to none of which fallen man is able to give it with certitude.

Certitude, in this fallen state, was therefore for Newman more than a question of epistemology. It was a question of healing grace which could not operate except in an ambience that constantly reverberated with the call: "your whole nature must be re-born, your passions, and your affections, and your aims, and your conscience, and your will, must all be bathed in a new element, and reconsecrated to your Maker, and, the last not the least, your intellect."[86] The call was the call of the Church that alone, among all churches, resembled the Church of the Apostles and of the Fathers. This is why Newman became a Catholic. Once a Catholic and a priest, he observed other priests closely and found two things about them: One was their unaffected, outspoken manners; the other was their certitude about all the mysteries of the Creed, a certitude that was never a burden for them.

[84] Ibid., p. 320.
[85] *Grammar*, p. 376.
[86] *Apologia*, p. 325.

Sharp-sighted an intellect as he was, Newman would even today spot the large number of priests, perhaps not in this or that particular country, but on a global scale, who still exude certitude and feel none the less healthy for it. He would also easily note the obvious, which is the certitude carried all over the world by the occupant of that chair which he apotheosized in one of his greatest sermons, entitled "Cathedra sempiterna."[87]

He would spot that obvious certitude partly because his perception was eminently visual. Although an excellent violinist, he celebrated the sense of sight throughout the *Grammar*. Its thirty or so analyses of particular cases of assent are so many

[87] He did so as Rector of the Catholic University of Ireland. The address is reprinted here as an Appendix for two reasons. One is the rarity of his posthumously published *My Campaign in Ireland. Part I. Catholic University Reports and Other Papers* (printed for private circulation only, by A. King & Co., Printers to the University, Aberdeen, 1896) in which it first appeared (pp. 211-14). The other reason relates to the striking anticipation in it of the substance and tone of his sermon, "The Pope and the Revolution" (*Sermons Preached on Various Occasions* [3rd ed.; London: Burns & Oates, 1870], pp. 263-98), preached on the feast of the Rosary, Oct. 7, 1866. This sermon, although easily available, has been systematically overlooked by "liberals," which is, of course, understandable as it casts in proper light a Newman, who at that time was just beginning his theologically mistaken foot-dragging about the advisability of the definition of papal infallibility (see on this my paper "Newman's Logic and the Logic of the Papacy," *Faith and Reason* 13 [1987], pp. 241-65, reproduced here as chapter 7). Far from being a quasi-rationalist sowing the seeds of disloyalty in the guise of specious distinctions, he was, as the sermon shows, consumed with a burning loyalty for the person sitting in the chair of Peter. It is doubtful that any Ultramontane has ever stated as touchingly as Newman did in that sermon that we Catholics have the duty "to look at his [the Pope's] formal deeds, and to follow him whither he goes, and never to desert him, however we may be tried, but to defend him at all hazards, and against all comers, as a son would a father, and as a wife a husband, knowing that his cause is the cause of God" (p. 269). The sermon also gives a priceless glimpse of the depth of Newman's Marian devotion, and in particular of his love for the Rosary. About the latter Father Neville, the Oratorian who was most closely associated with Newman during his last years, recalled "his ready reply to a condolence on his loss of the power to say it [the Breviary] being, that the Rosary more than made up for it; that the Rosary was to him the most beautiful of all devotions and that it contained all in itself. . . . From far back, in the long distance of time, memory brings him forward, when not engaged in writing or reading, as most frequently having the Rosary in his hand." Quoted in W. Ward, *The Life of John Henry Cardinal Newman* (London: Longmans, Green and Co., 1912), vol. 2, p. 533.

true-to-life graphic portrayals of psychological processes. Above all he paints his own mental portrait, and therein lies the lasting instructiveness of the *Grammar*. The picture shows him as a great mind, even in the ordinary sense. One of the first reviews of the *Grammar*, the one in the *Spectator*, a prominent and widely read British weekly, came to a close with an homage to that greatness: "The work of a really great man may fairly be allowed, for some at least, to speak for itself, before smaller men begin to praise or censure."[88]

Most of those who praised the *Grammar*, let alone those who censured it, failed to see Newman's greatness and the reason why the *Grammar* was to remain a great book. For the culture, national and ecclesiastic, into which Newman was born, which educated him, and which he hoped to restore to its ideal vigor, was vigorous only in producing opinions that could not encourage assent. Most of those who labored with Newman in the Oxford movement were unable to assent to the truth of that fatal symptom. Thus by the time Newman set forth in twelve public lectures, delivered in London in 1850, his penetrating diagnosis of the National Church,[89] it was clear that his hopes for a mass conversion among the intelligentsia were unrealistic. Men of unquestionably vigorous intellect and of more than average goodwill refused to follow him and his few dedicated associates on the path to Rome. They bemoaned Newman's conversion as

[88] *The Spectator*, Apr. 2, 1870, p. 439.

[89] Those twelve lectures constitute volume I of *Certain Difficulties Felt by Anglicans in Catholic Teaching* (London: Longmans, Green and Co., 1891). They were republished, with my Introduction (reproduced here as chapter 6) by Real View Books (Fraser, MI: 1994). If Newman felt any dislike in writing those lectures it was (as I argued in that Introduction) merely because he did not wish to waste any more time on the Church of England and not because, as is often alleged, he did not fully agree with the devastating portrayal there of the Church of England as a mere by-product of political and nationalistic, that is, essentially naturalist aspirations. Newman would be pained but not surprised by the compromise that the Lambeth Conference of Aug. 1988 adopted on polygamy. He would merely note the preservation of type, which he held high in the *Development*, evidenced in the courage of John Paul II, who fearlessly denounced polygamy a month later in the presence of an African head of state with four official wives, in addition to some unofficial ones.

the error of an overzealous conscience, without pondering the nature of their own zeal.

Others not so close to him, such as the undergraduates who had listened in awe to his University sermons in which several themes of the *Grammar* had been anticipated, conveniently forgot his message in the measure in which they became part of the Establishment. That the lay as well as clerical factors of that Establishment kept undermining genuine Christianity, however unwittingly at times, had become crystal clear to Newman by the time he finished the *Development*. But he, the *Apologia* is the witness, had to go through many shadows and free himself of many illusory images, such as the Via Media, before he could see the light. His chief accomplishment was that he could state with no touch of boasting that on that arduous quest for light he had never sinned against the Light, or the voice of God speaking through man's conscience. The epitaph—*ex umbris et imaginibus in veritatem*—he wrote for himself, could just as well be a reminder of his spiritual odyssey. Little of this was seen by the established order, which, steeped as it was in Locke's "common sense," had eyes only for opinions, however opinionated, but not for real assent even in worldly matters. Much less had it eyes for that assent which is to be given to the most challenging aspect of human existence, the voice of conscience speaking continually of matters otherworldly and eternal.

Newman's sensitivity to that voice was so great as to put him on the path to sainthood from his late teens on. On that path all signposts—actual and historical, personal and social—were reminders of a God who, if He is truly God, has to reveal above all His Holiness to sinful man. Hence Newman's search for that Church in which the standards of revealed holiness have always been held high, whatever the failures of those whose duty it is to proclaim those standards. If he said that the Fathers made him a Catholic, it was only because he had eyes for the holiness of the Fathers.[90]

---

[90] In Newman's reply to Pusey's *Eirenicon* in *Anglican Difficulties*, vol. 2, p. 24.

Newman's relentless quest for personal holiness is the explanation for the fact that in articulating his epistemology or grammar of assent he keeps going back to the reality of the voice of conscience. He would have been trapped in subjectivism had he centered on the voice itself and not on the objective moral content of that voice. No wonder that he always finds his way to the external objective world and even to that witness of the physical world which is the cosmological argument.[91] Though not particularly fond of it, he would have been the last to deny its validity. Yet for all his readiness to go to the objective external reality and to endorse, at least in principle, all that is implied in its knowledge, he failed to the end to see clearly the epistemological nature of that road.

Yet how close he could be to seeing the obvious! A passage in his *Philosophical Notebooks* has it in a nutshell. There he argues that the sense of consciousness is not immediate but "external" to his sensing it. From his hypothetical opponent, who sees in his insistence on consciousness a straight road into utter skepticism or solipsism, Newman asks but one concession: "You must allow *something*—and all I ask you to allow is *this*—that it is true that *I am*—or that my consciousness that I am represents the fact external to my consciousness (viz) of my existence. Now see what is involved in this one assumption. Viz My consciousness . . ."[92] Taken up so much with his consciousness, Newman could not see that he was mistaken in using the word "external" in this context. He was entitled to no more than to use the word "different." Most importantly, he did not see the obvious. The very fact of arguing with an opponent provided him with the external world as an indispensable condition for arguing at all; it

[91] See *Grammar*, p. 68.

[92] Entry dated Feb. 9, 1860, in *John Henry Newman: The Philosophical Notebooks*, vol. 2, p. 78. Tellingly, the context is Newman's reflections on his reading of the *Historical Development of Speculative Philosophy from Kant to Hegel*, by H. M. Chalybäus, professor of philosophy at the University of Kiel (trans. A. Edersheim; Edinburgh: T. T. Clark, 1854). Half of the pages of Newman's copy of Meiklejohn's translation of Kant's *Critique* were left uncut! See ibid., vol. 1, p. 229. The reason behind this was that, as Newman put it, "I do not think I am bound to read them [the German idealists] in spite of what Chalybäus says, for notoriously they have come to no conclusion." Ibid.

was an act securing him the external objective world and with it the only safe basis for working out one's philosopy.

This is not to suggest that Newman necessarily would have found that philosophy had he been born a Catholic. But philosophical clarity, which has never been a permanently widespread commodity even within the Church, may seem simply nonexistent in non-Catholic Christian ambiences. No less extraordinary should therefore seem the fact that he kept adhering to that clarity even though little enlightenment could come to him from inside that Church which was still to be reawakened to the teaching of Thomas Aquinas. A chief instructiveness of the *Grammar* may therefore lie in the disproportionality between Newman's philosophical resources and his philosophical achievement. This point has already been made elsewhere in far more graphic terms, which Newman, so keen on graphic portrayals, would have no doubt greatly cherished: He is described as "the genius who, following the gleam, cut his way through the undergrowth of a jungle where the weaker Pusey, with perhaps equal piety and goodwill, remained lost *in umbris*." His intellectual Odyssey, which is inseparable from his spiritual quest to find the proper place and object for a final and supreme assent, remains indeed "one of the most palpitating dramas in the history of the human soul. It tugs at the heart-strings like that of Augustine, and is surely not less beautiful because there is nowhere in the early background any trace of those aberrations which are so frankly revealed in the *Confession*."[93]

What remains to be done is to sketch briefly the bearing of all this for the intellectual aspects of our own ecclesiastical times. Seeing it with Newman's eyes, the first thing to be noted is the status of the Church of England. Today he would be immensely saddened, though not surprised, to see that Church go not so much the way of all flesh, but go all the way of the flesh. He

---

[93] J. Gannon, S.J., "Newman and Metaphysics," *The Irish Ecclesiastical Record* 69 (1947), p. 386. This article, possibly the best on the *Grammar* and on the various problems raised by Newman's philosophy, came to my knowledge only after this paper's conclusion has been reached. There is no reference to it in the works of Flanagan and Sillem, or in the editions of the *Grammar* quoted above.

would see in the utterances of the latest Lambeth conference on homosexuality and polygamy an illustration of a principal contention of the *Grammar*. Breaking with an assent is a proof that the assent has never been truly present. He would point out that it was for the same reason that the same Church could not see that its own male ordinations lost the last shred of credibility when the ordination of females was not seen above all as a question of validity.[94] Newman could certainly see the intimate connection between dissent from truth relating to sacramental ontology and dissent from truth relating to morals or holiness.

After that, Newman would direct his gaze to the Catholic Church. He would again be saddened, though not surprised, to see the assent to truth all too often replaced by disputes about inferences in order to justify dissent. As the author of the *Grammar*, he would engage in passionate controversy with many priests, theologians, nuns, and lay people. He would show them that they have destroyed the faith of much of an entire generation of Catholics. He would show them that by withholding their assent to the teaching of the Church, they have incapacitated themselves for the task of eliciting from their youthful charges that assent which is the backbone of faith. He would show them that their game with assent is the result of their unwillingness to give assent to the fact that there is sin in the strict spiritual sense, the very fact which, as he insisted in the *Grammar*, is the basis of natural as well as of revealed religion.

On one point he would cross swords again with the world at large, as he did when the moral integrity of the Catholic clergy was called in doubt. Just as he did not mind losing his case in the secularist court of his day, so he would not mind losing again today in the kangaroo courts of the media. He would be satisfied to make it clear that Catholics cannot obtain justice in the supreme courts of publicity. The darlings of those courts are those Catholic clergymen and religious (if they still have religion) who use his personalistic philosophy of assent as their noblest excuse for refusing their assent to legitimate Church authority.

[94] A position of the Archbishop of Canterbury himself. See *The Times*, Aug. 2, 1988, p. 28, col. 8.

He would challenge them to appear with him before the Court of Conscience which he rightly held high as the ultimate and supreme forum, provided it was not a mere fancy, whim, and social fashion. There he would ask them whether it was not he who wrote in connection with the See of Peter that, even when it speaks outside its special province and errs, "it still has in all cases a claim to our obedience."[95]

That Newman has become a battleground and possibly the great intellectual battleground within the Church shows more than anything else his greatness. Just as in Arian times, when both orthodox and unorthodox parties tried to secure the vote of Antony, *the* saint of the day, so today both parties try to claim Newman to themselves. It seems that the unorthodox Catholic and the non-Catholic parties have better perceived the monumentality of his vote. Newman was still to become a Cardinal when Gladstone, a chief Anglican opponent of his in the disputes about infallibility, admitted the monumentality of Newman's assent to it. "In my opinion," Gladstone wrote in 1876, "his secession from the Church of England has never yet been estimated among us at anything like the full measure of its calamitous importance. It has been said that the world does not know its greatest men; neither, I will add, is it aware of the power and weight carried by the words and by the acts of those among its greatest men it does know."[96]

---

[95] *An Essay on the Development of Christian Doctrine* (Image Book; Garden City, N. Y.: Doubleday, 1960), p. 104. Newman is quoted six times in defense of dissent from *Humanae vitae* in *Dissent in and for the Church: Theologians and Humanae vitae* by C. E. Curran *et al.*, (New York: Sheed & Ward, 1969). Of the four letters to the editor published in the Sunday, Sept. 14, 1986, issue of *The New York Times* in connection with the Vatican's declaration that Fr. Curran was no longer a Catholic theologian, two were in support of the Vatican. The writers of the two other letters buttressed their support of Fr. Curran with references to Newman! A detailed study of the exploitation of Newman by advocates of dissent would well pay the effort.

[96] Quoted from G. B. Smith, *The Life of the Right Honorable William Ewart Gladstone* (New York: G. P. Putnam, 1880), p. 499. Gladstone's words seem to have made no impression on Prof. Owen Chadwick's interpretation of Newman, in his eyes a chief among Roman Catholic modernists and, therefore, an Anglican *malgré lui*.

Today, on the eve of the centenary of Newman's death, his fellow Roman Catholics still have a long way to go toward realizing the magnitude of the gain they may derive from Newman's assent to reality, natural and supernatural. The closer they are to that realization, the better prepared they will be to play a constructive role in the great contestation between the Prince of lies and the Angel of truth. Newman's account about that contestation, or about the coming of the Antichrist, were prophetic because he, like any true prophet, gave his full assent to his God-given role to explain and implement assent to Truth.

10

Meditation on the
Grammar of Assent

Of Newman's three most widely read books two, the *Development* and the *Apologia*, were written in feverish haste. The third, the *Grammar of Assent*, took Newman three decades to write. This fact alone should caution one against expecting from the *Grammar* the same kind of intellectual drama which makes the reading of the two other works such a satisfying experience. The *Grammar* is often a very dry and in places perplexingly difficult book. It is indeed that book of Newman's which contains a set of phrases, a particular method, and a specific perspective that are still used today to support strategies of dissent, although Newman wanted rather to vindicate assent, taken in the strictest sense.

Of the many instances of this abuse of Newman's thought in general and of the message of the *Grammar* in particular, one is particularly eye-opening. It shows the shocking extent to which some think that Newman's thought can readily be referred to as justification for dissent in matters of faith and morals. In connection with the Vatican's declaration that Fr. Curran was no longer a Catholic theologian, the Sunday, September 14, 1986, issue of *The New York Times* carried on the subject four letters to the editor. Of the four two were in favor of the Vatican. One of these would have deserved to be photocopied and sent to every chancery, rectory, department of theology, teacher of Christian Doctrine, and promoter of renewal of any sort. For it contained a biblical phrase, possibly the most relevant biblical phrase for these times of ours when it has become "fashionable" to think that assent or dissent are mere matters for opinion polls. The phrase is from Exodus (23:2), where Moses warns: "Neither shall you allege the example of the many as an excuse for doing wrong." In the other two letters Fr. Curran's advocacy of dissent was supported with references to John Henry Newman.

There are indeed not a few phrases in the *Grammar* that appear to be graphic endorsements of sheer empiricism, which is the very opposite to the requirement for what St. Paul called in Romans (12:1) a reasoned worship of God. Then there is the *Grammar*'s method that looks very similar to what later took by storm the philosophical and theological scene under the name *phenomenology*. It stands for a systematic aversion, to use a Pauline phrase again, to reasoned assurance about things that do not appear, that is, are not phenomena. Finally, there is the perspective of the *Grammar*, a perspective of unabashed personalism. Newman states in the *Grammar* that although many books had been written on the subject of assent, he made no special study of them during all that time when the *Grammar* was being written and rewritten, with intermissions of course. This means that for over thirty years or so he deliberately ignored the primary and secondary literature on the subject. His reason for this procedure, most unscholarly on the face of it, was that had he been studying that vast literature, he might inadvertently have said something which was not strictly his own idea. One wonders whether with its disdain for primary and secondary literature the *Grammar* would have been accepted today by any prominent university press on either side of the Atlantic.

The *Grammar* was meant to be an account of Newman's way, emphatically *his own way* of giving to the challenge of truth, natural and supernatural, the kind of firm and irrevocable reply which he called assent. This is not to suggest that he did not expect that many, indeed all, should find congenial *his* way which, looked at superficially, is an amalgam of empiricism, phenomenology and personalism. But a not-too-long look at Newman's way should be enough to note the problems posed by his expectation. His way was that of an extraordinarily sensitive moral conscience, a conscience befitting a saint and not an ordinary Christian, let alone a run-of-the-mill non-Christian. That moral conscience let Newman constantly hear God speak to him and, if one may say so, out of a moral obligation on God's part. Newman called it an antecedent probability of the highest degree that if there is a God He should speak to man clearly and in three ways: through the evidence of nature (Newman means the cosmological argument), through the voice of conscience, and through revelation.

About the first way, the evidence of nature, he is never enthusiastic, though never doubtful either. It appears but fleetingly in the *Grammar*.[1] At any rate, in his time the cosmological argument was the victim of a philosophically atrophied natural theology in which the argument from design held the center stage. Newman knew, however, that the philosophical world at large looked askance at that argument, and for that reason alone it could not serve as a starting point.[2] What he failed to point out or to articulate was that the design argument could be turned into a most effective sequel to the cosmological argument. The third way of God's speaking to man, that is, special historical revelation, was of course of overwhelming importance to Newman, but only for one reason. Revelation for him is, in addition to being a set of intellectual propositions, the full unfolding of a most holy God's call to holiness in truth.

About the time when the *Grammar* was published Newman stated to a correspondent that he had become a Catholic because in the Catholics of the mid-19th century he found the same ethos or striving for holiness which was the mark of the Church of the Fathers.[3] Herein lies the clue to his declaration to Pusey in 1864:

[1] *An Essay in Aid of a Grammar of Assent* (Image Books; Garden City, NY: Doubleday, 1955), p. 68

[2] See his letter to W. R. Brownlow, Apr. 13, 1870, in *Letters and Diaries*, (Oxford: Clarendon Press, 1961), vol. 25, p. 97, where he refers to the *Grammar* and states: "I have not insisted on the argument from *design*, because I am writing for the 19th century, by which, as represented by its philosophers, design is not admitted as proved."

[3] "For myself, what made me a Catholic was the fact, as it came home to me, that the present Catholics are in all essential respects the successors and representatives of the first Christians, such a remarkable identity in position and character in ages so widely separated and so strikingly dissimilar, being at the same time the note of a supernatural origin and life." *Letters and Diaries*, vol. 25, p. 147.

"The Fathers made me a Catholic."[4] Newman did not mean arguments from patristic texts about this or that dispute between Anglicans and Catholics. He meant a striking parallel between two attitudes: One was the Fathers' refusal to conform to the thinking of the ancient pagan world. Newman had a special dislike for that urbane bishop, Eusebius, in whose sympathy toward Arianism he noticed the fatal pull of excessive respect for the cultural standards set by the world at large. This is why Newman had eyes to notice in the heretics of Patristic times the tendency to backslide into that world. The other attitude was that of the entire post-Patristic church, stretching from Gregory VII and Innocent III through the Council of Trent, and especially through its chief implementer, Saint Pius V, to Pius VI and Pius VII and, last but not least, to Pio Nono. This attitude was the refusal of the Church led by those popes to cave in to the relentless demands of an ever more aggressive secular world.

Reference to Pio Nono is an anathema nowadays among all Catholic thinkers aspiring to be accepted in Catholic academic circles, to say nothing of non-Catholic, let alone secular circles. Pio Nono is also a figure with whom even non-modernist Catholic thinkers are not too eager to appear nowadays. Newman was very proud to be a most loyal son of that much maligned pope. One proof among many is the sermon he preached on the feast of the Holy Rosary, on October 7, 1866. No less important is the fact that he preached that sermon at the request of Bishop Ullathorne, who was to be Newman's chief support in his campaign against the infallibilists. In that campaign Newman made many misjudgments,[5] but never to the extent of compromising the integrity of his assent to the pope, whoever he may be. His opposition to the advisability of the definition of papal infallibility always contained emphatic statements of his belief that the popes are infallible and therefore deserve an unreserved assent on our part to what they teach and not, to use some recent

---

[4] "A Letter addressed to the Rev. E. B. Pusey on Occasion of His Eirenicon," in *Certain Difficulties Felt by Anglicans* (London: Longmans, Green and Co., 1891), vol. 2, p. 24.

[5] For details, see my article, "Newman's Logic and the Logic of the Papacy," in *Faith and Reason* 13 (1987), pp. 241-65, reprinted here as chapter 7.

phrases of subtle evasiveness, some "critical obedience"[6] or "a measure of conservatism."[7]

In view of the rising revolutionary movements in Italy, where the *risorgimento* went hand in hand with aggressively secularist ideologies, Bishop Ullathorne asked every parish priest and the rector of every church run by religious in the Birmingham diocese to set forth to the faithful "our obligations to the Holy See." True to his fondness for the concrete, Newman began with a graphic parallel between the Church of the Apostles and the Fathers and the Church of his times: "Therefore, as it [the Church] was *in* the world, but not *of* the world, in the Apostles' times, so it is now: —as it was 'in honour and dishonour, in evil report and good report' . . . in the Apostles' times, so it is now:—as then it taught the truth, so it does now; as then it had the sacraments of grace, so has it now; as then it had a hierarchy or holy government of Bishops, priests, and deacons, so has it now; and as it had a Head then, so must it have a head now."[8]

Then Newman went on to describe that actual head in a series of questions that stood for so many aspects of that head's supreme power in the Church. "Who is that visible Head now? who is now the Vicar of Christ? who has now the keys of the kingdom of heaven, as St. Peter had then? Who is it who binds and looses on earth, that our Lord may bind and loose in heaven? Who, I say, if a successor to St. Peter there must be, who is that successor in his sovereign authority over the Church?"

Then came Newman's reply, a reply that should make speechless any Concilium theologian making studied appeals to

---

[6] The title of a chapter in *A Short Primer for Use of Unsettled Laymen*, by Hans Urs von Balthasar (San Francisco: Ignatius Press, 1985), pp. 110-14. One wonders whether such a phrase is suited to strengthen loyalty to the pope, the declared purpose of that book's illustrious author, who does not provide the unsettled layman with a guideline as to where criticism should stop lest it become the judge even of papal infallibility and a justification for endless filibusters.

[7] A phrase of Fr. A. Dulles, from his interview, "Fordham's New Theologian: A Flair for Diplomacy," *The New York Times*, Oct. 2, 1988, p. 50.

[8] For this and subsequent quotations from that sermon, "The Pope and the Revolution," see *Sermons Preached on Various Occasions* (3rd ed.; London: Burns, Oates and Co., 1870), pp. 263-98, especially pp. 266-69.

Newman, or theologians who fancy themselves to be bridges or bridge-makers[9] in the dispute between those in authority and those who claim for themselves the right to dissent from that authority. One could only wish that those self-appointed bridge-makers, who only ten years ago were still fomenting open dissent, would have a memory long enough to recall, if not their own recent doctrinaire record, at least the Latin origin of bridge-maker, that is, pontifex. Indeed, if there is so much trouble in the Church today it is because so many in it are pontificating and giving only lip-service to the tireless teaching of the only Pontiff or head in the Church. No wonder that the bridges they offer to heaven bend back to the earth before long, and at times to some of its smelly marshes.

Newman's reply to the question as to who is the head of the Church in 1866 reads as follows: "It is he who sits in St. Peter's Chair: it is the Bishop of Rome. We all know *this*; it is part of our *faith*." Lucky pre-Vatican I times, one may say, when the foremost expert on tradition could assume all this on the part of anyone sitting in the pews. Lucky times when a preacher could continue without a trace of apprehension that anyone in those pews would give less than full assent to the following:

> The visible headship of the Church, which was with St. Peter while he lived, has been lodged ever since in his Chair, that continuous line of Bishops of Rome, or Popes, as they are called, one after another, as years have rolled on, one dying and another coming, down to this day, when we see Pius the Ninth sustaining the weight of the glorious Apostolate, and that for twenty years past,—a tremendous weight, a ministry involving momentous duties, innumerable anxieties, and immense responsibilities, as it ever has done.

Then, since Newman's chief aim was to portray the measure of loyalty due to the one in that Chair, he had to list his prerogatives: "He can judge and he can acquit; he can pardon, and he can condemn; he can command, and he can permit; he can forbid, and he can punish. He has supreme jurisdiction over the people of God. He can stop the ordinary course of sacramental

---

[9] Fr. Dulles in the interview quoted in note 7 above.

mercies; he can excommunicate from the ordinary grace of redemption; and he can remove again the ban which he has inflicted. It is the rule of Christ's providence, that what His Vicar does in severity or in mercy upon earth, He Himself confirms in heaven." Newman then could raise the question:

> What need I say more to measure our own duty to it and to him who sits in it, than to say that, in his administration of Christ's kingdom, in his religious acts, we must never oppose his will, or dispute his word, or criticize his policy, or shrink from his side?

Concerning that measure of assent, Newman articulated it first in respect to what was implied in being a pope:

> There are kings of the earth who have despotic authority, which their subjects obey indeed but disown in their hearts; but we must never murmur at that absolute rule which the Sovereign Pontiff has over us, because it is given to him by Christ, and, in obeying him, we are obeying our Lord. We must never suffer ourselves to doubt, that, in his government of the Church, he is guided by an intelligence more than human. His yoke is the yoke of Christ, *he* has the responsibility of his own acts, not we; and to his *Lord* must he render account, not to us.

The thrust of this statement is, to put it crudely, similar to that of the old Roman saying about what is allowed respectively *Jovi* and *bovi*. For saying this no apology is required to those Newmanists who have spread the idea that Newman advocated a qualified loyalty, a limited assent.[10] Pointing out ignorance or plain abuse of plain texts is a charitable service and so it should be received with gratitude by all earnest inquirers after truth.

---

[10] Thus, for instance, P. Misner in his *Papacy and Development: Newman and the Primacy of the Pope* (Leiden: E. J. Brill, 1976). Misner makes much of the fact that his work was written as a doctoral dissertation under the guidance of Fr. K. Rahner. For this reason, too, it should seem to be no accident that Rahner, despite his having taken a solemn vow of loyalty to the pope as a Jesuit, took it upon himself to draft an Open Letter in which John Paul II was called upon to respect the "democratic rights" of Jesuits following his appointment of Fr. Dezza as a temporary General of the Society. For details, see my *Keys of the Kingdom: A Tool's Witness to Truth* (Chicago, Il.: Franciscan Herald Press, 1986), p. 205.

Then Newman portrayed the qualities which the pope's subjects must display in their assent to his teaching:

> Even in secular matters it is ever safe to be on his side, dangerous to be on the side of his enemies. Our duty is,—not indeed to mix up Christ's Vicar with this or that party of men, because he in his high station is above all parties,—but to look at his formal deeds, and to follow him whither he goes, and never to desert him, however we may be tried, but to defend him at all hazards, and against all comers, as a son would a father and as a wife or husband, knowing that his cause is the cause of God.

Catholic feminists may take note, as well as advocates of liberation theology. The Newman of the foregoing words cannot, even by the utmost stretch of the imagination, be pictured as someone in their corner.

Newman was not yet through. He now conjured up future popes:

> And so, as regards his successors, if we live to see them; it is our duty to give *them* in like manner our dutiful allegiance and our unfeigned service, and to follow them also whither-soever they go, having that same confidence that each in his turn and in his own day will do God's work and will, which we felt in their predecessors, now taken away to their eternal reward.

Clearly, if there was anything alien to Newman's thinking it was the expectation that a new pope might or would come who would be just a president, or a constitutional monarch, or a mere presiding bishop, or one whose temperament would make him slip into the tragic role of a Hamlet. For the last one cannot maintain the necessary momentum to lead, whereas the others are not even entitled to denounce, as the present pope recently did, that dissent whose chief aim is to legitimize assent to one's whims and fancy. If the latter was heatedly described by Newman as the counterfeit of genuine conscience,[11] it was only because in any attack on conscience he rightly saw an attack on

---

[11] In his famous reply to Gladstone on papal infallibility, *A Letter Addressed to His Grace the Duke of Norfolk on Occasion of Mr. Gladstone's Recent Expostulation* (London: B. M. Pickering, 1875), pp. 63-66.

the very essence of all his thinking and aspirations including the principal aim of the *Grammar*.

The latter had two aspects.[12] One was to demolish the claim of the equationists, for whom complete assent could rationally be given only when complete proofs were on hand. They were aptly called equationists because the equality they had in mind was the kind which is on hand in demonstrations of mathematics and physics. Newman showed that even there everything rested ultimately on common-sense evidence which could not be cast into mathematical forms. When Newman lampooned the infatuation that made mathematical physics the ultimate source of truth, he produced some sparkling phrases that illuminate even the present-day myths about artificial intelligence and related vagaries of the educated mind. Once common sense was vindicated, it was possible for Newman to argue that ordinary uneducated Catholics, blessed with common sense, were not unreasonable in giving unconditional assent to the teaching of the Church.

Newman gave in the *Grammar* extraordinarily graphic descriptions of the actual mental steps involved in giving assent on the basis of common sense, but never probed into the philosophy of common sense. He stuck to his way through thick and thin, a way which was a graphic grasp of reality. He extolled the sense of sight over all the other senses, including that of hearing, although it is the channel of the greatest marvel, the spoken word. No wonder that he sounds time and again like a rabid empiricist. He has more scorn than praise for the universals. He does not once take into consideration that every human word stands for a universal. Time and again he seems to give comfort to those who, then as now, take the view that the question of universals can be disposed of by labeling it a scholastic problem. And since he is all too ready to unfold the force of logic in initial premises, he comes in the *Grammar* time

---

[12] For details and documentations on this and subsequent topics relating to the *Grammar*, see my essay, "Newman's Assent to Reality, Natural and Supernatural," in *Newman Today* (San Francisco: Ignatius Press, 1989), pp. 189- 220, reprinted here as Chapter 9.

and again to the edge of a philosophical abyss which has engulfed countless others before and after him.

What saves Newman in those instances, about a dozen or so in the *Grammar*? What makes him, almost contrary to any expectation, suddenly pull back with statements, never properly articulated, that imply philosophical and theological orthodoxy? The answer is not to be found in Newman's reading of Thomas Aquinas or other scholastics, a reading rather limited. In fact, months after the promulgation of *Aeterni Patris,* he asked Fr. Robert Whitty, a Jesuit in Rome and sympathetic to him, what the whole encyclical was about. Fr. Whitty wrote back that the Encyclical came because "the Pope [Leo XIII] having himself been brought up in the Society's teaching—knowing that some of our Professors in Italy and France were leaving St. Thomas in certain points of *Philosophy*, and feeling that these were important points against the errors of the day—had expressed a wish that our teaching should return to the old lines."[13]

The answer is much less to be found in Newman's reading of modern philosophers which, with the exception of J. S. Mill, was not extensive at all. He showed much too great a sympathy for Bacon, Locke, and Bishop Butler, for him the *par excellence* British philosophers. Perhaps the saving grace for Newman was that he left uncut half the pages of his copy of Meiklejohn's translation of Kant's *Critique of Pure Reason.* At any rate, he saw through Kant and the German idealists. His comment on the monograph written on them by Chalybäus, professor of philosophy at the University of Kiel, was as brief as it was devastating: "I do not think I am bound to read them . . . for notoriously they have come to no conclusion."[14] Transcendental Thomists, better called Aquikantists, may take note. If conclusions to which assent is to be given can ever be the fruit of mere philosophical reasoning, however genuine, they certainly cannot issue from the miscegenation which transcendental Thomists try to bring about between Aquinas and Kant. It is the old story of the horse and the ass.

---

[13] See *Letters and Diaries*, vol. 28, p. 421.

[14] *John Henry Newman: The Philosophical Notebooks*, ed. E. J. Sillem (New York: Humanities Press, 1968), vol. 1, p. 229.

Newman indeed had an unusual measure of common sense. The *Grammar* instances time and again his wealth of insight about what he called in the *Apologia* "the wild living intellect of man."[15] He called it wild not because he approved of its innumerable and continual excesses but because he, more than any Catholic intellectual, with perhaps the sole exception of Chesterton, was convinced that wildness was in more than one sense a deep wound in the intellectual nature of man. He wrote more penetratingly than anyone else in modern times about the awesome reality of original sin.[16] No wonder. His was a saintly intellect that never failed to resonate to God's voice speaking through the voice of conscience and through natural and supernatural revelation. This is why he instinctively pulled back from the edge of each philosophical precipice. Before him he saw more than a conceptual chasm. He saw it for what it was: a continual rebellion of man's mind against the light.

If read in this light, the *Grammar* will serve, as intended by Newman, as a powerful source of assurance about objective and perennially valid truths. If not read in this light, it can be presented as a forerunner of Kuhnian paradigms, a scientifically coated form of radical irrationalism. Newman would turn in his grave were he to be told that this manhandling of his *Grammar* has been perpetrated with the help of the printing press of a prominent Catholic University in the USA.[17] In any case, for any unprepared reader, the *Grammar* can readily function as a storehouse of phrases that extol individual experience over objectively valid truths. I would not be surprised to find quotations from the *Grammar* in works promoting situation ethics. In other words, only if one shares something of Newman's intense quest for holiness will the *Grammar* become not a trap but an

---

[15] *Apologia pro vita sua* (Image Books; Garden City, N.Y.: Doubleday, 1956), p. 322.

[16] Ibid., pp. 320-26.

[17] I refer to the edition of the *Grammar* by the University of Notre Dame Press (1979) with an introduction by Nicholas Lash, who sets up Newman as a forerunner of such irrationalists as Thomas S. Kuhn, the champion of cognition in terms of accidental paradigm-shifts.

inspirational guide on the road toward a salvation which is, besides everything else, thoroughly intellectual.

The only point yet to be covered should relate to Newman, in particular to his various private utterances between 1869 and 1878, the last ten years of Pio Nono. Among other things, Newman expressed his hope, in strict privacy though, that Pio Nono might not live too long.[18] Do not those utterances, and many others made in connection with the infallibility debate, contradict his sermon of October 7, 1866, on assent to the pope and many similar statements of loyalty? One certainly should avoid the temptation to charge him with insincerity. It was that charge that brought down on Kingsley the most devastating defense of sincerity, the *Apologia*, ever produced in any major language.

It should seem much safer to follow another avenue. It leads to the inevitable human limitations in any human being, however extraordinary his stature may be. Newman was not only aware of his limitations but put up no defense when confronted with them. The most telling and possibly the least discussed instance of this relates to his desperate expectation that the definition of infallibility would not be endorsed with moral unanimity. No voice of dissent was heard, however, as August and September followed that fateful July 1870. But as he urged several correspondents to wait with patience for such voices, one of them wrote to him that his [Newman's] hopes were not different at all from the position he had once advocated in the *Via Media*. In his reply Newman had the honesty to admit that he could not refute the objection. Perhaps for the only time in his life, he, who almost every day in his life put thousands of words on paper, felt completely at a loss for words.[19] Though unable to see the advisability of the definition of infallibility he, being a saint, could bow his intellect and trust sincerely that, like anything else,

[18] See, for instance, Newman's letter (Nov. 7, 1870) to C. R. Poole, whom Newman wishfully reminded of the "common belief" that Pio Nono "will not live till that day" (June 17, 1871) when Poole expected to meet his son at the Oratory School in Birmingham. See *Letters and Diaries*, vol. 25, p. 226.

[19] See his admission in his letter of Nov. 1, 1870, to Bishop Moriarty of Kerry, ibid., p. 223.

that definition, too, could become an instrument of good in God's hands.

In this he believed with the utmost sincerity. Indeed, in 1877 when he wrote the long preface to the third edition of the *Via Media*, which was its first Catholic edition, Pio Nono was still alive. Nobody expected a Leo XIII. Among those who prognosticated was Ernest Renan, who conjured up a conclave electing a pope even more reactionary than Pio Nono and a subsequent revolt by progressive cardinals electing an antipope.[20] Renan confidently expected the demise of the papacy by the turn of the century. Clearly, what could Newman gain by writing in that preface that the image of the Church as a mystical body set forth in the *Via Media* was not to be seen as a softening up, however slightly, of the *imperial* notion of the Church. Much less did that image suggest any tampering with the total assent due to the one who is the supreme Sovereign and Ruler in that Church. In fact he stated nothing less than that the supreme power in question was "the Papacy and its Curia."[21]

This is not to suggest that Newman wished to be a curialist. He was very candid in begging for the privilege to remain in England and in Birmingham in particular, a city which he had chosen for his Oratory because of the large number of destitute Catholics there. But he could also say, in greeting Leo XIII's pontificate, that he did not expect the new pope's liberality to be taken for an excuse to give to the pope's teaching and rulings less than full assent. For a pivotal point in the *Grammar* is that assent is always a full assent. He could therefore also say that he remained consistent even when he hoped that Pio Nono would not live long.

A short year after his conversion, Newman recalled to Henry Wilberforce, one of those who wanted "absolute proofs," a passage in his first volume of Sermons "about the inconsistencies of good men," and added: "I have ever made consistency the

---

[20] For details see my *And on This Rock: The Witness of One Land and Two Covenants* (3d enlarged ed.; Front Royal, VA: Christendom Press, 1997), pp. 107-08.

[21] *The Via Media and the Anglican Church* (new ed.; London: Longmans, Green and Co., 1896), vol. 1, p. xl.

mark of a saint." In the same letter[22] he drew a brief comparison between the Church of England and the Roman Catholic Church in the same perspective. He then listed as a chief of those personal graces of which he had been the beneficiary since his conversion: "the natural intercourse and conversation" he had enjoyed with Catholics and pointedly noted his having been "extremely struck with their rigid purity. Evidence of this," he continued, "has come before me in a way not to be mistaken." His next words, "how low the Anglican church is here," tempt one to speculate on what Newman would say today on seeing two Churches: One yielding on each and every issue of sexual morality, the other standing firm, though only because it shares in the unyielding character of its Rock-foundation, the Papacy.

Yielding to that temptation to speculate should involve the task of doing justice to that letter in which Newman begins with the question of assent to the Papacy. He begins by pinpointing the essence of his disagreement with Wilberforce:

> My dear Henry . . . You do not seem to have apprehended, or rather I to have expressed what I said about 'the Church'. What I mean is this:—If we can get a tolerable notion which is the Church, and know (as we do) that it may be trusted because it is the Church, then comes the question why should not the Pope's supremacy be one of the points on which it may be trusted? For myself I have had so great experience of the correctness of the Roman view where once I thought otherwise that I should be a beast if I were unwilling to take the rest on faith, from a confidence that what is still obscure to me (if there be anything such, I am not alluding to anything) is explainable. And it seems to me extravagant or unreasonable in you to demand proof of one certain particular tenet which it so naturally comes to the Church to decide.

Here is another proof that in the back of his mind Newman was writing the *Grammar* already in 1846.

Even if at that time Newman had been less than a saint, it would not have occurred to him that one day a Pope, still two removed from Gregory XVI, would decide to create him a cardinal. On hearing about his being made a cardinal, his first words were *haec mutatio dexterae excelsi.* God, of course, does not change, but to those who remain consistent in the good cause to an apparently bitter end, God often reveals His own consistency by granting them an end that only grows in glory as time goes on.

11

Science

There are remarks and acts of Newman that may cast doubts on the merit of studying his views on science. He had, for instance, but a slightly disguised contempt for the British Association for the Advancement of Science. "I have shunned its presence from the first," he wrote to the Free Kirk theologian David Brown, on April 4, 1874, in implicit reference to the Association's meeting in Oxford in June 1832. "Doubtless," Newman continued in the same letter, "theologians have before now meddled with science—and now scientific men are paying them off by meddling with theology."[1]

That Oxford meeting was the second corporate appearance of the still fledgling Association on the British scene, on which it was to make afterwards a considerable impact with its annual gatherings. During the meeting the University conferred honorary degrees on John Dalton, Robert Brown, and Michael Faraday. Newman distanced himself from a meeting that showed a remarkable awareness of discoveries that were destined to be of crucial significance for the future of physical science.

Early September 1865 was the second time that the British Association had its annual meeting in a place, Birmingham, which was also Newman's domicile. He left town after writing to his old friend, William Kirby Sullivan, professor of chemistry at the Catholic University of Dublin, who wanted to stay in the

---

[1] *Letters and Diaries*, vol. 27, p. 43. His Diary has the terse entry for Monday, June 16, 1832: "Confirmation. This week, the meeting of Scientific Association" (ibid., vol. 3, p. 58).

Oratory during the meeting, that he hoped to be in the South by early September.[2] Newman did not get farther from Birmingham than Rednor while the Association was in session. Thirty-two years earlier his lack of interest in the Association might have been explained by his being utterly absorbed in the writing of his book on the Arians. This time there could be no mistaking his wish to keep at a safe distance from the Association.

Of course, Newman had planned for other reasons to have holidays on the Isle of Wight, where he arrived after spending a few days in the vicinity of Oxford. A slight contempt for science could be read into a passage of the letter he sent from the Isle of Wight to Ambrose St John in mid-September 1865. Newman referred in the letter to Pusey's being busy writing a sermon on science and religion.[3] Newman almost sounded as if he considered Pusey's effort to be largely a waste of time.

This would not only be a hasty conclusion but also a very wrong one. In 1832 Newman already felt what soon became widely suspected among Tractarians, namely, that the British Association was to meddle with theology, that is to do on a quasi-institutional basis[4] what individual scientists had already been busy doing for some time. As to the latter point, a memorable reminder has been served, in our times, by C. C. Gillispie's well-known survey of the theologically loaded controversies among two major schools of early-19th-century British geologists, the Neptunists and the Vulcanists. His considered judgment was that it was the geologists who meddled with the business of theologians, and not the other way around.[5]

In 1832 the Association was still dominated by the clergy, such as the Reverend Professors Sedgwick and Whewell of Cambridge and Buckland of Oxford. The latter delivered a major speech in which fossil anatomy was taken for a storehouse of

[2] Ibid., vol. 22, p. 35

[3] Ibid., p. 52.

[4] Its principal manifestation came in a long review by Newman's closest friend, Bowden, of the Reports of the first six meetings of the Association in *The British Critic* (then edited by Newman), January 1839, pp. 1-48.

[5] C. C. Gillispie, *Genesis and Geology* (1951; Harper Torchbooks, 1959).

data on design evincing the Creator.[6] This was anything but meddling. According to the published records of that meeting, nobody touched there upon the millions of years, so much at variance with biblical chronology, demanded by the geological record. Clearly, the meeting of 1832 provided no justification for Newman's fears. Yet that almost contemptuous concern of his about meddling proved to be on the right track.

Not a few of the annual meetings of the Association were to hear Presidential Addresses, delivered by leading British men of science, that were so many meddlings with theology, if not something far worse. They were prominently reported by the Press that certainly hailed Tyndall's Belfast address of 1870 in which matter was endowed with miraculous properties. In the late 1920s there came a triple salvo of pseudo-theologizing. It opened in 1927 with Sir Arthur Keith's claim about the purely animal origin and nature of man, followed two years later by General Smuts' endowing all of nature with the mysterious quality of emergence, duly extended to God himself. In 1932 Sir James Jeans graciously allowed the Creator to function as an impersonal mathematician. In our own times Sir Peter Medawar accorded, from the Presidential chair of the Association, quasi-divine honors to scientific progress.[7]

Newman would have contradicted his very soul had he not paid close attention to such exploitations of science for pseudo-theological purposes, whether within or without the British Association. In a series of sermons preached in 1835 on the Anti-christ, Newman explicitly referred to the trap which undue preoccupation with progress might pose to Christians.[8] He was prophetic in both respects. As to the idea of progress, it was within less than two decades to receive its apotheosis in the opening of the Crystal Palace on May 3, 1851. A future antagonist

[6] A summary of Buckland's speech is given in *Report of the First and Second Meetings of the British Association for the Advancement of Science* (London: John Murray, 1833), pp. 104-07.

[7] His address "On 'The Effecting of All Things Possible'," was reprinted in his *The Hope of Progress* (London: Methuen, 1972), pp. 110-27.

[8] See *Discussions and Arguments on Various Subjects* (London: Longmans, Green and Co., 1897), pp. 59-60.

of Newman's, Charles Kingsley, took, with tears in his eyes, that celebration of progress for the onset of the millennium. In the same year Herbert Spencer declared that Progress, writ large, was inevitable and necessary in the moral sense because it was such in technological and scientific respects.[9]

As to science, any warning about it could appear to be hollow rhetoric if not based on the sort competence in science which Newman possessed in larger measure than usually realized. Exhaustion due to overwork in two major fields caused his failure to earn, as he planned, "a first class in mathematics [including astronomy and mechanics] and second class in classics."[10] It was a setback, suffered in late November 1820, that almost ruined his prospects in Oxford. Still his excellence in mathematics and geometry played an important part in his competing, to the consternation of many in Oxford, with outstanding success for fellowship in Oriel in April 1822. Several years later, although busy with theology and pastoral work, Newman was still buying advanced books on mathematics and geometry. The dozen or so textbooks on science he used as an undergraduate contain topics that are offered nowadays only in graduate courses.[11] His lecture notes on Buckland's mineralogy course were recently found by a historian of geology to be the best summary of Buckland's ideas on the subject.[12] There was, in addition, the penetrating logical analysis which Newman displayed from early on. His first published writing, a long letter

---

[9] For details, see ch. 1 "Progress for no Purpose," in my *The Purpose of It All* (Washington: Regnery-Gateway; Edinburgh: Scottish Academic Press, 1990).

[10] *Letters and Diaries*, vol. 1, p. 93.

[11] They are available in the Oratory Library in Birmingham. They include two works by S. Vince, Plumian Professor of Astronomy and Experimental Philosophy, *A Treatise on Fluxions* (1818) and *The Elements of Astronomy* (4th ed. 1816). The latter includes such topics as a "New Method of Computing the Effect of Parallax, in accelerating or retarding the Time of the Beginning or End of a Transit of Venus or Mercury over the Sun's Disc" (pp. 238ff) in the form, of course, of differential geometry, a method more difficult to handle than ordinary calculus.

[12] Personal communication by Mr Gerald Tracey, Librarian and Archivist at the Oratory.

of May 1821 to the editor of *Christian Observer*, deals with the similarity of reasoning used in the sciences and in theology.[13]

All this is not to suggest that Newman included partiality for science among the factors that were responsible in the Church of England for the measure of worldliness that prompted Keble to preach his famous Assize sermon on National Apostasy in 1833. The Tracts that assured national attention to the Oxford Movement were almost invariably on theological and Church matters, and aimed above all at restoring the priority of the sacred over the secular. Anybody in sympathy with that aim looked to Newman to step in the breach when that priority seemed to be gravely compromised by one on whom the Tractarians counted heavily in their national polity.

He was none other than Sir Robert Peel, the leader of the Tories whose higher ranks for the most part still had High-Church sympathies around 1840. On a cursory reading nothing could be less objectionable than the speech with which Peel laid, on January 19, 1841, the cornerstone of a Public Library in Tamworth, his constituency. In the speech, first reported in *The Times* and quickly issued as a pamphlet,[14] the Prime Minister began by stressing the role of the Ministers of the Established Church in promoting moral conditions, partly through the spread of useful information. The nature of this role was not, however, to be their real role insofar as they were supposed to stand for religious truth. Books on theological controversies were not to be put in the Library. Its books had to promote knowledge useful for material benefits. Sir Robert dwelt at length on recent improvements in agriculture, drainage, and transportation. To the townsfolk of Tamworth, mostly agricultural laborers and mechanics, he held high the fame which men of science of low birth—among them he referred to Professor Farraday (sic)—had earned through their assiduous probings into the secrets of nature.

---

[13] Reprinted in *Letters and Diaries*, vol. 1, pp. 102-04.

[14] I would like to thank the Rev. Fr. Paul Chavasse, of Birmingham Oratory, for a photocopy of the pamphlet in the Oratory Library, *An Inaugural Address* . . . (London: James Bain, 1841), 31pp.

But since pursuit of fame could not be too far from seeking vainglory, Sir Robert felt the need to defend the aim of inexpensive public self-education. Acquisition of knowledge could not be contrary, he said, to the purposes of Providence, which "gave us faculties to distinguish us from the Beasts that perish and will demand from us a severe account of the manner in which we have employed them."[15] To further allay ecclesiastical apprehensions, Sir Robert quoted at length a recent sermon of the Bishop of London about the excellence of natural theology as derived from the study of the sciences. Sir Robert found in that sermon a proof on behalf of two points: The sagacity one acquires from scientific studies will cause one to lend the most unwilling ear to presumptions and objections against the Christian dispensation. Further, the same sagacity will greatly dispose one to recognize readily the perfect harmony of Christianity with all that one can conclude from reason, unaided by revelation, in regard to the constitution and course of nature, and the moral government of a Creator and Ruler of the world.[16]

Sir Robert's speech did not reveal any awareness of age-old and much agitated questions about the relation of the natural and the supernatural on the cognitive, let alone on the moral level. These were precisely the problems to which the Tracts time and again had made their readers sensitive. The Tracts certainly proved to be effective in that sense in the case of John Murray, editor of *The Times,* which had recently adopted a distinctly High-Church position. He quickly dispatched his son, an ardent Tractarian, to Oxford with an invitation to Newman to contribute a series of Letters on Sir Robert Peel's address. Newman was only too glad to comply with seven Letters that appeared between February 5 and February 27. They were signed "Catholicus," a pseudonym that kept Newman's identity a closely guarded secret for months.[17]

[15] Ibid., p. 24.

[16] Ibid., p. 30.

[17] As shown by Nina Fay Burgis, "An Edition of Newman's Tamworth Reading room, with Introduction and Textual and Expository Apparatus. Dissertation. University of London, 1964." The dissertation's chief concern is an analysis of Newman's method of rhetoric. It also contains valuable details

Not that Newman had to hide in February 1841 when he stood at the height of his influence as the leader of the Tractarians. He himself felt that he had clinched the cause with the argument set forth in Tract 90, that the Thirty-nine Articles allowed a Catholic interpretation. But on March 16 came the condemnation of that Tract by the Bishop of Oxford. Newman also got in trouble because of his series of Letters on Sir Robert Peel's speech, which was soon defended in a pamphlet signed "Protestant" and later that year by Sir Robert himself in Parliament. By then Newman's seven Letters had also appeared as a separate booklet of 42 pages, still under the pseudonym "Catholicus."[18] Whereas Tract 90 did not prove to be a prophecy of future developments as Newman had hoped, his series of Letters, published as "The Tamworth Reading Room" in booklet form, expressed his fears of a universal apostasy that would come, perhaps not in his lifetime but certainly within a century or so, and largely through an unjustified exploitation of science on behalf of agnosticism, scepticism, and materialism.

The apostasy was not to take the form of a drastic break, but of a gradual slipping from belief in the supernatural to rank naturalism, a process promoted whenever science was taken for the sole and ultimate source of truth and principles. The penetratingly prophetic character of Newman's "Tamworth Reading Room" lies precisely in his putting his finger on the most dangerous and most overlooked confrontation of science and religion. Were the two kept within their own competence, there would be little room for confrontation, a point which Newman was to develop in detail in one of his lectures to the Catholic University of Dublin, of which more later. But he unerringly

on the Public Library Movement of the 1820s and 1830s as spearheaded by Brougham, but is rather short on questions of science.

[18] The title page of the pamphlet of 42 pages is headed by the line, "The Tamworth Reading Room," followed by "Letters on an Address delivered by Sir Robert Peel, Bart. M.P. on the Establishment of a Reading Room at Tamworth. By Catholicus. Originally published in *The Times,* and since revised and corrected by the Author" (London: John Mortimer, 1841). Its text is readily available in *Discussions and Arguments,* pp. 254-305. Subsequent quotations from the text there can easily be identified by looking up the respective Letters referred to.

sensed that the confrontation was to be between a science turned
into a pseudo-religion and a revealed religion degraded to a mere
natural science that as such had no right to speak of the
supernatural known only by Revelation.

This is why in the "Tamworth Reading Room" Newman
viewed science, or rather the ideological misuse of science, as a
preamble of disbelief. This theme he developed in its positive
aspects in the first and last of the Letters. There he answered the
question of what is secular, that is, mostly scientific education.
He did so with an eye on Lord (Henry Peter) Brougham's by
then almost two-decade long crusade on behalf of what came to
be spoken of, a century later, as scientism. Newman rightly saw
that Peel's ambivalent position on the relation between the
natural and the supernatural represented that unstable equilib-
rium that was bound to gravitate to the strictly deistic, if not
covertly naturalist position which Brougham had been advocat-
ing with much success.

Since 1825 Brougham had traveled up and down the country
to establish public libraries and mechanics' institutes. He became
the founder, in 1832, of the *Penny Magazine* and launched a year
later the *Penny Encyclopedia*. His *Discourse of the Objects,
Advantages, and Pleasures of Science*, a densely printed pamphlet
of 48 pages,[19] was the first of cheap propaganda works on behalf
of the contention that proficiency in practical (scientific) knowledge leads to the practice of moral virtues. Although Brougham
admitted that "by direct interposition, through miraculous
agency, we become acquainted with his [God's] will, and are
made more certain of his existence," he made the flat claim (not
spelled out directly by Peel) that God's "peculiar attributes are
nearly the same in the volume of Nature and in that of his
Revealed word."[20]

---

[19] London: Baldwin, Craddock, and Joy, 1827. Again I would like to thank
Fr. Chavasse for a photocopy of the examplar in the Oratory Library. Far
more accessible is the text in Vol. VII (pp. 291-370) of Brougham's *Works*
(Edinburgh: Adam and Charles Black, 1872), which contains Brougham's
writings on natural theology.

[20]   Ibid., p. 135.

Perhaps because of the notoriety of Brougham's views Newman did not quote this crucial passage from Brougham's pamphlet. For the very same reason he did not have to document his claim that according to Brougham scientific education purifies, motivates, provides intellectual adventure, imparts wisdom, provides the highest level of learning, banishes ignorance, and frees one from mental slavery in the broadest sense. Christian theologians, Newman kept suggesting between the lines, had always ascribed such effects to supernatural religion.

Newman's portrayal of scientific education as a dangerous substitute for religious education becomes most explicit in the seventh Letter. There he gathers the features of that pseudo- or ersatz apologetics from Sir Robert's encomium of scientific education. In that pseudo-apologetics, which should have an eery timeliness for those familiar with recent writings about the scientific priesthood, the question of *whence* or ultimate causation is replaced by the *why* of mechanistic connections; the question *for what purpose* is replaced by the question of the *how*. With no small psychological finesse Newman also notes that misguided Christian advocates of this new theology based on the physical sciences, like Sir Robert, merely read their own Christian mind into a subject which is essentially indifferent to religious matters. A further instance of psychological finesse is Newman's remark in the same Letter that "as the soldier is tempted to dissipation, and the merchant to acquisitiveness . . . , yet there are good . . . merchants and soldiers, notwithstanding; so there are religious experimentalists [physicists], though physicists, taken by themselves, tend to infidelity; but to have recourse to physics to *make* men religious is like recommending a canonry as a cure for the gout."

Another remark of Newman's on the tendency of physicists "to take their formulas for [Divine] fiats" should appear a prophecy in retrospect. One need only be modestly familiar with some preposterous claims of Hawking, Penrose, Guth, and other luminaries who think that their arcane equations can make the Creator superfluous. In the same seventh Letter Newman also observes that while Nature prompts awe in the religious mind, it becomes a mere machine for the scientist who can satisfy therefore only his curiosity by analyzing it. A further danger for the scientist is to admire the mere creation but overlook the wonder of its being truly created.

Wonder, taken for a product of curiosity, Newman notes, is not a religious act, "or we should be worshipping our railroads," the wonders of the 1840s. Today he would refer to space rockets, the great technical wonders of our times. In this scientific age which has seen so many theologians to be overawed by science and lose their hold on religion proper, there is an ominous ring to Newman's remark: "What the physical creation presents to us in itself is a piece of machinery, and when men speak of a Divine Intelligence as its Author, this god of theirs is not the Living and True, unless the spring is the god of a watch, or steam the creator of the engine." And further, still in the same seventh Letter: "What we seek is what concerns us, the traces of a Moral Governor; even religious minds cannot discern these in the physical sciences." Which physics or astronomy, asked Newman, "teaches of divine holiness, truth, justice, or mercy? Is that much of a Religion which is silent about duty, sin, and its remedies?"

The five other Letters are devoted to the negative side of the subject, namely, what scientific education is not. First, far from being a source of moral improvement, it is at most a travesty of it in the form of mere intellectual charm, seduction and diversion (Letter II). In the next Letter Newman points out that knowledge is not a spiritual power. It can at most keep out bad thoughts, but not destroy them. In fact by placing emphasis on intellectual fascination, scientific education conditions the mind or the psyche, Newman would say today, to seek ever stronger forms of it. Or analogously, "Stop cigars, they will take to drinking parties; stop drinking, they gamble; stop gambling, and a worse license follows." One cannot help thinking of the process that in the last thirty years devolved, in universities and colleges, from intellectual titillation (the cultivation of scepticism) to sexual titillation, and from there to the charms of marijuana and ever stronger drugs.

Regardless of whether this awful logic has or has not run its full course, Newman was right in stating that "if we attempt to effect moral improvement by means of poetry, we shall but mature into a mawkish, frivolous, and fastidious sentimentalism." Further, if we try to achieve the same improvement "through experimental science," we shall but mature "into an uppish, supercilious temper, much inclined to scepticism." Spending a day in any larger department of physics, or chemistry, or molecular biology would provide much evidence on behalf of the truth of Newman's observation.

Scientific education, so Newman makes his next negative point in Letter IV, is not a propedeutics to Christianity. First it distracts the mind from the proper propedeutics. What these are can be gathered from Newman's question: "What *is* Christianity? Universal benevolence? Exalted morality? Supremacy of law? Conservatism? An age of light? An age of reason?—Which of them all?" When in the same Letter Newman states that in those Letters "not a word has been uttered or intended . . . against Science," he says the truth. Nothing in those Letters contradicts his assertion: "I treat science . . . with respect and gratitude. . . . I do not nickname science infidelity." His target is not science but a scientistic ideology.

Newman lists in Letters V and VI two more negative characteristics of that ideology: It is not a principle of social utility, and it is not a church for modern times, with scientists as its priests. The precipitous collapse under our very eyes of the Marxist efforts to organize society scientifically would provide much grist today for Newman's mill. No less effectively could he use today the growing number of sociological and psychological studies on scientists who take a Nobel or even smaller prize for a justification to pontificate on matters that have nothing to do with their scientific expertise.

In Letter VI Newman discusses the fifth negative feature, namely, that physical science is not a principle of action. He offers in some gem-like phrases the gist of what he was to set forth years later in the *Grammar of Assent*. Take, for instance, the phrase, "No one, I say, will die for his own calculations; he dies for realities." Did Newman have in mind Galileo? Or even better, does not this phrase apply to those hardly heroic admirers of Galileo who deplore his having recoiled from taking a martyr's stand? Or the phrase, "Logicians are more set upon concluding rightly, than on right conclusions," which puts in a nutshell the debacle of logical positivism. Professor A. J. Ayer gave but an unwitting commentary when he admitted on the BBC that the major error of logical positivism was that almost all of it was wrong.[21] Newman was far more logical than all logical positivists, who claimed to be scientific philosophers, when he remarked: "If we commence with scientific knowledge and argumentative proof, or lay any great stress upon it as the basis of personal Christianity, or attempt to make man moral and religious by Libraries and Museums, let us in consistency take chemists for our cooks, and mineralogists for our masons." Compared with what religion offers to the real man, Newman could rightly speak of "the small beer of science."

In all this, historians and philosophers of science may find powerful pointers that could be given extensive illustrations from the history of physics. Biographies of great physicists, for instance a recent one on Schrödinger with its luridly hedonistic details, would be a mine of such illustrations. Einstein derived no strength from physics to prevent him, in the words of a major biographer of his, Abraham Pais, from treating shabbily two women, his first and second wives. Great physicists though they were, Lenard championed Nazism and Heisenberg quietly served it. After the War, and in the face of the colossal rape of Eastern Europe, Bohr had words of praise for Stalinist Russia. Oppenheimer opened up frightful vistas of unconscionability when he defended the making of the atom bomb with the remark: "When you see something that is technically sweet, you go ahead and do it and you argue about what to do about it only after you have had your technical success."[22] Max Born earned himself the resentment of not a few prominent physicists when he extended in 1955 a forgiving hand to the University and town of Göttingen.

So much for some secular saints of physics in the way of a latter-day commentary on Newman's observations on the

---

[21] B. Magee, *Men of Ideas: Some Creators of Contemporary Philosophy* (London: British Broadcasting Corporation, 1978), p. 131.

[22] *In the Matter of J. Robert Oppenheimer* (Washington, D.C.: US Government Printing Office, 1954), p. 81.

profound and crucial difference between science and morality. Of course, those observations will not be meaningful for a latter-day theology in which morality is reduced to protests about racial discrimination and threats to the environment while it condones everything else and proclaims the motto: "prayerfully pro-choice."

Let us now turn to a theoretical consideration of the relation between physics and religion, as discussed by Newman in a lecture given in Dublin in 1855 which later became part of his book *The Idea of a University*. The lecture shows Newman the logician at his best and also as a most perceptive observer of how certain theoretical positions drive the mind in certain directions. In the lecture Newman considered two questions: Is a conflict possible between physical science and religion? and if not, why did there arise a conflict between them time and again?

The impossibility of the conflict rested, according to Newman, on the fact that while theology is a deductive science, physics is inductive. To define physics as simply inductive was the standard idea in the middle of the 19th century. Today the method of of physics is usually called empirio-deductive because of the greater awareness of the various suppositions which the physicist must assume in looking for facts. Still fully valid remains Newman's far more important remark about physics: "With matter it began, with matter it will end; it will never trespass into the province of mind." In the same breath he added a reference to a Hindu myth which in various books written by 20th-century physicists appears only as a stab at a philosophical concern about an Ultimate Cause. In Newman's reporting it, the myth is a stab at some scientific mythmakers: "The Hindoo notion is said to be that the earth stands upon a tortoise, but the physicist, as such, will never ask himself by what influence, external to the universe, the universe is sustained, simply because he is a physicist."[23] The sad fact is, however, that even more than in Newman's time, physicists are not satisfied being simply physicists. They find it more interesting to take on the role of a guru. No wonder that conflicts continue to arise.

[23] "Christianity and Physical Science," in *The Idea of a University* (Garden City, N.Y.: Doubleday, 1959), p. 394.

Indeed this is what Newman himself found as the principal cause of conflicts between religion and science. Of course, he was fully aware that theologians at times trespassed outside their domain. Newman recalled how some theologians had endowed the Ptolemaic system with a sacred validity. On occasion they did the same with the story of the six-day creation. That these trespasses were relatively few is also the gist of Newman's remark, elsewhere in the same book, about the Galileo case as a one-stock argument.

The trespasses of physicists were, according to Newman, far more systematic and sinister. They consisted in the sustained insistence that unless theology becomes empirical or inductive, it will not become a science. It was due to that insistence, Newman notes, that physico-theologies had usurped much of theology in his time and in the previous century.

Not being a historian of science, Newman did not exploit the tremendous demonstrative possibilities contained in his foregoing remark about physics as starting with matter and ending with matter. This exceedingly sound principle, which echoes the Ash Wednesday words of "remember man that thou art dust and unto dust thou shalt return," could have been used by him, for instance, against those physicists, Newton included, who saw a convenient place for God in the gaps of their knowledge of the physical world. In doing so they sinned not only against good theology, but also against good physics. The latter, so goes a priceless remark of Newman's, "may be dissatisfied with its own combinations, hypotheses, systems; and leave Ptolemy for Newton, the alchemists for Lavoisier and Davy; that is, it [physics] may decide that it has not yet touched the bottom of its own subject, but still its aim will be to get to the bottom, and nothing more."[24] And nothing less, if I may add. Whether it will ever get there is another matter. But if it gets there, and this is Newman's principal claim, it will touch on matter and nothing more.

Newman's point has a timeliness that cannot be emphasized and valued highly enough. It should suffice to think of the

---

[24] Ibid., pp. 393-4.

headlines, especially numerous in connection with the launching of the Hubble orbital telescope, that physicists will soon be spotting the first moment of creation. The latter is not a moment, precisely because in ontological priority it precedes all time. A physicist, with or without the Hubble telescope, can only observe an actually existing material configuration, from which one can refer only to another such configuration, but never to the nothing. Only the intrinsically impossible observation of the nothing could ever give the physicist empirical justification for speaking about the first moment of creation.

This is, of course, a mere matter of logic, a matter very dear to Newman and on which he was always very keen, perhaps at times all too keen. At any rate, had he lived in the 20th century he would have almost certainly spotted the tragic illogicality which is at the basis of the "scientific" disproof of causality. I mean the Copenhagen interpretation of quantum mechanics, according to which an interaction that cannot be measured exactly in the operational sense, cannot take place exactly in the very different ontological sense.[25]

It was the primacy of sound reasoning on which Newman set the greatest store in the controversies sparked by Darwin's *Origin of Species*, a subject that demands a separate treatment.[26] Solidity of reasoning ultimately decided, in Newman's view, between science and religion. To that point Newman devoted his attention for over thirty years, as proven by the history of his writing the *Grammar of Assent*. He tried to help in particular a prominent engineer friend of his, William Froude, who expected theology to deliver the same strict, that is, quantitative proofs as did Newtonian mathematical physics. But when Newman treated the readers of the *Grammar* to a theme that had for long been a favorite with him, he showed that mathematics itself rested on

---

[25] I argued this point on many occasions over a period of twenty years, most recently in ch. 5 of my *God and the Cosmologists* (Edinburgh: Scottish Academic Press, 1989; second revised and enlarged edition, 1998) and in my essay "Determinism and Reality," in *Great Ideas Today 1990* (Chicago: Encyclopaedia Britannica, 1990), pp. 277-302.

[26] As given in the next chapter.

non-quantitative considerations and as such shared in the "probabilistic" aspects of all human knowledge.[27]

In the *Grammar* Newman also called attention to the psychological conditionings that underlies many scientific claims. As an illustration he referred to what is holding the center stage today as SETI or Search for Extra-Terrestrial Intelligence. There should be much food for thought in a little-noticed passage in the *Grammar* for those who by looking for signals from outer space take for facts enormously high improbabilites:

> Facts cannot be proved by presumptions, yet it is remarkable that in cases where nothing stronger than presumption was even professed, scientific men have sometimes acted as if they thought this kind of argument, taken by itself, decisive of a fact which was in debate. Thus in the controversy about the Plurality of worlds, it has been considered, on purely anteced-ent grounds, as far as I see, to be so necessary that the Creator should have filled with living beings the luminaries which we see in the sky and other cosmical bodies which we imagine there, that it almost amounts to a blasphemy to doubt it.[28]

Today Newman would refer to SETI as a case of infatuation that can pose the most serious damage to the faith of ill-informed Christians. The information they need, Newman would say, is not more science but a keen ability to see through a maze of undefined terms, tacit presuppositions, and gratuitous inferences. For the Christian it is enough to know two things. One is that only God can create intelligent beings and that He is free to create them or not to create them in every nook and cranny of the universe. The second is that on the basis of standard evolu-tionary theory, it is most inconsistent and also most dangerous to look for extraterrestrials. Inconsistent because on the basis of that theory, one cannot expect a universality of intellect through-

[27] This parallel between the exact sciences and theology is the principal theme of the carefully researched essay of G. R. Evans, "Science and Mathematics in Newman's Thought," *Downside Review*, October, 1978, pp. 247-66, in which, however, little is made of Newman's emphasis on the non-probabilistic character of man's immediate registering of external reality. This latter point is discussed in chapter 9.

[28] *Grammar of Assent* (Garden City, N. Y.: Doubleday, 1955), pp. 298-99.

out the cosmos, throughout the Milky Way, or even throughout the solar system. And also most dangerous, because extraterrestrials from different parts of the galaxy would represent different species, or perhaps genera, all of them in grim struggle for existence with one another, and with us, were we so unlucky as to bump into them or they into us.

It should be no surprise that Newman, so keen on what the human intellect is, should come up in the *Grammar of Assent* with gemlike phrases applicable to the artificial intelligence mythology.[29] That book is, of course, a powerful rebuttal of the misconception, even more widespread today than in Newman's day, that scientific demonstrations are the only valid forms of rigorous reasoning. What Newman showed in that book goes to the very heart of the proper understanding of the relation between science and theology or faith. The gist is that real assent cannot be given to logic in general, or to mere identity relations in particular, which are the propositions and conclusions of physics, but only to propositions that put one face to face with material, historical and social realities.

It is on this and similar epistemological or philosophical points that hinges the outcome of the debate between science and religion.[30] Such a debate can be carried on with no reference to revealed religion in general and to Christian Revelation in particular. At a time when the historiography of science had no inkling about the medieval Christian provenance of Newton's first law, and about the medieval breakthroughs in technology,[31] Newman's horizons on the relation of Christianity and science had to be restricted indeed. By and large, he confined his dicta, as he did in *The Idea of a University*,[32] to insistence on the limits of what can be learned by the scientific method and dismissed the

---

[29] Especially in subsection 3 of the chapter on "The Range of Illative Sense."

[30] The remainder of this paragraph and the following three paragraphs are additions to the original text of this chapter.

[31] These topics are fully treated in my *The Savior of Science* (Edinburgh: Scottish Academic Press, 1988) and in my essay, "Medieval Christianity: Its Inventiveness in Science and Technology" (1993); reprinted in my *Patterns or Principles and Other Essays* (Bryn Mawr, PA: Intercollegiate Studies Institute, 1995), pp. 63-86.

[32] Especially in the chapter on physical science.

dwelling of agnostics and rationalists on the Galileo case as a
one-stock argument.

The utter honesty of his penetrating intellect was, however,
displayed to an astonishing degree when he took up in early
September 1876 the question posed by a correspondent about the
respective measure of the contribution made by Catholics and
Protestants to science. He began by distinguishing between basic
science and its application. Concerning the latter, he readily
recognized that the pragmatic bent of mind of the Anglo-Saxons
gave them a dominant role in exploiting the industrial possibilities of science. He granted that "this special characteristic of
activity, independence, boldness, and utilitarianism has also had
something to do with their being Protestants, as indisposing them
to listen to the claims whether of Authority or of Dogmatic Faith,
which are the prime instruments of Catholic training." Newman
unflinchingly drew the implication of this, namely, "that the
Catholic Church having for its province exclusively religion and
morals, does in fact so earnestly enforce the claims of the unseen
world as to put a wet blanket on the energetic enthusiasm with
which men who are not Catholics, that is, who have not vivid
faith or definite practical creed, pursue purely secular ends."[33]

But then he turned the tables on Anglo-Saxons insofar as
they were Protestants. Inasmuch as they shared this supernatural
anxiety of the Catholic Church, "the Church of England and the
Puritans have been as jealous of physical research as monks and
inquisitors have been; and have only succeeded less in their
resistance to it, because they have had less power." He then was
free to dispute a direct connection between Protestantism and
this or that specific scientific discovery, such as "the electric
telegraph." Further, he could point out that genius, scientific or
not, is rare, and "Protestants certainly have not a monopoly of
it."[34]

[33] Letter of September 6, 1876, in *Letters and Diaries,* vol. 28, p. 109.
[34] Ibid. "Thus among Catholics we find on the first blush of the matter,
inventor of printing Guttemberg [sic] 1450, Bacon 1250, Copernicus 1500,
Linacre 1500, Vesalius 1560, Galileo 1600, Kepler 1600, Torricelli 1640,
Gassendi 1650, Malpighi 1660, Galvani 1760, Volta 1800, Ampere 1800, Secchi
1870, all Catholics." For listing Kepler as a Catholic, Newman had indeed to

Newman, who was ready to give to ideas and persons their due, was therefore fully entitled to deny to men of science a right they had no lawful claim to, namely, the right to pontificate about matters non-scientific, especially about religion. In what may be his last utterance on the relation between science and religion, he delivered a broadside, though only in private, on precisely that type of pontificating. The context was his set of reflections on an article about secular progress published by his nephew, John Rickards Mozley, at that time Professor of Mathematics in Manchester.[35] Once more Newman did not apologize for the fact that the primary mission of the Church was to seek first the Kingdom of God. But he disputed Mozley's claim that "now, any more than in the middle age the Church makes light of secular progress." He also referred to his lectures on the idea of a university where, as he now put it, he insisted on an equity: Neither was attention to secular subjects, such as the sciences, to sideline interest in theology, nor was interest in "physical science or other departments of knowledge to be sacrificed to theology. I said that theology must not encroach upon their provinces any more than they upon its."[36]

Newman was now free to aim a broadside at scientific gurus who pontificated in matters of religion. He did so in order to explain his feelings about secular progress. He began with a reference to his long-standing dislike of that British Association which originated, according to Newman, in a movement, Benthamism—and here, as the author of the essays on the Tamworth Reading Room, Newman could speak with authority—that aimed at the exclusion of religion from public education. But the British Association "never has been able . . . to keep its hands off religion." Furthermore, it could not resist its inner logic: "It began with preaching Deism—it has ended in preaching

---

blush. Some others in that list were, of course, but nominal Catholics, but merely nominal was also the Protestantism of many an eminent man of science during Newman's times as well as before and after.

[35] For more on Mozley, see chapter 8.

[36] *Letters and Diaries*, vol. 28, pp. 265-66.

Atheism. 'Why cannot it let religion alone?' I have all along said, but it can't."[37]

In this age, when any Nobel-laureate scientist can get up and perorate on anything under the sun, without being reminded of *ne sutor ultra crepidam*, which Newman quoted right there and then, there is an eery timeliness in his words: "I am indignant that men, whose line is Science, relying by paralogism on the prestige of their scientific reputation, as if because they are great in one line, they must be great in another." Worse, Newman found that "in scientific matters [they] go out of their way to make preachments against Catholic truths," while denying their platforms to Catholics who would take exception to this abuse of science. This abuse of science and of Catholics was, Newman argued, "no accident with them, they have been from the first to last consistent certainly. I have felt it as a Protestant as strongly as when a Catholic."[38]

What Newman said on science should seem, therefore, to have its gist not so much in his exemplary readiness to give credit where it belongs and deny credit where it does not, as in his principle that man's highest duty is to seek the supernatural. This principle was his guiding light all the time and he derived it from his lifelong, unwavering commitment to the highest Christian idea of holiness, the chief motivating force of his long life that came to an edifying close a hundred years ago.

[37] Ibid., p. 267.
[38] Ibid.

12

Evolution

As the year of the centenary of Newman's death approached many voiced the hope that it might speed up the process of his canonization. Not a few of Newman's admirers may have been startled, however, by the claim in an editorial in *The Times* that Newman's canonization would promote ecumenism in England on account of his endorsement of an evolutionary outlook particularly acceptable in his country. Newman, to quote the same editorial, "was a particularly English cardinal, and it was in a particularly English way that he got his red hat—members of the aristocracy, including the then Duke of Norfolk, used their influence. The novelist A. N. Wilson has said of Newman that he was the only Victorian intellectual of the first rank who had not been disabused of Christian faith by the theories of Charles Darwin: and Newman himself said he was happy 'to go the whole hog' with Darwin's hypothesis of natural selection."[1]

Whether Newman's canonization will come soon is rather doubtful, in spite of the announcement in August 1990 that the first phase of the process has been taken by Rome as completed. Largely because of the absence of miracles obtained through his intercession, a hundred years after his death Newman still cannot be called Blessed, and much less a Saint. A firm believer in miracles obtained by saints, Newman himself would not approve from Heaven those admirers of his who try to downplay the crucial role of miracles in the process of beatification and

[1] C. Langley, "Lead Kindly Light, amidst the Encircling Gloom," *The Times*, Feb. 7, 1989, p. 12.

canonization. Their minimalist approach to miracles would be countered by him with a recall of a phrase of his *Apologia*: "It is not at all easy (humanly speaking) to wind up an Englishman to a dogmatic level."[2] In fact, as will be seen, he took the acceptance of the possibility and reality of miracles as the most concrete litmus test for Christians in the great antagonism which Darwin and Darwinism fostered, and still does, against the supernatural.

Newman's expression of his readiness "to go the whole hog with Darwin" first saw print in 1934, in an article by Father Humphrey Johnson, a member of the Birmingham Oratory. As such, Fr. Johnson had ready access to Newman's then still unpublished Philosophical Notebooks from which he quoted an entry, dated December 9, 1863, as follows: "There is as much want of simplicity in the idea of the creation of distinct species as in that of the creation of trees in full growth, whose seed is [in] themselves, or of rocks with fossils in them. I mean that it is as strange that monkeys should be so like men with no *historical* connexion between them, as the notion that there should be no course of history by which fossil bones got into rocks. The one idea stands to the other as fluxions to differentials. Differentials are fluxions with the condition of time eliminated. I will either go the whole hog with Darwin, or, dispensing with time and history altogether, hold not only the theory of distinct species but also of the creation of fossil-bearing rocks. If a minute was once equivalent to a million years now relatively to the forces of nature, there would be little difference between the two hypotheses. If time was not, there would be none, if the work of creation varied as to F.T., force being indefinitely great as time was indefinitely small."[3]

Such is the immediate context of Newman's obviously conditional readiness "to go the whole hog with Darwin." On the basis of that context alone one is not entitled to impute to Newman more than a thorough appreciation of the parameter of time. He stated that he would line up with Darwin if the alternative

---

[2] *Apologia pro vita sua* (Garden City, N. Y.: Image Books, 1956), p. 291.

[3] H. Johnson, "The Origin of Man in the Light of Recent Research," *The Dublin Review* (July, August, September, 1934), pp. 46-65. For the passage in question see p. 46. The passage is reproduced with slight editorial variations in *The Philosophical Notebook of John Henry Newman*, edited by E. Sillem and revised by A. J. Boekraad (Louvain: Nauwelaerts, 1970), vol. 2, p. 158.

was that time had to be ignored. To ignore time would hardly have been to the liking of Newman who loved to be "deep in history" if for no less important a reason than to "cease to be a Protestant."[4] Whatever the true nature of Newman's stated sympathy for Darwin, Newman did not cease holding some timeless truths dearer than life just because he cherished the parameter of time.

Oversight of these differences between Darwin and Newman —that were impossible not to see in 1863, let alone in 1934, and certainly not today—can greatly mislead one concerning Newman's views on evolution in general and Darwin in particular. A case in point is Fr. Johnson's article. There one finds, immediately after the foregoing passage, Newman contrasted with his "contemporaries in the religious world" as ones who "were far from sharing his belief in the antecedent probability of an 'historical' connexion between the origin of monkeys and the origin of men."[5] To exemplify those contemporaries Fr. Johnson quoted the views of Newman's bishop, Ullathorne, as being more typical on the subject. Ullathorne's view is all the more worth quoting as it appeared in print a few months before Newman jotted down that passage. The context was the bishop's pastoral denunciation of the *Rambler* for giving space to views which seemed to imply that man was a mere product of apes.

The views denounced by the bishop were such that Newman himself would have certainly denounced them just as strongly. If Newman had reservations about the bishop's statement, they would have been about the bishop's imputation of a specific motive to leading physiologists. According to the bishop it was "out of a grudge against man's spiritual liberty" that "physiology has undertaken to prove that man is the product of an ape." Without citing from the works of Lord Monboddo and Lamarck, the bishop referred to them as the originators of the "degrading notions" of man's descent from the apes, which are "now revived by Darwin and the *Rambler*."[6] Whatever the

---

[4] *An Essay on the Development of Christian Doctrine* (Garden City, N. Y.: Image Books, 1960), p. 35.

[5] H. Johnson, "The Origin of Man," pp. 46-47.

[6] Ibid., p. 47.

ideological motivations of Lord Monboddo and Lamarck, Newman was ready to give the benefit of the doubt to Darwin concerning ulterior motivations. More of this later.

Newman would have been the last to disagree with the emphasis laid by his bishop, in the same context, on the spiritual, supernatural component in man: "Man, says the Apostle, is the glory of God, His glory, for He made him, and made him in His likeness. And men can be found to say, and other men beneath the canopy of Heaven to repeat, that not to God belongs the authorship, the fatherhood, the glory of man, but to the one of all creatures that one fears to name without the guilt of mockery in such connexion."[7] Fr. Johnson hardly did justice to the bishop as he introduced this passage with the remark that "in the suggestion of a genetic connection between men and the ape Ullathorne saw so peculiar an impiety that he found it hard to contain himself." Fr. Johnson's remark would have been misplaced even if he had spoken of a bodily connexion instead of a genetic one, which in Ullathorne's time was totally unknown. To compound the confusion, Fr. Johnson added in a footnote: "Throughout this article, when the phrase 'Evolution of Man' is used, nothing more is meant than the evolution of man considered as a physical organism. Man, considered as a rational being, cannot have been a product of evolution."[8]

But then who were to be really deplored by Fr. Johnson? Most of Newman's Catholic contemporaries and possibly many of those of Fr. Johnson, or rather the *leading* Darwinists pontificating about a wholly animal descent of man's spiritual faculties? Never, or hardly ever, did those scientific gurus present their evolutionary views as restricted to man's physical background, though such a restriction should have been required by their very scientific method. The disregard of such restriction had found a crusading champion in Fr. Johnson's most often quoted authority, Sir Arthur Keith. Was it therefore justified on Fr. Johnson's part to ignore Sir Arthur's encomiums of evolutionary materialism with which he had regaled, in the form of a

---

[7] Ibid.
[8] Ibid.

Presidential Address, the 1927 meeting of the British Association?[9]

In 1934, or half a century earlier and later, leading experts on man's ancestry would not have given a hoot for the essentially theological claim which Fr. Johnson and many other Catholic theologians before and after him hung on the slender tree of highly revisable scientific data. Even when such data are well established, they have no bearing on value judgments and metaphysical issues, among them man's spiritual descent. Fr. Johnson, as many others before and after him, stated and muddled the issue in the same breath:

> The progress of human palaeontology has eliminated the necessity of invoking a 'mutation' to account for the origin of man. We need not, however, deny, though the question is necessarily one of great obscurity, that some final modification of the brain and nervous system brought about by direct divine action was necessary before the most highly organized and progressive of the hominids was elevated into a true man by being united to a spiritual soul. At all events the orthodoxy of such a theory is now being admitted by an increasing number of representatives of the scholastic tradition in theology.[10]

Whether that "final modification" will ever be found, and in an unmistakably unequivocal way, is not at all certain. At any rate, what Fr. Johnson could find in 1934 about man's simian ancestry constituted a very complex and in not a few places a most conjectural dossier. His recount of that dossier showed on his part an extensive study of human palaeontology, a study which Newman never made. But unlike Fr. Johnson, Newman could make, in spite of the meagerness of his knowledge of biology and paleontology as they stood in the 1860s and later, appropriate comments that are instructive in a positive way even today.

The source of that difference consists largely in Newman's proverbially deep respect for the dictates of logic. Partly because

[9] A. Keith, "Darwin's Theory of Man's Descent as it Stands Today," *British Association for the Advancement of Science. Leeds Meeting. August 21-28, 1927* (London: British Association for the Advancement of Science, 1928), pp. 3-18.

[10] H. Johnson, "The Origin of Man," p. 65.

of this, Newman had a keen sense of the revisability of the actually available scientific data, a reversability that was then even greater than it is today. This is not to suggest that Fr. Johnson was entirely gullible in agreeing with Sir Arthur Keith's interpretation of the Piltdown Man or *Eoanthropus Dawsoni*, named after Charles Dawson, a country lawyer and amateur geologist, who "discovered" its few fragments outside the village of Piltdown, in Sussex, between 1908 and 1912. According to that interpretation the Piltdown Man did exactly the opposite of contradicting Darwinian evolution as some anti-evolutionists first asserted. Rather, by making man's evolutionary lineage a most complex matter, that lineage could be seen as matching the very complicated simian family tree. This had to be so if apes and men were equally subject to the randomness of Darwinian evolution. Such a bearing of the Piltdown Man had, of course, to be a foregone conclusion, in view of the fact, suspected for some time and now shown well-nigh conclusively, that the very fragmentary remains of the Piltdown Man were forged and planted for that very purpose by Sir Arthur Keith himself.[11]

Newman who knew much about the vagaries of theological history would not have been surprised. As one who traced the "wild living intellect of man" to "some terrible aboriginal calamity in which the human race is implicated,"[12] Newman knew that mere interest in science would not turn anyone into a paragon of virtue and intellectual honesty. He was fully aware of the narrowness of the scientific or quantitative method ("calculations never made a hero" and "no one will die for his own calculations," he wrote in the *Development* [13] and in the *Grammar*[14] respectively). He therefore might not disagree with this observation that cheating is far less frequent in science than in other

[11] See F. Spencer, *Piltdown: A Scientific Forgery* (London: Oxford University Press, 1990), and J. N. Wilford's front-page pre-publication report, "Mastermind of Piltdown Hoax Unmasked?" *The New York Times*, June 5, 1990, p. A1 (continued on p. C1).

[12] *Apologia*, pp. 320 and 322.

[13] *Development*, p. 314.

[14] *An Essay in Aid of a Grammar of Assent* (Garden City, N. Y.: Image Books, 1955), p. 89. This statement is part of a several-page-long quotation from Newman's "Tamworth Reading Room," written in 1841.

fields for the simple reason that cheating with the usually quantitative data of science is easy to unmask. Nor are the monetary rewards high for cheating in science. Since the contrary is true about business transactions, swindling there with quantities is so frequent as to make our prisons burst at the seams.

The one who could say without boasting that he "did not sin against light",[15] never cheated in the form of trying to appear more learned in any branch of learning (not excepting Darwinian evolution) than he actually was. Yet in the 1860s and 1870s, when hardly anyone could appear learned without wading into the heated disputes about Darwin, Newman referred not once to him in his publications. Only a lesser character would have resisted such a temptation offered in the opportunity of writing an intellectual odyssey similar to Newman's Apologia. The Apologia, written four short years after the publication of the Origin, contains no reference to Darwin's theory either, although in its conclusion Newman took a most anti-Darwinian stance. He did so by being most emphatic on the reality of original sin,[16] which the Darwinians were already busy reducing to a nature "red in tooth and claw." Again, when posturing as a forerunner of Darwin became fashionable, it would have been tempting for any lesser character than Newman to refer to his Development, republished with a new preface in 1878, as an anticipation of at least some basic perspective of Darwin's.

An even better and more specific opportunity was provided by the subject he treated at length in the Grammar. There he surveyed a wide variety of propositions from the perspective of the kind of adherence they merit. As he took up the certitude of theological propositions, he faced the objection that those propositions might, in the latter part of the nineteenth century,

[15] See Letters and Correspondence of John Henry Newman during His Life in the English Church, ed. A. Mozley (London: Longmans, Green and Co., 1890), vol. 1, pp. 365-66. This phrase of Newman's is part of his first reminiscences on his almost fatal sickness in Sicily, but is applicable to his subsequent quest for full truth.

[16] On the basis of a purely empirical survey of society as he found it, Newman felt entitled to conclude: "Thus the doctrine of what is theologically called original sin becomes to me almost as certain as that the world exists, and as the existence of God." Apologia, pp. 320-21.

obtain no higher status than the propositions of early science. In listing some of these, Newman added, as if in an aside, some contemporary scientific propositions that were but mere probabilities: "About such doctrines [such as the basic elements, the distribution of heavenly bodies etc] there was no certitude no more than there is *now* certitude about the origin of languages, the age of man, or *the evolution of species*, considered as philosophical questions"[17] (Italics added). Newman did not care to confront and pick to pieces the certitude of Darwin and the Darwinians a mere ten years after the publication of the *Origin*.

A few years later, when asked to explain and defend papal infallibility, he could have found more than one excuse to hold high to ridicule, as did George Bernard Shaw half a century later, the infallible Church of the Darwinists.[18] Still another few years later, in 1879, when on receiving the red hat he took for his target moral liberalism, Newman could have added a sideswipe at its new Darwinist underpinning, or the claim that all is flux in ethics because there are no stable forms in nature.

Against the background of such opportunities, Newman's public silence on Darwin may make him look like a man from a distant planet or from a bygone age. In private, in the course of writing between 1859 and 1890 thousands of letters that now fill over four thousand pages in twelve large volumes,[19] he mentioned Darwin only six times and rather briefly in all cases. The first came almost a full decade after the publication of the *Origin*, in a letter Newman wrote on August 22, 1868, to Canon J. Walker,[20] who had called his attention to a new commentary on the Pentateuch.[21] The Canon was instrumental in arranging for a

[17] *Grammar of Assent*, p. 329. See also p. 166, 299 and 376.

[18] G. B. Shaw, *Saint Joan* (Penguin Books, 1946), p. 29 (Preface).

[19] Volumes 19 to 31 of *The Letters and Diaries of John Henry Newman* published between 1961 and 1984.

[20] *Letters and Diaries*, vol. 24, p. 77.

[21] Contrary to the usually very careful practice of the editors of *Letters and Diaries*, the author of the book was not W. Smith, but R. Payne Smith, Dean of Canterbury. The first part, dealing with Genesis, of his commentary on the Pentateuch bcame widely available in 1885 as a volume in *The Handy Commentary* series under the title, *The First Book of Moses, called Genesis* (London: Cassel and Co.).

courtesy copy of the second edition of R. M. Beverley's anony-
mously published critique of Darwin's theory, followed shortly
by a supplementary chapter to it.[22] Newman's comment on the
former, "I got Smith on the Pentateuch at once on your suggestion,
and have been much interested in what I have read of it —
but have not read enough to get into it as a whole," reflected his
resolve to reserve his spare time as much as possible for the
completion, at long last, of his *Grammar of Assent*.

The rest of his letter dealt with his reflections on Beverley's
book which, apart from its preface and the supplementary
chapter, he left uncut! Still, his comments on it were anything
but an exercise in vague words or something worse. The reason
for this is that Newman, obviously familiar with the philosophical
foundations of Darwin's theory, could restrict himself to some
fundamental issues it had raised. One was a defense of what
Newman called not the principle of evolution but "the principle
of development," which he still qualified with the remark, "or
what I have called [the principle] of construction." It is enough
to think of Darwin's emphatic claim about the non-teleological
character of evolution to sense the enormous extent to which
Newman has thereby distanced himself from Darwinism.
Introductory to that remark of Newman's was his praise of
Beverley's book as "a careful and severe examination of the
theory of Darwin—and it shows, as is most certain he would be
able to do, the various points which are to be made good before
it can cohere." Newman was insistent on giving logic its full due
even when confronted with Darwin's theory.

Once Newman made logic confine within strict limits the
competence of Darwinian theory, he could be generous on
secondary issues. One was the great merit of the view (compati-
ble with evolutionary theory and even endorsed by Darwin, only
to regret this later[23]) that the Creator worked through secondary

---

[22] The reference was to the second edition of Beverley's *The Darwinian
Theory of the Transmutation of Species*, first published in 1866. Like Canon
Walker, Beverley too was a resident of Scarborough. Two years older than
Newman, Beverley allied himself with the Oxford Movement by writing a
critique on the corrupt state of the Church of England.

[23] "But I have long regretted," wrote Darwin to J. D. Hooker, on March 29,

causes over large periods of time. But the particular argument Newman attached to this general remark was most un-Darwinian. The Creator's power to let His work unfold through secondary causes "we do not deny or circumscribe when we hold he has created the self acting originating human mind, which has almost a creative gift." Newman's remark, aimed on its face value at some foot-dragging theologians, hit Darwin before hitting them. The remark implied a view of the mind as the "citadel of theism," the very view which Darwin tried to demolish by not meeting its challenge head-on, that is, with genuinely philosophical arguments.[24]

It was with a similar tactic that Newman granted something to Darwin about "design" while denying him something very central to his purposes. Starting from the admiration of "Divine *Design*" that imparted "certain laws to matter millions of ages ago, which have surely and precisely worked out, in the course of those long ages, those   effects which He from the first proposed," Newman could offer the concession: "Mr Darwin's theory *need* not be atheistical, be it true or not; it may simply be suggesting a larger idea of Divine Prescience and Skill."[25]

On that "Prescience and Skill," Newman would never yield an inch. One at most could deplore that Newman never went on public record with grippingly graphic "antievolutionist" remarks such as the one which Baron von Hügel, visiting him in Edgbaston, recorded for posterity: "Newman took me to the Botanical Gardens, all gloriously abloom with rhododendrons and azaleas, and as he dived in and out behind and around the plants, full of ecstasies of admiration, he exclaimed: 'But what argument could Evolution[ist]s bring against this as evidence of the work of Mind?'"[26]

1863, "that I truckled to public opinion, and used the Pentateuchal term of creation, by which I really meant 'appeared' by some wholly unknown process." See *The Life and Letters of Charles Darwin*, edited by F. Darwin (London: Murray, 1888), vol. 3, p. 18.

[24] For details, see my *Angels, Apes and Men* (La Salle, IL: Sherwood Sugden, 1983), p. 52.

[25] *Letters and Diaries*, vol. 24, p. 77.

[26] Von Hügel, *The Reality of God and Religion and Agnosticism* (London: J. M. Dent, 1931), pp. 53-54. The visit took place in mid-June 1876. According to von Hügel's notebooks, now at the library of St Andrews University, he had

With such reservations about Darwinian evolution, reservations unacceptable to Darwin and most Darwinists, Newman could be generous toward Darwin to the extent of asking Canon Walker to urge Mr Beverley not to be "hard on Darwin sometimes, which [whereas] he might have interpreted him kindly." Looking at Darwinian theory from the heights of sound theology and consummate logic it could not appear terribly dangerous: "I do not fear," Newman added, "the theory so much as he [Mr Beverley] seems to do." Newman certainly did not fear the prospect of millions of years, nor the word "evolution," though he resorted to it only once in the form of a quote from Beverley as he asked Canon Walker once more to convey to Beverley his view that a theist did not necessarily have to hold that "'the *accidental* evolution of organic beings' is inconsistent with divine design."[27]

Whereas a Darwinist could see in this a verbal latitude that might accommodate him provided he was not virulently materialistic, he could derive no comfort from the devastatingly simple observation Newman added in the same breath: "It is accidental to *us*, not to *God*." On this distinction hangs in balance the truth of evolution as distinct from materialistic ideology. By letting a "theistic logic," that is a logic ready to go the whole hog not so much with Darwin as with reason, it was not self-defeating on Newman's part to admit in the same letter a plain ignorance about scientific specifics. He did not want to oppose Beverley's critique of Darwin's theory as being incompatible with design: "Perhaps your friend," he wrote to Canon Walker, "has got a surer clue to guide him than I have, who have never studied the question, and I do not like to put my opinion against his."[28]

talks with Newman on 14, 16 and 18 June, discussing 'the vicariousness of our Lord's suffering,' 'the possibility of invincible ignorance in matters of natural religion,' 'certainty,' 'Scholastic Philosophy,' 'Infallibility,' and 'Temporal Power' of the Pope." See R. K. Browne, "Newman and Von Hügel," *The Month* (July 1961), pp. 27-32, and H. Tristram, "Cardinal Newman and Baron von Hügel," *Dublin Review* (Autumn 1966), pp. 295-302. The material given in this paragraph and note is additional to the original form of this chapter.

[27] *Letters and Diaries*, vol. 24, p. 77.
[28] Ibid.

Newman's next reference to Darwin came in his letter of June 5, 1870, to Pusey. The letter was prompted by Pusey's report about the disputes that arose in Oxford after Darwin had been offered an Honorary Degree to be conferred on him at the June Commemoration. Darwin declined the honor on the ground that he could not cope with the strain of the ceremony. Most likely he did not want to be discomfited by being in the company of orthodox divines such as Pusey.

At any rate, few could have guessed in Oxford in the Spring of 1870 that Darwin was completing a book far more ominous for divines, a book published on February 24, 1871, under the hybrid-looking title, *The Descent of Man, and Selection in Relation to Sex*. Darwin himself was surprised at the equanimity with which his book was received: "Everybody is talking about it without being shocked," he wrote to a friend three months later.[29] Only two groups of competent readers took exception to man's descent as proposed by Darwin. One group was made up of theologians with convictions similar to Pusey's, a group of no consequence for Darwin. He had in mind members of the other group as he registered with no small disappointment that the argument of the *Descent* failed to meet with "the approval of hardly any naturalists as far as I know."[30]

While the naturalists disagreed with Darwin about the lineage he traced out for man, they did not object to the broader claim of the *Descent* that man, not only in body but in mind too, was a purely random product of strictly natural forces.[31] Although some passages in the *Descent* smacked of plain materialism,[32] only a hundred years later did it become clear that by 1871 Darwin had been a rank materialist for over thirty years. The evidence came with the publication, in the 1960s, of Darwin's early notebooks dating from 1837-39. Those notebooks, from

[29] A statement of Darwin to a visitor in early 1871. See *The Life and Letters of Charles Darwin*, vol. 3, p. 133.

[30] Darwin to Dohrn, on Feb. 3, 1872; ibid.

[31] Even Alfred Russell Wallace dissented only insofar as he found it illogical that a still non-existent mental activity (invariably connected with a large brain) be credited with the prompting of the evolution of such a brain.

[32] One such detail is Darwin's approving reference to a naturalist's equation of a dog's intent look at his master with a worshiper's face.

which many passages entered the *Origin*, contain rudely materialistic remarks such as, "Why is thought, being the secretion of
brain, more wonderful than gravity, a property of matter?" and
"if all men were dead, then monkeys may make men," and that
"the Devil under form of Baboon is our grandfather."[33] In the
1860s one could merely state on reading the *Origin* that it
allowed no exception for a special creation of man's mind (soul).
Darwin himself greeted the publication in 1868 of Ernst Haeckel's
unabashedly materialistic *History of Creation* as being the logical
extension of the *Origin*, in which Darwin spoke of man with
studied reticence. It is against this background that one should
ponder Newman's letter to Pusey:

> I have not fallen in with Darwin's book. I conceive it
> to be an advocacy of the theory that that principle of propaga-
> tion, which we are accustomed to believe began with Adam,
> and with the patriarchs of the brute species, began in some
> common ancestor millions of years before.
>
> 1. Is this against the distinct teaching of the inspired
> text? if it is, then he advocates an antichristian theory. For
> myself, speaking under correction, I don't see that it does—
> contradict it.
>
> 2. Is it against Theism (putting Revelation aside)—I
> don't see how it can be. Else, the fact of a propagation from
> Adam is against Theism. If second causes are conceivable at
> all, an Almighty Agent being supposed, I don't see why the
> series should not last for millions of years as well as for
> thousands.
>
> The former question is the more critical. Does Scripture
> contradict the theory?—was Adam *not* immediately taken
> from the dust of the earth? '*All* are of dust'—Eccles iii, 20
> —yet *we* never *were* dust—we are from fathers, why may not
> the same be the case with Adam? I don't say that it *is* so—
> but, if the sun does not go round the earth and the earth
> stand still, as Scripture seems to say, I don't know why Adam
> needs be immediately out of dust—Formavit Deus hominem
> de limo terrae—i.e. out of what really was dust and mud in its
> nature, before He made it what it was, living. But I speak
> under correction. Darwin does not *profess* to oppose Religion.
> I think he deserves a degree as much as many others, who
> have had one.[34]

[33] For details, see my *Angels, Apes and Men*, p. 53
[34] *Letters and Diaries*, vol. 25, pp. 137-38.

Newman's letter calls for several comments. First, he does not refer to the fact that Darwin's theory, if taken consistently, has a bearing on the question of the origin of man's mind or soul. Second, in proposing a non-literal interpretation of the origin of man's body Newman twice voices deference to ecclesiastical authority. Third, he takes Darwin's theory merely for an emphasis on the length of time necessary for natural forces to work and voices no concern for the theory of natural selection as a theory full of logical inadequacies that had, by 1870, been extensively aired. This may appear a damaging omission on the part of a master logician eager to seize on any misstep in logic! In view of this, one might be tempted to say, taking Newman's letter by itself, that Newman could not have fallen in with Darwin's book for a reason that had little to do with logic. It seems indeed that if and when that book fell in his hands he merely thumbed through it. Great collector of books though he was, Newman never owned a copy of the *Origin!*[35]

Still it was the primacy of logic in dealing with Darwin's theory that formed the gist of Newman's third epistolary reference to Darwin. This time the recipient of Newman's letter was an accomplished biologist, St George Mivart, who had just become the leading critic of Darwin's *Origin* with a book, *The Genesis of Species,*[36] the importance of which Darwin himself keenly felt. In registering St George Mivart's note of thanks for the first two volumes of his *Essays Critical and Historical,* Newman wrote with commendable self-effacement:

> Let me say that I shall be abundantly satisfied and pleased if my essays do a quarter of the good which I hear your volume is doing. Those who have a right to judge speak of it as a first rate book—and it is pleasant to find that the first real exposition of the logical insufficiency of Mr Darwin's theory comes from a Catholic. In saying this, you must not suppose that I have personally any great dislike or dread of his theory,

[35] A conjecture further strengthened by the catalogue of Newman's books in the Birmingham Oratory Library.

[36] London: Macmillan, 1871. Mivart's arguments against natural selection are listed in detail in *A Conscience in Conflict: The Life of St. George Jackson Mivart,* by J. W. Gruber (New York: Columbia University Press, 1960), pp. 52-56.

but many good people are much troubled at it—and at all events, without any disrespect to him, it is well to show that Catholics may be better reasoners than philosophers.[37]

More than a hundred years later, Newman's satisfaction over the fact that Catholics, scientists or not, can handle logic better than some scientists who are not Catholic, may have an eery relevance. One wonders if it was not a carefully cultivated distrust (couched in profuse references to the Church Fathers) of logic and of Thomist realism that prepared the slippery ground on which so many Catholic intellectuals fell head over heels once exposed to Fr. Teilhard's evolutionary metaphors apt to trip up clear thinking. At any rate, Newman's silence on Darwin's *Descent of Man*, already out for nine months, should seem surprising. Nor is it clear from Newman's letter that he had perused Mivart's *Genesis*. Newman, however, in a letter he wrote to Mivart almost two years later (Nov. 10, 1873), explicitly stated that he had read "with great interest as far as I was up to the matter of it," Mivart's latest book, *Man and Apes*, a critique of Darwin's *Descent*, and continued: "I suppose the key to the whole inquiry which it contains lies in your statement towards the end that the phenomena which Comparative Anatomy presents to us is a net and not a ladder—and that Darwin's hypothesis with its supplements is not warranted by them, when you come close to them and catalogue them, however much they may promise in his favour on the first rough view of them."[38]

Mivart actually wrote that "the lines of affinity existing between the different Primates construct rather a network than a ladder" and that the "network" was a "tangled web, the meshes of which no naturalist has as yet unravelled by the aid of natural selection."[39] There was much more to Mivart's remark, the scientific truth of which is fully intact more than a hundred years after

---

[37] *Letters and Diaries*, vol. 25, p. 446.

[38] Ibid., vol. 26, p. 384.

[39] See American edition (New York: D. Appleton, 1874), p. 176. Mivart continued, "Nay, more, these complex affinities form such a net for the use of the teleological retiarius as it will be difficult for his Lucretian antagonist to evade, even with the countless turnings and doublings of Darwinian evolutions."

it saw print. The surplus latent in Mivart's contrast of a network with a ladder was, however, noticed by Newman, in witness to his sensitivity to matters ontological. He loved logic not for its own sake but as an indispensable tool for doing justice to reality, natural and supernatural.[40] In fact the whole history of the critique of Darwinism would have been far more convincing if non-Darwinist evolutionary scientists (whose number and weight is far greater than generally believed[41]) had hammered away at the critical issue or the question of whether one is justified in taking chance for a cause. Newman put the matter tersely as he continued his letter to Mivart: "I am not so well satisfied with your own hypothesis, but I hardly think you mean it for one, but only as an indication for the direction in which to look for one— I mean the hypothesis, that chance variations are the ultimate resolution of the phenomenon, which meets our eyes, of distinct species. Of course, *chance is not a cause.*"[42]

To this remark (whose italicized part should be engraved over the entrance of every department of biology, anthropology, philosophy of science, particle physics, and natural history museum[43]) Newman added, by way of illustration, a reference to a by then classic in anthropology, James Cowles Prichard's *Natural History of Man*, whose first edition of 1843 had once been in his hands. Newman seems to have spoken of it from memory in recalling it as "Physical History of Man." However, memory served Newman right in recalling that Prichard's theory attributing anthropological variations to chance, a point Newman could not leave uncensored: "But what seems chance must be the result of existing laws as yet undiscovered." Finally, he asked Mivart: "Why though mentioning the Mexican eft, do you not speak of worms becoming butterflies?" Newman knew how to turn the

[40] As discussed in chapter 8.

[41] As recognized and documented even by some leading Darwinists around the turn of the century. For details, see my *The Purpose of It All* (Washington D. C.: Regnery Gateway, 1990), pp. 34-35.

[42] See note 34 above.

[43] The antirational and antiontological results of attributing to chance a crypto-causal role in physics are set forth in my essay "Determinism and Reality," in *Great Ideas Today 1990* (Chicago: Encyclopedia Britannica, 1990), pp. 276-302.

table on advocates, Darwinist or not, of chance by a simple reference to a most palpable biological process, one of the myriads of such, whose extraordinary phases, defying all chance, are still to be accounted for by Darwinists in a quantitatively illustrated sequence of random variations.[44]

Clearly, a good argument on secondary points against Darwin did not make Newman overlook the danger of siding with Darwin on very basic points. One such point was the taking of a probable proposition for certainty both in science and in biblical exegesis, a carelessness breeding phantom conflicts between science and theology. It was with an eye on the origin of man that Newman gave a general warning against such carelessness: "For myself I should lay down as a Catholic, that mere probability of a scientific fact should not be allowed to tell against a received interpretation of Scripture. It ought not to be allowed, it has no right, to be brought into court. Many things are probable which are eventually proved to be false. Evolution of vegetable and animal life is not proved—but it may be probable, and that without being in the way to be proved."

Newman turned to Prichard's anthropology book for an illustration of how a good reasoning can possibly lead to an unwarranted conclusion: "Dr Prichard wrote to prove the descent of mankind from one pair. It was, as I recollect, a beautiful instance of close reasoning. It had one defect—it made Adam a negro," which, of course, was a wholly gratuitous conclusion. And he drew the moral for his correspondent: "This will illustrate what I mean when I say that we have no need, we are not called, to meet probable cases, which may, as time goes, be refuted by other probabilities."[45]

Newman's last reference to Darwin dates from 1887 or 1888. It was occasioned by his having received from William S. Lilly the proofs of ch. iv of his forthcoming book dealing with the impact of the ideology of the French Revolution.[46] In that chapter,

---

[44] As I further argued in my *The Purpose of It All*, pp. 78-79.

[45] Letter of March 21, 1882, to Henry S. Bellairs, in *Letters and Diaries*, vol. 30, pp. 69-70.

[46] That Newman did indeed receive a copy of the proofs of the book and not the book itself is also clear from the fact that the book was published (London: Chapman and Hall) only in 1889.

"The Revolution and Science," Lilly showed among other things that the ideology presupposed and bred by Darwinism, or the doctrine that everything was in endless flux, was incompatible with the sacred dogma of nineteenth-century liberalism, or its attribution of inalienable rights to each and every individual. But then Lilly, who took great care to distance Darwin from Darwinism, quoted with approval the concluding page of *The Descent* where man is derived without further ado, "from a hairy quadruped, furnished with a tail and pointed ears, probably arboreal in its habits." While Newman was delighted with Lilly's setting forth the incompatibility in question, he was troubled by Lilly's uncritical citing of a full page from the *Descent*. "The more I was pleased, the more I was frightened as you proceed to express your belief that the first men had tails. I think this temerarious."[47] Owing to the weakness of his fingers, Newman had to make his letter very short, but even so he seems to have provided much food for thought for those latter-day admirers of his who set him up as the prophet of a perennial evolution in matters anthropological, theological, and exegetical.

Were he to brand them as temerarious or something worse, he would not do so out of intellectual timidity. He was ready to comfort Mivart when the latter became subject to rash criticism on the part of those who confused fidelity with immobility. It was natural, Newman wrote to Mivart on May 28, 1876, "to incur the jealous narrowness of those who think no latitude of opinion, reasoning, or thought is allowable on theological questions."[48] As one who knew that in the present condition of man truth can be kept only by fighting for it, he appreciated that Mivart's forthcoming *Lessons from Nature as Manifested in Mind and Matter* would be dedicated to him.[49] "I truly rejoice," Newman wrote to Mivart on September 29, 1875, "that you are collecting your various pieces of artillery into one battery, for the destruction of our enemies. Their arrogant notes of triumph have been very

---

[47] *Letters and Diaries*, vol. 31, p. 179.
[48] *Letters and Diaries*, vol. 28, pp. 71-72 (May 28, 1876).
[49] *Letters and Diaries*, vol. 27, p. 390 (Dec. 6, 1875).

hard to bear, and have been borne by Catholics quite long enough."[50]

But Newman had to address Mivart less than ten years later not as a valuable ally but as one drifting into that camp which Newman already in 1834 described as the front office of the Antichrist himself.[51] That camp swore by reason, science, and progress, all writ large. Catholics straying into that camp had no choice but to urge the Church to accommodate herself to the new findings, as other churches were doing. Such was the "ecumenism" of the late nineteenth century, an ecumenism that would give rise to modernism and be revived in our day in the form of neomodernism. In England it was most logical to take the doctrinally drifting Established Church for the firstfruits of the new ecumenism, and this is what Mivart tried to justify to Newman. He did so in the guise of the question of whether Newman saw any good in the Church of England.

In his reply of March 25, 1884, to Mivart, Newman could, of course, easily show Mivart that both before his conversion and after it he saw much good in that Church. But precisely because he had learned as an Anglican about the foremost good, or the fact that "our Lord has set up a church," he had to join the Catholic Church as the only one that dared to remain a "teaching Church." His next phrase is one of his most fearfully prophetic utterances ever and should greatly help in seeing that no ecumenical syncretism was implied in his utterance, reported at the start of this essay, "to go the whole hog with Darwin."

With an eye on the Church of England, Newman stated that "an experiment is going on; whether a Christian Church can be without a definite, recognized Creed. It is a problem that cannot be worked out within a generation."[52] A little over three generations later the experiment seems now to have reached a fateful dénouement within the Church of England where the principle

---

[50] Ibid., vol. 27, p. 363.

[51] Newman made that inference repeatedly in his "The Patristical Idea of Antichrist in Four Lectures" (1834). See *Discussions and Arguments on Various Subjects* (London: Longmans, Green and Co., 1897), pp. 59-61.

[52] *Letters and Diaries*, vol. 30, p. 338.

of religious evolution is held high as the supreme dogma to believe in.

The deepest aspect, the one that best reveals the very depths of Newman's attitude toward evolution, comes from his essay, "Inspiration in Its Relation to Revelation," written in 1884. The very fact that it begins with a reference to a recent publication of Renan, a chief champion of evolutionary naturalism, guarantees its applicability to our subject. Newman was not yet one third through writing his essay when he pointed out that Catholic intellectuals are bound to be silent or exceedingly reticent even when faith does not impose on them the duty to oppose some very novel proposition:

> It [the novelty] need not be heretical, yet at a particular time or place it may be so contrary to the prevalent opinion in the Catholic body, as in Galileo's case, that zeal for the supremacy of the Divine Word, deference to existing authorities, charity towards the weak and ignorant, and distrust of self, should keep a man from being impetuous or careless in circulating what nevertheless he holds to be true, and what, if indeed asked about, he cannot deny. The household of God has claims upon our tenderness in such matters which criticism and history have not.[53]

The same household had to be protected, though in a very different way, from the threat of naturalism as it took on new life in terms of Darwinian or evolutionary ideology. In order to fight it more effectively Newman welcomed, for instance, Mivart's anti-Darwinian battery. Newman was a fighter who could be at home in the Catholic Church chiefly because, as he put it in the *Grammar*, its Founder came to launch a spiritual warfare which would go on until the end of time.[54] This aspect of Newman's Catholicism calls for a special treatment both because it is central to his spiritual physiognomy and also because it goes particularly against the grain in these days when an obligatory smile has become the feature of a "face-lifted" Catholicism. Here let it

---

[53] See the critical edition of Newman's essay in D. J. Holmes and R. Murray, *On the Inspiration of Scripture. John Henry Newman* (London: G. Chapman, 1967), p. 103.

[54] *Grammar*, p. 344. In the *Apologia* Newman spoke of "that awful never dying duel" (p. 328).

suffice to register Newman's view that the Darwinian ideology was nothing short of an "epidemic" taking a disastrous toll among Christians. What prompted Newman to use that weighty word was a critique of the evolutionary ideology sent to him by the Rev. David Brown, a prominent Free Kirk minister, who later fondly recalled his two visits with Newman at the Birmingham Oratory.[55]

In the first paragraph of his letter written to Dr. Brown on Easter Eve, 1874, Newman recalled his long standing dislike of the pontifications often taking place at the annual meetings of the British Association. Then he diagnosed the epidemic fostered by men of science: "Doubtless theologians have meddled with science, and now scientific men are paying them off by meddling with theology. With you, I see nothing in the theory of evolution inconsistent with an Almighty Creator and Protector; but these men assume, assume with an abundant scorn of us and supercil-iousness, that religion and science are on this point contradictory, and on this audacious assumption they proceed dogmatically to conclude that there is no truth in religion. It is dreadful to think of the number of souls that will suffer while the epidemic lasts; but truth is too powerful not in the end to get the upper hand."[56]

One wonders whether Newman expected that the epidemic not only would last for another century but also would gain enormously in strength. Etienne Gilson was a good observer in noting that in almost every case when a Catholic became infected with even such a spiritually coated "evolutionism" as the one in Teilhard's poetry in prose, the germs of a spiritual demise began to operate.[57] To all those who today take Newman for a forerun-ner of Darwin, he would repeat that he asked Mivart long ago not to take his idea of dogmatic development as something even remotely similar to Darwin's evolutionary views. Apart from this

---

[55] See W. G. Blaikie, *David Brown: A Memoir* (London: Hodder and Stoughton, 1898), pp. 244 and 246. The two visits took place in 1877 and 1882.

[56] Ibid., p. 241, in *Letters and Diaries*, vol. 27, p. 43.

[57] "You cannot get any benefit or any enlightenment from thinking about Teilhard. The ravages he had wrought, that I have witnessed, are horrifying." *Letters of Etienne Gilson to Henry de Lubac*, tr. M. E. Hamilton (San Francisco: Ignatius Press, 1988), p. 136.

disclaimer of Newman's, the arguments of the *Development* are so many rebuttals of efforts to tie him to Darwin.

In the *Development* the word evolution occurs only once.[58] There, when on a few occasions Newman uses a metaphor taken from organic life, he has in mind the unfolding of the full potentialities of a single organism.[59] He never speaks there of the transformation, let alone of the random evolution, of one organism into another. Of the seven notes whereby he distinguishes genuine developments from mere corruptions, already the very first, "the preservation of type," flies in the face of Darwinian perspectives. Only some sleepwalkers would see a touch of Darwinism in such other notes as "the logical sequence" and "the conservative action on its past" evident in genuine development.

Most importantly, the one who in the Introduction of the *Development* held high change and indeed frequent change as the hallmark of life, physical and spiritual,[60] saw those changes as so many means serving one single objective truth. In the *Development* Newman took the Incarnation for the central truth of the Gospel[61] and spoke of the Church as "the pillar and ground of the Truth,"[62] because it was authorized from above to arbitrate infallibly in religious disputes:

> And if the very claim to infallible arbitration in religious disputes is of so weighty importance and interest in all ages of the world, much more is it welcome at a time like this present, when the human intellect is so busy, and thought so fertile, and opinion so manifold. The absolute need of a spiritual supremacy is at present the strongest of arguments in favour of the fact of its supply. Surely, either an objective revelation has not been given, or it has been provided with means for impressing its objectiveness on the world.[63]

---

[58] *Development*, p. 61.

[59] See ibid., especially pp. 107, 177, 179, 359, 395.

[60] "Here below to live is to change, and to be perfect is to have changed often," ibid., p. 63.

[61] Ibid., p. 310.

[62] Ibid., p. 107.

[63] Ibid.

One of the exercises of that ecclesial infallibility relates to judgments on healing performed through the intercession of candidates for canonization. And, as Newman would add, this is why a Church conscious of her teaching infallibility cannot become ecumenical to the point where she would have to part with that consciousness of hers, let alone to the point where she would be required by Darwinian ideology to give up her faith in miracles objectively performed and in a Revelation objectively imparted. This is also what Newman, in two letters he wrote to Mivart on consecutive days in May 1884, singled out as the ultimate line of demarcation between the Catholic Church and evolutionary ideology. Failing an agreement on at least the possibility of miracles, he warned Mivart, all dialogues between Christians and evolutionists were to bog down in matters of secondary importance or in matters of no consequence at all, or in arguing in a circle. Or to quote Newman's very words:

> I can fancy a really Catholic, really scientific article doing much good, but it strikes me that the first step which an author ought to take, before he asks for information from the Church on additional points, is to show that he believes what is propounded already. Most writers ignore the question whether miracles are possible, or admissible in argument. . . He [such a writer] may have many good reasons for thinking so strange an event [the Deluge] improbable, or not to be taken literally—but if he begins with the avowal that it is too great a matter to accept on faith, I don't see how good can come of arguing.[64]

A day earlier, on May 8, Newman wrote to Mivart:

> What is the good of argument unless opponents can join issue on some certain general principle? how can a priest combat a man of science when the latter virtually denies the possibility of miracles and the former holds that the most stupendous have actually occurred? The man of science ought to know that he has not proved that miracles are not possible, yet he uses that assumption as confidently against the Catholics, as if it was the most necessary of truths. Why am I to deny that the Lord rose again the third day because Professor A or B says it is impossible? He brings no facts.[65]

[64] *Letters and Diaries*, vol. 30, p. 360 (May 9, 1884).
[65] Ibid., p. 359.

One could only wish that Newman had enlarged on two points, closely related as they are to the issue on hand. First, he should have probed into what the "Professor" actually brings into the discussion. He could have easily unmasked it as a furtive reliance on genuine metaphysics. If one argues against the impossibility of miracles with an eye on the universal validity of physical laws, he lays himself open to questions about the epistemological grounds on which he holds the notion of physical laws, let alone their universality across an empirically unverifiable totality, or the universe. He then can be forced to admit the inadequacy of empiricism, Humean and other. Second, Newman should have elaborated on that greatest of all miracles, greater than all physical healings, which is the human mind.

He failed on both counts because he was hampered by his insistence, especially in the *Grammar*, on the individually concrete fact.[66] Yet, it is not so much the perception of the concrete single fact that reveals the miraculous powers of the mind, but its ability to register the universal in the singular. It is precisely through that power of the mind that one can see the particular literary data attesting a biblical miracle, or the various medical data attesting a particular healing, really imply something beyond purely physical forces at work.

If a Hume and a Huxley could "creditably" claim that no miracle had ever been proven, it is only because they were allowed to hide their empiricism. But if one is an empiricist, one cannot even become an evolutionist. Darwin was already warned, though in vain, by no less a naturalist than Agassiz, that it took metaphysical eyes to see species,[67] to say nothing of genera, families, orders, classes, phyla, and kingdoms—so many genuine universals. Even more metaphysics is needed to see the demonstrative force of the fossil record and of the geological distribution of living forms, two of Darwin's most persuasive points. The furtive exploitation by Darwin of metaphysical assumptions in his theory, insofar as it is distinct from disreputable ideology, never becomes the target of Newman's dicta on evolution. This

---

[66] See the chapter referred to in note 36 above.

[67] L. Agassiz did so in an essay review of Darwin's *Origin* in *American Journal of Science and Arts* 30 (July 1860), p. 143.

failing on Newman's part is possibly due to the fact that trusting too much his personalistic motto, *unusquisque in sensu suo abundet*,[68] he presented in the *Grammar* a rather incomplete epistemology and metaphysics. Still, his sensing crucial issues about evolution abounds in insights worth pondering.

<hr />

[68] *The Grammar of Assent* (Doubleday Image Books, 1955), pp. 234, 272, 278, 319.

13

Newman: a Mystic?

The question of whether Newman was a mystic is a minor one among the many debates relating to him, though not at all inappropriate about one so fond of clarity, however nuanced. The question was not found worth pursuing by any of Newman's major biographers, such as Ward, Trevor, and Ker. In his *John Henry Newman: His Inner Life*, the Capuchin Father Zeno states that Newman "seems to have enjoyed only very seldom, if at all, the experiential perception of God's presence . . . which is bestowed on the mystics." He also found, on the basis of a decades-long study of Newman's intimate biographical writings, confidential letters, and most self-revealing sermons that they "do not contain a single passage that can be explained solely as a mystical experience in the strict sense of the word."[1]

Even more negative was the conclusion of an equally competent student of Newman's prayer life, the Birmingham Oratorian Henry Tristram. In support, he quoted Newman's own admission about an almost habitual aridity he experienced in prayer and devotions. In a letter written at the height (Feb. 11, 1850) of his fresh enthusiasm over having become a Catholic, Newman referred to the mystical way when he disclosed to a correspondent: "I have nothing of a saint about me." Newman found this to be "a severe (and salutary) mortification" to keep in mind. Very significant should seem what he added: "I may have a high view of many things, but it is the consequence of educa-

---

[1] San Francisco, Ignatius Press, 1986, p. 276.

tion and a peculiar cast of intellect—but this is a very different thing from *being* what I admire. . . . I may be well enough in my way, but it is not the 'high line'."[2]

Undoubtedly, H. Bremond, the famed author of a vast history of spirituality and mysticism in France, could have been expected to magnify any evidence of a mystic strain, in his study of Newman's religious psychology. Bremond was compelled to write: "I have no intention of presenting, as an adequate representative of Catholic mysticism a man who, as a matter of fact, never deviated from the beaten track [of spiritual life]."[3]

Only a very few Newmanists have claimed that Newman should be spoken of as a mystic. The most extensive presentation of this claim is the dissertation, *Newman mistico,* by G. Velocci.[4] Undoubtedly, Newman voiced most impressively his sense of the presence of God and of the reality of the "unseen world," a favorite expression of his. His posthumously published *Meditations and Devotions* have inspired countless readers searching for solid spiritual sustenance.

But to speak of Newman as a mystic is to run into problems of plain semantics. No deep spiritual life, not even the heroic practice of virtues (which is now officially established about Newman), not even a total surrender to God's will, are tantamount to mystical experiences. Otherwise every saint, perhaps every great spiritual writer, should be spoken of as a mystic. Again, mysticism should be evaluated in terms set by the most authoritative mystics, above all Saint Teresa of Avila and Saint John of the Cross.

With an eye on those terms the most that can be said about Newman the mystic was stated by the Cistercian R. Hodge.[5] He sought support in the dictum of Saint John of the Cross, according to whom "the commencement of contemplation is in general

---

[2] H. Tristram, "With Newman at Prayer," in *John Henry Newman: Centenary Essays* [Westminster MD: The Newman Bookshop, 1945), p. 111; subsequently edited in *Letters and Diaries,* Feb. 11, 1850. vol. 13, p. 419.

[3] *The Mystery of Newman,* tr. H. C. Corrance (London: Williams and Norgate, 1907), p. 280.

[4] Roma: Pont. Univ. Lateranense, 1964.

[5] "Cardinal Newman: Contemplative," *Cistercian Studies* 11 (1976), pp. 193-227.

secret, and unknown to him who is admitted to it."[6] This means that even if Newman had reached the initial stage of mysticism, he might not have been aware of this. But Hodge himself admitted that Newman certainly would not fit into the initial phase of the mystical (contemplative) state as specified by Saint Teresa of Avila.

Newman's was not the "high line," but he never failed to direct the vision of others to truly supernatural heights. Even the greatest mystic cannot take greater credit as far as most others are concerned.

[6] *Dark Night of the Soul*, Bk. 1, ch. 9.

14

Priestly Celibacy

It was in the 1820s that Johann Adam Moehler, the earliest great Catholic theologian of the nineteenth century, was regaining, as he himself put it, his Christian soul through reading the Fathers. Shortly afterwards something akin happened to Newman, who was to become, in chronological order, the second of theological giants of that century, with Matthias Joseph Scheeben being the third of them.[1] Newman referred to the writings of the Fathers as having been "simply and solely the one intellectual cause" of his having converted to Roman Catholicism."[2] In the same context Newman also epitomized the supreme motive of his conversion. He found the ethos of the Catholic Church of his day remarkably similar to the ethos animating the Church of the Fathers, many of whom were great theologians as well great saints. He had therefore no choice but to exclaim: "Be my soul with the saints!"[3] No wonder that Newman, another patron saint of the "new" theology, spoke as emphatically and approvingly as did Moehler about priestly celibacy, a fact which both the chief and the secondary figures of the "new" theology have preferred to be silent about.

Newman has been often referred to as the theologian of

---

[1] The views which these three held on priestly celibacy are presented as the background to the "new" theology on that subject in the chapter, "A New Theology?" in my book, *Theology of Priestly Celibacy* (Front Royal, VA: Christendom Press, 1997).

[2] J. H. Newman, *Anglican Difficulties*, with an introduction by S. L. Jaki (Fraser, MI: Real View Books, 1994), pp. 244-45 (Lecture XII, 2).

[3] Ibid., p. 259.

Vatican II.[4] Newman himself might wonder about the appropriateness of this halo accorded to him. As one who prophesied
about a deluge of hostility in store for the Church, he would
certainly wonder, or rub his eyes in disbelief, that Vatican II
contains only five lines on what, according to the Council, is a
permanent condition of the Church through all history. That
condition is a permanent state of struggle against the powers of
Evil. Such a struggle, since it is permanent, clearly has to be an
always uphill struggle. The struggle involves the individual
Christian on the most personal moral level.[5] Hardly anything
more appropriate could have been stated about the basic predicament within which celibacy, or any other virtue for that matter,
remains a struggle to be taken up at every new day's dawning.

Yet not much more than a couple of lines have been written
about that permanent condition (including its very personal
component) by "progressive" theologians who dominated that
Council as far as publicity-control was concerned. They certainly
celebrated, in accord with the false optimism of the 1960s, the
glorious material and cultural progress in store for humanity.
They therefore did much to sublimate the awful reality of
original sin and of its consequences, although Newman saw there
the very starting point of a theology appropriate for modern
man.[6]

Of course, Newman tried to help save that fallen man,
including his modern kind, as he warned him that it is the

---

[4] Thus, in reminiscing about Vatican II, where he was a prominent figure,
Cardinal Gracias of Bombay wrote: "Representatives of the Hierarchy from
all over the world, theologians, philosophers, faithful from everywhere, and
from all ranks, see in Newman a guide in their sincere search for the truth."
"The Friends of Cardinal Newman," *The Examiner* 128 (May 21, 1977), p. 278.

[5] "A monumental struggle against the powers of darkness pervades the
whole history of man. The battle was joined from the very origins of the
world and will continue until the last day, as the Lord attested. Caught in this
conflict man is obliged to wrestle constantly if he is to cling to what is good.
Nor can he achieve his own integrity without valiant efforts and the help of
God's grace." Pastoral Constitution on the Church in the Modern World
(#37), in *The Documents of Vatican II*, ed. W. M. Abbott (New York: Guild
Press, 1966), p. 235.

[6] See my article, "A Gentleman [Newman] and Original Sin," *Downside
Review* July 1996, pp. 192-215, reprinted here as chapter 2.

Antichrist himself who uses material progress most effectively for his very purposes.[7] Newman, who refused to be an evolutionist,[8] would have been the last to suggest to fellow Catholics that they are caught up in a gigantic forward and upward moving stream of progressive evolution that would raise mankind one day, and still on this very earth, into a new, unimaginably superior noosphere. A Newman, who rightly deplored that it amounted "almost to a blasphemy to doubt"[9] the existence of people on other planets, would weep today on hearing an educated Catholic layman refer to his "cousins in other galaxies" as the source of his comfort and inspiration enabling him to cope with life on earth.[10] Yet, it is partly by taking cover with profuse references to Newman that champions of the new theology have sown the seeds of a strange spiritual flora and fauna wherein nothing old is tolerated and everything new is blithely endorsed. He would hardly be pleased to be invoked as a justification of a theology replete with hollow phrases and catchy words, all larded with quotations from him, quotations at times brazenly truncated, lest the true Newman should appear.[11] In that theological jungle there is clearly no place for the cultivation of Newman's views on celibacy.

Those views are all the more telling because they appear spontaneously here and there in Newman's diaries and published

[7] Particularly telling are the four lectures Newman delivered in 1835 on the patristic idea of the Antichrist, reprinted in his *Discussions and Arguments On Various Subjects* (London: Longmans, Green and Co., 1897). See especially pp. 60-61.

[8] See my essay, "Newman and Evolution," *Downside Review* 108 (January 1991), pp. 16-34; reprinted here as chapter 12.

[9] *Grammar of Assent* (Doubleday Image Book, 1955), p. 299. See also pp. 166, 329 and 376 for further strictures of Newman's on the logical fallacies involved in that belief.

[10] The case, which I know personally, is all the stranger, as the life of the Catholic in question was blessed with all the amenities that devolve to a successful Madison Avenue executive. Only when one morning his older son blew his head to pieces did the father's eyes open to the crucifix which alone can provide meaning and strength in such circumstances.

[11] For details, see my article, "Newman's Logic and the Logic of the Papacy," *Faith and Reason* 13 (1987), p. 261 and note 89 there; reprinted here as chapter 7.

works, and show thereby all the more forcefully how decisive was in his eyes the theological import of priestly celibacy. Yet Newman never wanted to be considered a theologian; he emphatically looked upon himself as a controversialist, although the topics he controverted almost always related to the very core of theology. In his eyes the chief task was to articulate the following assertion: God gave about himself and his aim with mankind a revelation over and above what man can learn about God by looking into himself or at the great nature around him. In other words, Newman's principal concern was the vindication of the supernatural dispensation.

This is why Newman never went to any length in articulating the cosmological argument, although he firmly held it.[12] He had reservations about the design argument, partly because of the form Paley gave it, and partly because it did not say anything about God's supernatural design for man. This does not mean that Newman lacked keen eyes and appreciation for the natural. Indeed, it was a very empirical fact, an existential experience available to any and all, that made the supernaturally revealing God loom obvious in Newman's eyes. He loved to describe that fact or experience as a proof that mankind became involved in "some terrible aboriginal calamity."[13] His views on Revelation, on grace, on sacraments, on Church were all conditioned by that huge reality of man's fallenness.

Telling glimpses of this are given in the introductory part of Section III of the *Development*, where he states why there has to be a growth of a truth initially revealed by God and why God had to build into that revealed truth a factor whereby it is saved from gradual corruption. The growth, if it is truly one, has to be organic, which means the ever growing interconnectedness of theological doctrines: "These doctrines are members of one family, and suggestive, or correlative, or confirmatory, or illustrative of each other. One furnishes evidence to another, and all to each of them; if this is proved, that becomes probable." He then turns to the logical order between some dogmas: "The

[12] *Grammar of Assent*, pp. 275 and 383.
[13] *Apologia pro vita sua* (Doubleday Image Books, 1956), p. 320.

Incarnation is antecedent of the doctrine of Mediation, and the archetype both of the Sacramental principle and of the merits of Saints." A little later, but still in this context, Newman lists instances of one doctrine leading to another. Among them is the following chain: "The doctrine of the Sacraments leads to the doctrine of Justification; Justification to that of Original Sin; Original Sin to the merit of celibacy."[14]

A most momentous chain, which gives the fundamental perspective for a theology of priestly celibacy. The priest is a model, yes, a reminder of higher realities, and many other things in addition. But all these are secondary, or second-story facets of what basically constitutes a priest. The only empirical and there- fore also logical starting point towards the rationale of the priesthood is original sin, the fallen human nature, that nowhere fell so deep as in relation to the proper use of sex. To mediate man's redemption from this disorderly, sinful state is the essential role of priesthood. Therefore, as Newman listed chapter headings to illustrate which dogma includes another dogma, he logically ended with the caption: "Celibacy is the characteristic mark of Monachism and the Priesthood."[15]

The foregoing details are a lead-up to Newman's grand conclusion about the organic growth of doctrine, in which there is nothing stated about priesthood and celibacy. Yet the fact that the conclusion immediately follows upon his remark that celibacy is characteristic of the priesthood, conveys something of New- man's profound conviction about celibacy as an indispensable, integral part of priesthood, and indeed of the entire system of Christian dispensation and doctrine: "You must accept the whole or reject the whole; attenuation does but enfeeble, and amputa- tion mutilate. It is trifling to receive all but something which is as integral as any other portion; and on the other hand, it is a solemn thing to accept any part, for, before you know where you are, you may be carried on by a stern logical necessity to accept the whole."[16]

---

[14] *An Essay on the Development of Christian Doctrine* (London: Basil Montagu Pickering, 1878), p. 94.
[15] Ibid.
[16] Ibid.

To defend that whole, insofar as priestly celibacy was an integral part of it, was most dear to Newman. As one born and raised within a thoroughly Protestant ambience, and as one who knew full well its ingrained anti-Catholic prejudices, he, the consummate logician, learned to know fully the logical holes in them. In devoting an entire lecture series to those illogicalities, he had to deal with the ones that characterized Protestant views on the Catholic clergy in general and on their celibacy in particular. In general, he laid it down that nobody has proven that there are fewer improprieties within the Protestant clergy than among the Catholic. He meant all sorts of improprieties, such as love of money, thirst for power, arrogance, insensitivity and so forth. With respect to celibacy, he was not to stress much the fact that, certainly in the England of his time, the Catholic Church took great caution in selecting and educating future priests. Much less was he willing to hold high the example of the few very virtuous to offset the weight of the weaknesses of many others. He turned the tables on Protestants by stating: "I am very skeptical indeed that in matter of fact a married clergy *is* adorned, in any special and singular way, with the grace of purity; and this is just the thing which Protestants take for granted." Inevitable was then Newman's question: "What is the use of speaking against our discipline, till they have proved their own to be better?"[17]

Such a question, which sounds ominous in view of the present-day approval by most Protestant clergy of contraception,[18] had, to use the modern theological parlance, much more phenomenological justification to it than do modern efforts to evaluate priestly celibacy on a phenomenological basis. Newman's question is therefore to be pondered most carefully by latter-day advocates of optional celibacy as long as they have a truly spiritual concern at heart and want to be in Newman's camp. And if they do, they can derive much help from pondering

---

[17] *The Present Position of Catholics in England* (London: Longmans, Green and Co., 1903), p. 134.

[18] With Karl Barth giving them the "dogmatic" lead in his *Church Dogmatics, Vol. III, The Doctrine of Creation*, Part Four (Edinburgh: T & T. Clark, 1961), pp. 273-75. There Barth rejects the inflexible doctrine of *Casti connubii* and endorses the Lambeth Conference of 1930!

Newman's emphatic declaration: "Now I deny that they [Protest-ants] succeed with their rule of matrimony [for the clergy] better than we do with our rule of celibacy." Newman was denying this on a ground which is as valid today to any reasonable reader of newspapers and magazines as it was in Newman's time: "The public prints and the conversation of the world, by means of many shocking instances, which of course are only specimens of many others, heavier or lighter, which do *not* come before the world, bring home to me the fact, that a Protestant rector or a dissenting preacher is not necessarily kept from the sins I am speaking of, because he happens to be married." But something even worse was in store for a married minister: "When he offends, whether in a grave way or less seriously, still in all cases he has by matrimony but exchanged a bad sin for a worse, and has become an adulterer instead of being a seducer." After this, almost anticlimactic was Newman's observation that matrimony does only one thing for a married minister: "His purity is at once less protected and less suspected."[19]

Newman today would, of course, probe into the theological reasons why the media revels in the sexual scandals of Catholic clergy, but shows far less interest in similar failures of Protestant ministers.[20] After all, the media finds many allies in ministers of main-line Churches, where the sixth and the ninth com-mandments impose nothing more than indignation about what the media too condemns, though not on moral grounds, such as the sexual abuse of children and the sexual harrassment of women.[21] Quite different is the attitude of the media toward

---

[19] *The Present Position of Catholics in England*, pp. 134-35.

[20] Thus, for instance, hardly anything is reported about the far larger number of Protestant ministers charged with pedophilia.

[21] The situation in the Armed Forces is a perfect illustration of modern man's truly fallen predicament. Although most male soldiers will forever harrass women soldiers and other women as well, who in turn will forever entice the male, they all are expected to display a high measure of self-discipline without reliance on God's grace, in a matter which poses great difficulties even with full reliance on it. Thus a legal system that bars God from the premises, while it lets them be flooded over with pornography and opens them to gays and lesbians, wants those living there to function as if they were in monasteries and nunneries. Of course, that legal system would not endorse Christ's warning about lustful looks that alone goes to the root of the

revivalist ministers who still preach the supernatural, whatever their addiction to biblical literalism. Newman would find the reason for this difference in the fact that the media, as part of a fallen world which refuses to recognize its fallenness, finds nothing so inconveniencing as being presented with the supernatural, and especially as it is witnessed by the celibacy of Catholic priesthood. Indeed for a fallen world which glories in taking its sexual failures, and even perversities, for natural virtues, nothing can appear more embarrassing than the mere sight of celibate priests.

About that media and world it is even more true what Newman wrote in reference to a married Protestant clergy: "The married state is no testimonial for moral correctness, no safeguard whether against scandalous offences, or (much less) against minor forms of the same general sin [of impurity]." What he said next could serve as a most needed warning to those new theologians who describe marital love as the rose-strewn highroad to the highest virtue: "Purity is not a virtue which comes merely as a matter of course to the married any more than to the single, though of course there is a great difference between man and man."[22]

Newman would not have been a theologian of celibacy had he bogged down in matters of fact translatable into statistics. Of course, in this age when Catholic theologians almost apologize for priestly celibacy by suggesting, directly or indirectly, optional celibacy as a panacea, it is not amiss to take for a much needed shock treatment Newman's blunt words: "I have as much right to my opinion as another to his, when I state my deliberate conviction that there are, to say the least, as many offences against the marriage vow among Protestant ministers, as there are against the vow of celibacy among Catholic priests."[23] And in an age when theologians love circumlocutions more than plain words and straight logic, it should seem refreshing and instruc-

matter. In sum, a society that does not believe in angels has no right to expect its soldiers, policemen, politicians and clergymen to boot, to behave like angels.

[22] *The Present Position of Catholics in England*, p. 135.

[23] Ibid.

tive to hear a logician such as Newman state the obvious: "But if matrimony does not prevent cases of immorality among Protestant ministers, it is not celibacy which causes them among Catholic priests." Objectors to priestly celibacy achieve nothing until they come to terms with Newman's terse appraisal of the case: "Till, then, you can prove that celibacy causes what matrimony certainly does not prevent, you do nothing at all."[24]

Newman could say something still far more profound, though still very obvious. The root of the problem, within celibacy or marriage, is fallen human nature: "It is not what the Catholic Church imposes, but what human nature prompts, which leads a portion of her ecclesiastics into sin. Human nature will break out, like some wild and raging element, under any system; it bursts out under the Protestant system; it bursts out under the Catholic; passion will carry away the married minister as well as the unmarried priest."[25] To describe human nature as infested with "some wild and raging element" is hardly to the liking of new theologians, who at times quote in support of their wild reasoning Newman's words about "the wild living intellect of man."[26] Far from recommending wild innovations, Newman deplored reckless instability in reasoning and the capricious espousal of anything novel, seeing as he did in all this the impact of original sin on man's mind. Some new theological thinking about priestly celibacy, to be discussed later in this chapter, fully deserves the *caveat* which he delivered as if he had been a thundering Old Testament prophet: "It is the world, the flesh, and the devil, not celibacy, which is the ruin of those who fall."[27]

It is not possible to state more clearly and to demonstrate more strongly that the theology of priestly celibacy must start with a courageous statement on original sin and its effects. Apart from such a statement, that theology will have no foundations steeped in reality. At any rate, only a Newman unspoiled by ecumenical "good feeling" could have the courage to raise a question about "slothful priests," a question directed at Anglicans:

[24] Ibid., p. 136.
[25] Ibid.
[26] *Apologia pro vita sua*, p. 322.
[27] *The Present Position of Catholics in England*, p. 136.

"Why, where was there any religion whatever, established and endowed, in which bishops, canons, and wealthy rectors were not exposed to the temptation of pride and sensuality?"[28] Today one need only read the British newspapers to see the appropriateness of Newman's words as far as the clergy of the Church of England is concerned. Although almost all of them are married, they are still sorely tempted and at times do fall with a crashing noise, which the media picks up with its contorted seismograph calibrated to suit an increasingly amoral public.

Newman indeed would be the last to say that he had not been tempted. In fact, being a deeply introspective soul and in love with his diary, he made it all too clear that he had been tempted again and again. But, most importantly, he also insisted that purity was a virtue, that is, a disposition acquired through hard practice of readily doing the good. This has yet to gain wide currency in order to balance the endless references to Newman's early realization, when he was only 16, that God had called him to a single life. He never considered this calling of his as a talisman, or a charisma, that disposed of temptations. In fact, when three years later he gained "the unshakable resolve to live and die single," he qualified it with the words: "with divine aid."[29] In 1824 he jotted down in his diary that he should "pray for purity, sobriety, chastity, temperance . . . pray against excess, uncleanness, worldly-mindedness, lying, insincerity."[30] In 1826, the year of his Anglican ordination, he noted that during the previous year he had been particularly saved from sins against purity.

For Newman purity was an asset to be won and not to be taken for granted, a sacrifice, though one which "strengthened one's feeling of separation from the visible world."[31] Nor was the virtue of celibate purity to be less appreciated because it did not eliminate the feeling of being in need of that natural sympathy that marriage satisfies best.[32] Nor did it imply the wearing of a

---

[28] Ibid.

[29] Quoted in J. Tollhurst, "The Interchange of Love: John Henry Newman's Teaching on Celibacy," *The Irish Theological Quarterly* 59 (1933), p. 218.

[30] Ibid.

[31] *Apologia pro vita sua*, p. 130.

[32] *Autobiographical Writings*, pp. 137-38, quoted by Tollhurst, p. 221.

blindfold in the presence of truly Christian married life.[33] Still the virtue of celibate purity (especially when combined with Catholic priesthood) was something which Newman valued most intensely. Otherwise he would not have risked initiating and losing a lawsuit (which he indeed lost) against a notorious detractor of the Catholic priesthood and its celibacy.[34] Nor could Newman fail to see that the honesty of Catholic priests with respect to their vow of celibacy was a tacit target of Kingsley's charge, that it was customary with Catholic priests to be less than honest, because it was impossible to be honest and celibate.[35]

Kingsley, an early champion of Darwin, did not have to worry about his branding of priestly celibacy as rank duplicity. For he did this at a time when applause greeted Darwin who made the same charge, though, of course, in a roundabout way. Darwin saw nothing immoral in "the greatest intemperance" among the savages and the prevalence among them, "to an astonishing degree, of utter licentiousness and unnatural crime." No wonder that he deplored the raising of "the senseless law of [priestly] celibacy" to the rank of a virtue.[36] Soon to second Darwin came Francis Galton, the father of eugenics, who denounced the Church for having "brutalised the breed of our forefathers" by its resolve to "preach and exact celibacy" from those who by their "gentle nature" were fitted "to the deeds of charity, to meditation, to literature, or to art," and who, because "of the social condition of the time, . . . found no refuge elsewhere than in the bosom of the Church." Of this "policy, so brutal and suicidal" Galton was "hardly able to speak . . . without impatience."[37] The latter expression was a classic in the art of understatement for which the British have a special fondness.

[33] Following John Bowden's death Newman wrote to his widow, saying that in visiting his late friend at home, he felt he was in the midst of the Holy Family. See Tollhurst, p. 220.

[34] An excellent account of the Achilli case is in M. Trevor's *Newman: The Pillar of the Cloud* (London: Macmillan, 1962), pp. 546-59.

[35] A view widely entertained then as now in Western society.

[36] Charles Darwin, *Descent of Man* (1871; 3rd ed.; London: Murray, 1876), p. 182.

[37] D. W. Forest, *Francis Galton: Hereditary Genius* (New York: Taplinger, 1974), p. 100.

In this respect, too, as in many others, Newman refused to be mislead by the art of "patriotic" preferences. He did not engage in that art when he deplored the difficulty of winding up the English "to a dogmatic level."[38] Today he would add, and bluntly, that the same is true of all too many theologians and educated lay people in all the "developed" parts of the world. Those parts include all the countries that, unlike his beloved England, did not fall prey to the lures of a Reformation that was actually a tragic deformation of all that true reform has meant throughout the entire history of the Church. In the dispiriting growth of insensitivity to dogma he would see the very opposite to what he set forth in his nominally last Anglican, but in actuality his first Catholic book, *The Development of Christian Doctrine.* No wonder that, as this chapter showed, Newman set forth in that book, too, priestly celibacy as a hallmark of true development and put thereby the conceivably most concrete capstone on his challenge to Catholics of today and of all times.

[38] *Apologia pro vita sua* (Doubleday Image Books, 1956), p. 291.

Appendix

John Henry Newman
"Cathedra Sempiterna"

Deeply do I feel, ever will I protest, for I can appeal to the ample testimony of history to bear me out, that, in questions of right and wrong, there is nothing really strong in the whole world, nothing decisive and operative, but the voice of him, to whom have been committed the keys of the kingdom and the oversight of Christ's flock. The voice of Peter is now, as it ever has been, a real authority, infallible when it teaches, prosperous when it commands, ever taking the lead wisely and distinctly in its own province, adding certainty to what is probable, and persuasion to what is certain. Before it speaks, the most saintly may mistake; and after it has spoken, the most gifted must obey.

Peter is no recluse, no abstracted student, no dreamer about the past, no doter upon the dead and gone, no projector of the visionary. Peter for eighteen hundred years has lived in the world; he has seen all fortunes, he has encountered all adversaries, he has shaped himself for all emergencies. If there ever was a power on earth who had an eye for the times, who has confined himself to the practicable, and has been happy in his anticipations, whose words have been deeds, and whose commands prophecies, such is he in the history of ages, who sits from generation to generation in the Chair of the Apostles, as the Vicar of Christ and Doctor of His Church.

It was said by an old philosopher, who declined to reply to an emperor's arguments, "It is not safe controverting with the master of twenty legions." What Augustus had in the temporal order, that, and much more, has Peter in the spiritual. When was he ever unequal to the occasion? When has he not risen with the crisis? What dangers have ever daunted him? What sophistry foiled him? What uncertainties misled him? When did ever any power go to war with Peter, material or moral, civilized or savage, and got the better? When did the whole world ever band together against him solitary, and not find him too many for it?

All who take part with Peter are on the winning side. The Apostle of Christ says not in order to unsay; for he has inherited that word which is with power. From the first he looked through the wide world, of which he has the burden; and according to the need of the day, and the inspirations of his Lord, he has set himself, now to one thing, now to another, but to all in season and to nothing in vain. He came first upon an age of refinement and luxury like our own; and in spite of the persecutor, fertile in the resources of his cruelty, he soon gathered, out of all classes of society, the slave, the soldier, the high-born lady, and the sophist, to form a people for his Master's honour. The savage hordes came down in torrents from the north, hideous even to look upon; and Peter went out with holy water and with benison, and by his very eye he sobered them and backed them in full career. They turned aside and flooded the whole earth, but only to be more surely civilized by him, and to be made ten times more his children even than the older populations they had overwhelmed. Lawless kings arose, sagacious as the Roman, passionate as the Hun, yet in him they found their match, and were shattered, and he lived on. The gates of the earth were opened to the east and west, and men poured out to take possession; and he and his went with them; swept along by zeal and charity, as far as they by enterprise, covetousness, or ambition. Has he failed in his enterprises up to this hour? Did he, on our fathers' day, fail in his struggle with Joseph of Germany and his confederates—with Napoleon, a greater name, and his dependent kings—that, though in another kind of fight, he should fail in ours? What grey hairs are on the head of Judah, whose youth is renewed as the eagle's, whose feet are like the feet of harts, and underneath the Everlasting Arms?

"Thus saith the Lord that created thee, O Jacob, and formed thee, O Israel. Fear not, for I have redeemed thee, and called thee by thy name! Thou art Mine.

"When thou shalt pass through the waters, I will be with thee, and the rivers shall not cover thee.

"When thou shalt walk in the fire, thou shalt not be burned, and the flame shall not kindle against thee.

"For I am the Lord thy God, the Holy One of Israel, thy Saviour.

"Fear not, for I am with thee, I am the first, and I am the last, and besides me there is no God."

***

This sermon, which Newman preached as Rector of the Catholic University of Dublin in 1853, first appeared in print only in 1896 as part of his *My Campaign in Ireland. Part I. Catholic University Reports and Other Papers* (printed for private circulation only by A. King & Co., Printers to the University Aberdeen, 1896, pp. 211-14). Fr. Neville, Newman's fellow Oratorian and his literary executor, added a note, which is equally worth reprinting here:

It is not altogether irrelevant to mention here that in January, 1856, Dr. Newman, having occasion to go to Rome on business of very great anxiety, he at once, on alighting from the diligence, went with Father St. John to make a visit of devotion to the shrine of St. Peter, going the whole way barefoot. The time was the middle of the day, when, as was the case in those years, the streets were very empty, and thus, and screened by his large Roman cloak, he was able to do so unrecognized and unnoticed—nor was it ever known except to Father St. John and another.[1]

His friend Dr. Clifford (the Hon. William J. H. Clifford, late Bishop of Clifton), who with his father Lord Clifford, had travelled with him from Siena, and with whom he dined that day in Rome, knew nothing of this until it was mentioned to him on occasion of his preaching the Cardinal's funeral sermon in 1890.

[1] This other person was Fr. Neville himself. See M. Trevor, *Newman. Light in Winter* (London: Macmillan, 1962), p. 103.

Index of Names

Gutenberg, J., 262
Guth, A., 253

Haeckel, E., 277
Hanmer, A. J., 89-91
Harper, T. N., 210
Harris, R., 139
Hawking, S., 253
Hegel, G. F. W., 184
Heisenberg, W., 256
Henry VIII, 23
Hergenröther, J., 195
Hey, J., 46
Hinds, S., 58
Hodge, R., 292-93
Hollis, C., 7, 62
Holmes, A., 128
Holmes, D. J., 284
Hooker, J. D., 273
Hope, J., 59, 103, 110, 120
Hügel, Baron von, 15, 123, 274
Hume, D., 46, 51-52, 288
Hurter, F., 189
Husband, E., 136, 167
Hutton, R. H., 125-27, 144, 151-52, 197
Huxley, T. H., 60-61, 199, 288
Huygens, C., 208

Innocent III, pope, 232

Jaki, S. L., 59-60, 77, 169, 206, 208, 212, 259, 261
James, J., 247
Janssen, J., 195
Januarius, saint, 64
Jedin, H., 195
John of the Cross, saint, 292
John XXIII, pope, 170
John Paul II, pope 64, 136-37, 221, 235
Johnson, H., 266-69
Johnson, M., 88

Kant, I., 32, 76, 77, 194, 215, 223, 238
Keble, J., 109, 249
Keith, A., 247, 268-70
Kepler, J., 262
Ker, I. T., 50, 63, 79, 129, 211, 291
Kingsley, C., 5, 31, 59, 61, 121, 126, 146, 150, 240, 248, 305
Kuhn, T. S., 211, 239
Küng, H., 58

Lakatos, I., 212
Lamarck, J.-B., 267-68
Langley, C., 265
Lash, N., 211, 239
Laski, H. J., 187
Latimer, H., 133
Lavoisier, A.-L., 258
Lebreton, J., 195
Lenard, P., 256
Leo XIII, pope, 136, 139, 214, 241
Leonard, G., 139
Liberatore, M., 204
Lilly, W. S., 281-82
Linacre, T., 262
Locke, J., 207-09, 222, 238
Loyson, H., 168
Lyell, C., 199

Magee, B., 256
Maitland, O., 139
Malpighi, M., 262
Manning, H. E., card., 1, 79, 86, 109-10, 120, 122, 150, 166
Maritain, J., 11
Martin, V., 195
Mascall, E., 140
Maskell, W., 104-05
Maskell, Mrs. W., 39
Maurice, F. D., 187
Medaware, P., 247

Index of Subjects

(continued from p. ii)

The Savior of Science
(Wethersfield Institute Lectures, 1987)

Miracles and Physics

God and the Cosmologists
(Farmington Institute Lectures, Oxford, 1988)

The Only Chaos and Other Essays

The Purpose of It All
(Farmington Institute Lectures, Oxford, 1989)

Catholic Essays

Cosmos in Transition: Studies in the History of Cosmology

Olbers Studies

Scientist and Catholic: Pierre Duhem

Is There a Universe?

Universe and Creed

Reluctant Heroine: The Life and Work of Hélène Duhem

Patterns or Principles and Other Essays

Bible and Science

Theology of Priestly Celibacy

Means to Message: A Treatise on Truth

God and the Sun at Fatima

* * *

Translations with introduction and notes:

The Ash Wednesday Supper (Giordano Bruno)

*Cosmological Letters on the Arrangement
of the World Edifice* (J.-H. Lambert)

*Universal Natural History
and Theory of the Heavens* (I. Kant)

[322]

Note on the Author

Stanley L. Jaki, a Hungarian-born Catholic priest of the Benedictine Order, is Distinguished University Professor at Seton Hall University, South Orange, New Jersey. With doctorates in theology and physics, he has for the past thirty years specialized in the history and philosophy of science. The author of forty books and over a hundred articles, he served as Gifford Lecturer at the University of Edinburgh and as Fremantle Lecturer at Balliol College, Oxford. He has lectured at major universities in the United States, Europe, and Australia. He is an honorary member of the Pontifical Academy of Sciences, *membre correspondant* of the Académie Nationale des Sciences, Belles-Lettres et Arts de Bordeaux, and the recipient of the Lecomte du Nouy Prize for 1970 and of the Templeton Prize for 1987